MONTGOMERY COLLEGE LIBRARY
GERMANTOWN CAMPUS

THE AMERICAN FEDERAL EXECUTIVE

THE AMERICAN

FEDERAL EXECUTIVE

A Study of the Social and Personal Characteristics
of the Civilian and Military Leaders of the United States
Federal Government

by

W. LLOYD WARNER

PAUL P. VAN·RIPER

NORMAN H. MARTIN

ORVIS F. COLLINS

GREENWOOD PRESS, PUBLISHERS
WESTPORT, CONNECTICUT

Library of Congress Cataloging in Publication Data

Warner, William Lloyd, 1898-1970.
   The American Federal executive.

   Reprint of the ed. published by Yale University Press, New Haven, Conn.
   1. Government executives--United States. I. Title.
[JK723.E9W3   1975]   301.44'47'0973   75-11487
ISBN 0-8371-8207-7

Copyright © 1963 by Yale University.

All rights reserved. This book may not be reproduced, in whole or in part, in any form (except by reviewers for the public press), without written permission from the publishers.

Originally published in 1963 by Yale University Press, New Haven

Reprinted with the permission of Yale University Press

Reprinted in 1975 by Greenwood Press, a division of Williamhouse-Regency Inc.

Library of Congress Catalog Card Number 75-11487

ISBN 0-8371-8207-7

Printed in the United States of America

To the Memory of
W. I. Thomas

Contents

Preface

PART I. INTRODUCTION

1. Image of the Bureaucrat — 1
   What the Book Is About — 1
   The Purposes of the Research — 2
   Representative Bureaucracy: The Problem of Consequences — 4
   The Research on Civilian and Military Leaders — 6
   Profiles of the Civilian Executives — 10
   Profiles of the Military Executives — 15
   Comparison of the Civilian and Military Services — 17
   The Executives of American Big Business and Big Government — 18

PART II. SOCIAL ORIGINS: HOW REPRESENTATIVE OF AMERICA ARE THEY?

2. Fathers and Sons: Occupational Origins — 27
   The Origins of Civilian Federal Executives — 28
   The Origins of Military Leaders — 31
   The Professions as Sources of Federal Executives — 33
   Comparative Analysis of the Origins of the Several Services — 35
3. The States and Regions That Produce Executives — 39
   State and Regional Representation — 41
   State and Regional Mobility — 49
4. The Urban, Rural, and Foreign-Born Executives — 56
   The Contribution of Big Cities, Small Towns, and Rural Villages — 56
   Region, Community, and Occupational Background — 57
   Government Leaders Who Are Foreign Born — 60
   The Occupational Origins of the Foreign Born — 63

Part III. The Influence of Family

5. Three Generations: Marriage, Descent, and Occupation 71
   The Father's Father's Influence on the Movement of Men into the Federal Executive 71
   The Occupational Routes through the Generations to the Federal Executive 73
   The Military: Three Generations of Mobility 77
   The General Routes of Mobility: A Comparative Analysis 81
6. Mothers and Sons 84
   The Mother's Lineage: Kinship Certainty and Occupational Ambiguity 84
   The Status Relations of the Mother's and Father's Lineages 86
7. The Wives of Government Leaders 90
   Wives and Husbands 90
   Education, Marriage, and Occupational Mobility 96
   Marriage and Achievement 101
   Nativity, Geographic Origins, and Marriage 101

Part IV. Education

8. The Education of Federal Executives 107
   College Training and the Federal Elites 107
   Father's Occupation and College Education 110
   Education Levels of Executives and Their Fathers 113
   Education Levels of Federal and Business Executives 113
   What Kind of Higher Education Do They Get? 115
   Advanced Degrees and Father's Occupation 116
   Academic Areas in Which They Took Degrees 120
9. The Colleges and Universities That Produce Executives 126
   The Colleges and Universities Where They Were Trained 131
   Occupational Mobility and Individual Institutions 141

Part V. The Careers of Federal Executives

10. Career Lines 149
    Career Patterns of Business and Federal Executives 154
    Career Pattern and Father's Occupation 156
    Father's Occupation and Scalar Position 161
    Achievement Time in Careers of Executives 164

Contents ix

11. The Careers of Women in the Federal Executive 177
　　The Jobs They Do 180
　　The Occupational Background from Which They Come 182
　　The Nativity of Women Executives 183
　　The Education of Women Executives 184

PART VI. THE PRIVATE AND PUBLIC WORLDS OF THE FEDERAL EXECUTIVES

12. Personalities of Federal Executives 191
　　Method for Evaluating Personality Data 191
　　Personality and Its Variations 193
　　Variations in Style 195
　　The Federal Executive by Grade Classification 201
　　Three Personality Profiles 205
　　His Family 211
13. Professional Pride and the Value of Service 221
　　Career: Its Ideals and Ideas 223
　　The Social Image—An Elite 229
　　They View Themselves 230
14. The World of the Civilian Executive 237
　　The World of Civilian Executives: An Abstraction 238
　　The Conflicting Demands of the Executive Role 243

APPENDIX A. THEORY AND METHOD 253

　　Theory and Literature 253
　　Methods and Techniques 262
　　The Final 1959 Questionnaires 265
　　The Questionnaire Returns and Their Accuracy 288
　　The Selection of Population to Be Studied 297
　　The Use of Census Data in the Study 308

APPENDIX B. SUPPLEMENTARY TABLES

　　(see page 315 for listing)

INDEX 401

Text Tables

	Page
1. Occupations of Fathers of 1959 Civilian Federal Executives	29
2. Occupations of Fathers of 1952 Business Leaders	36
3. Distribution of 1959 Civilian Federal Executives by Region of Birth and 1910 Adult Population by Region of Residence	43
4. Comparison of Geographical Mobility and Size of Birthplace of 1952 Business Leaders and 1959 Federal Executives	53
5. Ratio of Size of Birthplace of 1952 Business Leaders and 1959 Federal Executives and Size of Community of Residence of U.S. Population	58
6. Comparison of Nativity of 1959 Federal Executives and U.S. Population in 1950 with 1952 Business Leaders and U.S. Population in 1940	62
7. Place of Birth as a Factor in Occupational Mobility: Ratio of Proportion of U.S. Adult Males in Occupation to Proportion of Fathers of 1952 and 1959 Executives in Occupation, by Two Nativity Groups	66
8. Patterns of Occupational Mobility for 1959 Civilian Federal Executives: Mobility Ratios of Six Occupational Groups	74
9. Patterns of Occupational Mobility for 1959 Military Executives: Mobility Ratios of Seven Occupational Groups	79
10. Ratios of Stability and Occupational Continuity for the Several Services (from Executive's Paternal Grandfather to His Father)	82
11. Comparison of Occupation of Father's Father and Mother's Father for All Services	87

Text Tables

Page

12. Occupational Origins of Executives' Wives and Mothers (for the Several Services) — 93
13. Education and Marriage by the Occupation of Spouse's Father — 98
14. Ratios of Educational Levels of Men in the Elites to Educational Levels of U.S. Adult Males — 109
15. Percentages, by Father's Occupation, of Men in the Elites at Four Levels of Education — 111
16. Areas of Specialization by Type of Service at the Four-Year Level — 121
17. Types of Institutions from Which Four-Year Degrees Were Received — 128
18. Summary of Men at Each of the Education Levels Who Reported Degrees from Public and Private Institutions — 129
19. Thirty Institutions Which Produced the Largest Number of Four-Year Degrees Reported by Civilian Executives — 132
20. Thirty Institutions Which Produced the Largest Number of Federal Executives with Doctoral Degrees — 138
21. Civilian Executives from Each Occupational Origin Group Who Received Four-Year Degrees from Twenty Institutions, in Rank Order — 142
22. Proportions of Men from Three Occupational Origin Groups Who Received Doctor of Philosophy Degrees from Twenty Institutions — 145
23. Career Sequence of 1959 Civilian Federal Executives — 150
24. Fathers' Occupations and Career Patterns of Civilian Federal Executives — 157
25. Occupations of Fathers of 1959 Civilian Federal Executives at Several GS Levels or Equivalent — 163
26. Average Age of Entering Public Service or Business and Father's Occupation for the Several Elites — 166
27. Total Number of Organizations During Executive's Career — 170
28. Women in the Higher and Lower Ranks of Federal Government in 1959 — 179
29. Career Sequence of 1959 Federal Women Executives — 185

Preface

Between the original idea for the study of the federal executives and the published report as it appears in this volume, the time and work of many people—members of the research team and people in other organizations—supported the research. Not all can be mentioned in this brief review, and simple naming of them here is insufficient recognition of the long hours of devoted work they gave to the study. Neither is it sufficient compensation for their ideas and solutions of problems which have been interwoven into the finished product.

The Carnegie Corporation of New York granted the funds which made the research possible, but the contribution of the Carnegie Corporation did not end there. Their people, and especially John Honey, through careful and considered attention to the development of the research, contributed much to the study.

Five men whose names are widely known in American life agreed to stand as sponsors of the research:

> Chester I. Barnard, New York City
> John Jay Corson, Arlington, Virginia
> Lewis Douglas, New York City
> Clarence Francis, New York City
> Otto L. Nelson, Jr., New York City.

The willingness of these men to vouch for the value of the work contributed greatly to the willingness of federal employees to participate. (Chester Barnard's recent death was a great shock to all of us; some of us knew him intimately, all of us knew him professionally and greatly admired the man and his work.)

Some of the people to whom we are most deeply indebted

are members of the federal government who aided us throughout all stages of the research and assisted in many ways in solving some of our most difficult problems. It is impossible to name all or most of them; however, we feel that some names, because of the important contributions they made to the success of our enterprise must be mentioned. Our liaison officers were O. Glenn Stahl, Director of the Bureau of Programs and Standards for the Civil Service Commission; Ross Pollock, Chief of the Career Development Section, for the U.S. Civil Service Commission; Joseph E. Winslow, for the White House, representing the office of Rocco C. Siciliano, Presidential Special Assistant for Personnel Management. For military liaison we express thanks to the Office of the Assistant Secretary of Defense for Manpower, Personnel and Reserve, and especially Major General Ned D. Moore, U.S.A., Director of the Office of Personnel Policy; Leon L. Wheeless, Staff Director, Civilian Personnel Policy Division, and his assistant William C. Valdes; Rear Admiral Bernard J. Clarey, U.S.N., Staff Director, Military Personnel Policy Division, together with Colonel Paul V. Tuttle, Jr., U.S.A., and Lieutenant Colonel Elizabeth C. Smith, U.S.A.

Others in Washington were of major assistance to our work, among them Roger W. Jones, Chairman of the U.S. Civil Service Commission; its Executive Director and present Chairman of the Commission, John W. Macy, Jr.; Warren B. Irons, Executive Director of the Commission; Flora M. Nicholson, Chief, Employment Statistics Office, U.S. Civil Service Commission; Ida F. Fugett, Administrative Assistant to Dr. Stahl; and Harold H. Leich, Chief of the Program Planning Division. Although we do not present the individual names of the personnel directors of the various federal agencies, we wish to express publicly our gratitude for the decisive help they gave us during the planning of the field period of our research. Many of them placed information concerning our project in their departmental and agency publications; others provided essential names to complement our listings and still others contributed understanding to significant issues and problems. We want to

Preface

speak particularly of Melville Hosch, Director, Department of Health, Education, and Welfare, Regional Office, Chicago, Illinois.

Originally the research was begun under the joint aegis of Cornell University and the University of Chicago, where it was based. Lawrence Kimpton, then Chancellor of the University of Chicago, and Chauncey Harris, Dean of the Division of the Social Sciences, gave active and sympathetic support to the undertaking. In the autumn of 1959 the research group moved from Chicago to Michigan State University. Alfred Seelye, Dean of the College of Business and Public Administration, and Associate Dean Kullervo Louhi became active and forceful administrative associates of the undertaking. Throughout the research, President Deane W. Malott of Cornell University actively cooperated with our work and was of assistance in helping with our list of advisory board members.

The field staff and those who worked on the analysis made the progress and completion of the work possible. We wish to acknowledge their contributions by mentioning the names of those who were of assistance in preparing and collecting the data. At the University of Chicago the following people were involved in the field work and the analysis: Cyril W. Brosnan, Anne Brown, John T. Brown, James A. Blumberg, Eleanor A. Coup, Thomas N. Jones, Harold Kooden, Millicent Lentz, John D. McCaffrey, Joyce McCaffrey, Stanley J. Schechter, Kirpal Singh, Suse Singh, Hildegard Sletteland, Madelaine Smothers, Isabella Steinberg, Lawrence Steinberg, John R. Terwinkle, Hilda Weissman, and John K. White. Students at Cornell University helped work up some of the literature and history of the federal executive. They were Roger H. Jones, Mary Helen McClanahan, and Emile S. Shihadeh. The officers of the Cornell ROTC staff helped with a pilot study. At the latter part of the research, after it moved to Michigan State, a number of young social scientists helped us with the analysis of the materials. They were: Bobara Barr, Terry B. Clark, Kenneth D. Eerwin, Arnold D. Gooder, John Maurer, John C. Moffett, Paul Sands, John H. Trimm, Gary E. Warriner, and Edward A. Woods.

The four colleagues who planned and directed the research and wrote the results functioned variously. The first three authors originated and planned the research. Orvis Collins soon joined as director of field operations and analysis. There was close collaboration of the four throughout the study, so that all parts of it were directly aided by the thought and work of each. However, each chapter, as indicated on its first page, was written by the appropriate individual or team. All chapters were first read, criticized, and edited by each; all were then given to the senior author for final editing. (He had the assistance of a professional editor, see below.) The final draft is thus a joint product.

The present work is built directly on the previous study of business leaders. We wish to thank Dr. James Abegglen, now with the firm of McKinsey and Co., for his earlier contributions to the business leader study and for his criticism and advice about the present research on federal executives.

Two very able professional men, Professors William E. Henry and Benjamin Wright, of the University of Chicago, aided as consultants on special problems. John H. Simms and Roger Coup did the bulk of the analysis of the Thematic Apperception Test protocols, under the close guidance of Professor Henry. Dr. Wright acted as statistical consultant and aided in clarifying a method of statistical analysis and reporting which is simple and direct.

Dr. Darab B. Unwalla joined the research group after the data-gathering process was completed and assumed an important role in helping with the undertaking. Ruth Maki worked on the statistical analysis. While the research was at the University of Chicago, Alice Chandler participated in the formulation of the questionnaire, its circulation to federal executives, and in many other capacities. Paul Lunt, an old colleague and one of the authors of the Yankee City series, greatly assisted us by interviewing certain members of the Cabinet and other high officials in Washington.

Mildred Hall Warner edited first drafts of the manuscript, later those that went to the publisher, and thereafter helped prepare the final one used for the present volume.

During the latter part of the writing the Yale University Press and its talented editors gave valuable counsel, excellent editorial advice, and materially aided in making the final results a better document.

We wish to thank all of these competent and helpful colleagues. Writing acknowledgments is never a satisfactory task. As we indicated at the beginning, each name and others that might have been mentioned could only be justly dealt with by a long statement telling what each did and his high significance for the completion of the research. All we can do here is to say once again thank you, and thank you very much.

THE AUTHORS

PART I

Introduction

CHAPTER 1

Image of the Bureaucrat

What the Book Is About

Americans are often suspicious of the people who hold bureaucratic offices. Sitting in a distant city, removed and insulated from reality, the bureaucrat, it is sometimes believed, can make only wrong decisions in terms of individual and local needs. Associated with this view is the idea that he is probably working for the government because he cannot hold his own in the rough world of free competition, the business world; his government position is a refuge. The fact that the American commonwealth underpays many officials is used as an indictment of their qualifications. Because a government employee may be earning $15,000 a year while his business counterpart is earning $30,000, the inference is freely drawn that the government man is not capable of performing at a $30,000-a-year level.

These men who occupy high position in the great civilian and military hierarchies of the federal government of the United States, for good or evil, exercise increasing power. They are far more influential, now and potentially, than their nineteenth-century predecessors and even those of only three or four decades ago.

Americans may argue the merits and necessities of this trend, but all would agree that the increased military and political

Authors of this chapter: W. Lloyd Warner and Paul P. Van Riper.

strength of their country in world affairs, supported by an expanding domestic economy, a rising population, and an advancing scientific technology, is swiftly changing both the environment and function of government as well as the requirements for the effective administration of public affairs. This is especially true at the national level. New international obligations and forces are requiring action in national terms; new kinds of federal laws are regulating our local commerce for national purposes; new concepts of taxation are supporting immense national civil and military establishments; and new interpretations are governing the rights and privileges of all citizens throughout our nation-state. Despite the great diversity and heterogeneity in American society and the increasing division of labor, a growing integration of our regional life into a unified social system has tended to move ultimate authority toward the central government. All this has vastly added to the responsibilities, duties, authority, and power of the men who manage our nation.

This increasingly great impact of government and public affairs upon almost all aspects of American life suggests, in turn, the importance of further attention to the crucial role of all government executives, particularly those in the federal government. However, this role cannot be fully understood, much less carefully considered in terms of the future, without more knowledge concerning the social origin, education, mobility, attitude, and personality structure of those who occupy these positions of trust and responsibility.

The Purposes of the Research

The first of several primary purposes was to find out what kinds of men and women are in the highest civilian and military positions of the federal government: who they and their families are; what they are like as individuals; where they come from; whether they are representative of the kinds of citizens ordinarily found in America.

The second purpose was to discover how government leaders

reached their positions, what routes they took, and what career lines were formed by their movement to the top.

The third was to learn how the leaders of the federal government compare in these respects with American big business leaders. Does the spirit of equality and democracy, characteristic of citizenship in America, operate in such a way that sons of men modestly placed have more opportunity to reach the top in government hierarchies than in big business?

An earlier study of big business leaders[1] demonstrated that higher education plays an increasingly important role in helping men climb to the top and in aiding those born to high position to stay there. Do government men use education as often and in the same way? Are they more or less highly educated than men in big business? Certain colleges and universities are reputed to be reserved primarily for sons and daughters of the American elite. Are government leaders likely to attend these institutions or those run by states and cities and private enterprise whose reputations are based primarily on other grounds?[2]

From a broad base of knowledge about the education of big business and government executives, it seemed possible that general inferences about our higher educational system could be drawn.

For both business and federal executives, nativity was studied—foreign or native, proportions by state and region, distribution by cities, towns, and rural areas—so that broad generalizations could be made. Family and family position, important to a career, were studied for occupational background of the father, the father's father, and the mother's father to learn about influences of several generations of marriage, descent, and occupation.

The personalities of civilian federal executives (as of busi-

---

1. Warner and Abegglen, *Occupational Mobility in American Business and Industry* (University of Minnesota Press, 1955) and *Big Business Leaders in America* (New York, Harper, 1955). The present study was based on this previous study of all varieties of big business leaders in the United States. Exact comparisons can be made between government and business elites.
2. See Orvis F. Collins, "The Education of Federal Executives" (unpublished M.A. thesis, University of Chicago, 1961).

ness leaders) were examined through projective techniques, depth interviews, and other procedures for common psychological characteristics and variances within the group and between the two groups. These findings are significant in the career and in the decisions the executives make for their organizations and for the country.

What is the relation of the social backgrounds and personalities of federal executives to the kinds of beliefs, values, and ideologies they hold? Are their beliefs and values fundamentally like those of big business leaders and other Americans who hold high positions of responsibility and authority?

Our first objectives reached, we could then move toward our basic purpose: to draw broad generalizations about the representative character of the American federal bureaucracy and, in turn, about the nature of occupational mobility and succession in American society as a whole.

Although this report does not directly concern itself with such matters, it was expected that fulfillment of these prior objectives would result in information and insights, comparative and otherwise, relevant not only to education in our universities for public service but also to such basic and continuing administrative problems as executive recruitment, management development, and the definition of career perspectives and opportunities.

Finally, whatever the answers to these questions, what broad scientific and social significances about America can be derived from the two bodies of evidence about these important elites? What does the evidence about federal executives tell us concerning the conflicting theories of occupational and social mobility in this country? Is this a rigid society where there is little opportunity for the modestly placed to rise? All such broad questions of policy and fact necessarily relate to our values and beliefs about a representative bureaucracy.

Representative Bureaucracy: The Problem of Consequences

The concept of representative bureaucracy is important to this study because it is concerned with the institutional consequences of the mobility process, particularly as applied to government. Its importance stems primarily from a growing concern among political scientists with theories of responsibility: how vast civil and military bureaucracies can be kept responsive and responsible to the general public and its elected representatives. The idea that the social composition and the outlook of a civil or military bureaucracy have an important bearing upon its actions is by no means new; nor do advocates of this approach propose a civil or military establishment which in social origins, skills, and abilities would copy the total society. But they do imply that, to achieve democratic ideals, recruitment and promotion of personnel should be from all social, racial, and religious groups on the basis of ability.

Considerations of the institutional effects of increased representativeness in government and other hierarchies vary in their conclusions; much work must be done in the study of the consequences of various degrees and types of opportunity as they may affect the upper and lower levels of particular hierarchies. Consideration must also be given to the effects upon occupational and social mobility of the many renovations proposed for various elite groups by social, political, and administrative theorists or of the existing and developing programs in career lines, recruitment, promotion, and training.

The federal structure provides an especially significant field of inquiry into the problem of representative bureaucracy since, in both the civilian and (to a lesser degree) the military establishments, statutes and regulations attempt to keep them free of the typical barriers to occupational mobility. This suggests that the personnel at the top of these hierarchies—the civil and military elites—would be at least as representative of American society, in terms of both social characteristics and social ideals, as any elite group in the nation. Whether this is a fact in our national government, with respect to both the opportunity for upward mobility and the representativeness of the existing elite groups as we have defined them, is a basic question of this research.

Exact answers to this fundamental question, beginning with

the profiles that follow, are to be found in all chapters throughout the book. Ratios of the exact amount of representation of all kinds of populations, including economic and territorial, are given so that the reader can find how often and how much the kinds of people who make up the American population are over- or under-represented in the federal government.

The Research on Civilian and Military Leaders

The present volume reports on the careers of 12,929 civilian and military executives. The men and women of the career civil service, the foreign service, and those who have political appointments hold positions from Cabinet level to General Schedule (GS) grade level 14 or equivalent: 7,640 from the career civil service, 1,269 from the foreign service, and 1,865 with political appointments (plus 77 unclassifiable)—a total of 10,851 civilian employees. The military men are from the top levels of command, reaching from admirals and generals down to captains in the Navy and colonels in the Army, Air Force, and Marine Corps: 2,078 officers. The elite of all departments and all agencies, old and new, from State, Treasury, and Defense to Health, Education, and Welfare, from TVA to the Small Business Administration, in and out of Washington, were asked to supply evidence about themselves and their careers. Over 69 per cent of those receiving schedules filled them out and returned them.[3]

Quick insight into the enormous elaboration of the federal government's structure and functions and the huge expansion of its body of employees, particularly those in the executive branch, can be gained by a summary review of the civil and military personnel employed at different periods in our nation's history. Such information also assists in understanding the changing nature of the role and milieu of the federal executive

3. For a full description of the sample, field, and analytical procedures; for definitions of grade levels, and other distinctions; and for many other qualifications and operational procedures, see Appendix A. For supplementary tabular material, see Appendix B.

through time and helps to place in perspective the data of the present study, which relate to federal executives in the central months of 1959.

In 1792, when our government was three years old and the executive departments could be counted on the fingers of one hand, there were, excluding postmasters, nearly 800 civil officers in the executive service. Of these, more than 600 were in the Treasury Department, which also contained the largest field office in the government, that of the Collector of Customs in New York City, with nearly 40 employees.[4]

By 1801 the total had risen to some 3,000, of whom about 1,700 were in the Treasury and nearly 900 were postmasters. There were then only 35 civilians in the headquarters of the War and Navy Departments combined, and the main office of the Department of State in the capital employed only 9 people including the Secretary and a messenger. Then, as now, less than 10 per cent of federal office holders worked in Washington, D.C. or vicinity, representing a ratio which has remained fairly constant over a century and a half.[5] Despite its relatively small size, the federal government of 1801 was rivaled by only a few state governments and no business enterprises, which were quite small, few employing more than 100 persons. Even so, the entire federal establishment then comprised less than one-half of one per cent of the adult population; and the average annual federal budget for the previous decade was a bare five million dollars.

Throughout the nineteenth century our central government's organizational structure was simple. During this period there were never more than eight departments of cabinet rank, and

4. Calculated from "List of Civil Officers of the United States, except Judges, with Their Emoluments, for the Year Ending October 1, 1792," *American State Papers, Miscellaneous*, 1, 57–68. This is the first year for which there is reasonably accurate information, although it should be noted that all federal employment statistics prior to the 1880's, and some since, are approximate at best.

5. For 1801 see "Roll of the Officers, Civil, Military, and Naval, of the United States," ibid., pp. 260–319.

by 1900 there were still just a baker's dozen of agencies reporting directly to the President, whose "White House staff" was slightly increased in 1901 to three secretaries, six clerks, and a number of doorkeepers and messengers.[6] But the line of communications from top to bottom was steadily increasing, and by the Civil War the managerial levels of Assistant Secretary and Bureau Chief had been interposed between the Secretaries and their Chief Clerks. The creation of the Civil Service Commission in 1883 foreshadowed the need for better control and coordination of a growing number of differentiated functional activities. Indeed, it was only a few more years until the creation of the modern Army General Staff, the expansion of the concept of the independent regulatory commission, the adoption of the corporate form for the management of certain business-type government enterprises, the creation of the post of Under Secretary, and the submission of the detailed administrative analysis of President Taft's Commission on Economy and Efficiency of 1912, from which later derived the Bureau of the Budget and the General Accounting Office.[7]

The greatest expansion of governmental agencies, functions, and personnel began during the Great Depression. This story is well known. Total civil employment rose to about 950,000 just prior to World War II, mushroomed to over 3,800,000 in 1945, and then dropped back to approximately 2,000,000 between 1947 and 1950. The Korean War occasioned a rise to 2,600,000, followed by a plateau of around 2,350,000 for the executive branch plus another 27,000 or so for the com-

6. Leonard D. White, *The Republican Era* (New York, Macmillan, 1958), p. 102.
7. For details see Leonard D. White's well-known series of administrative histories and his *Trends in Public Administration* (New York, McGraw-Hill, 1933) and Paul P. Van Riper, *History of the United States Civil Service* (Evanston, Ill., Row, Peterson, 1958). The General Staff was created in 1903; the Interstate Commerce Commission was created in 1887, followed by the Federal Trade Commission in 1914; the Panama Railroad Co. was acquired in 1904; the first position of Under Secretary was created in 1919; and the Bureau of the Budget and the General Accounting Office were created by an act of 1921.

Image of the Bureaucrat 9

bined legislative and judicial services.[8] Agencies proliferated on a similar scale, and by 1937 the President's Committee on Administrative Management noted that the span of control represented by separate organizations reporting directly to the President had passed the 100 mark. Despite some further growth of agencies during World War II, various reorganization acts and orders have reduced this number to its present figure of 60 to 65 agencies of some importance. As of 1959, these could be classified as including at least 6 distinct units in the "executive office of the President," the 10 "departments," and approximately 45 "independent agencies"—some 61 in all. Executives from almost all of these agencies are included in the study.

The growth of our uniformed military services, representing the other great wing of the total "executive service," presents a somewhat different pattern. Like their civil counterparts, the military services were vastly expanded during wartime; but during peace they were cut back much more. Between 1800 and 1897 the Army grew from about 5,000 officers and enlisted men to 2,000 or so officers and 25,000 enlisted men, while the Navy and Marine Corps together expanded to less than 15,000. After the Spanish-American War the Navy grew proportionately much more rapidly during peacetime than the Army. By 1935 the former contained 95,500 men and the latter 138,000. Since World War II the combined military services—Army, Navy, Air Force, and Marine Corps—have never totaled less than something over 1,400,000 officers and

8. See U. S. Civil Service Commission, *76th Annual Report, 1959* (Washington, Government Printing Office, 1959), pp. 68–69, Table A–6, "Paid civilian employment of the Federal Government, 1816–1959." (Hereafter the U. S. Civil Service Commission will be cited as USCSC and its reports as, for example, *Annual Report, 1959.*) This and most other historical series on federal civil employment lump legislative and judicial in with executive employees; but the effect on totals is negligible since, between 1904 and 1959, for example, judicial employment expanded from about 2,900 to only 4,900 and legislative employment from about 1,750 to nearly 23,000. See Van Riper, pp. 198–200; USCSC, *Monthly Report of Federal Employment, July 1959,* p. 3.

men. By the spring of 1959 these four services were composed of 318,437 officers and 2,187,262 officer candidates and enlisted men, for a total of 2,505,699 men and women on active duty.[9] Thus, by the time of this study, the grand total of federal employment of all types had reached nearly 5,000,000 persons, engaged in a vast multitude of tasks at an annual expenditure of close to 80 billion dollars.

Civil and military government employment at all levels—federal, state, and local—approached by the end of the fifties a total of 10,500,000 persons; more than 90 per cent of whom were serving full time. That is, about 15 per cent of our total work force of nearly 70 million were serving our various governmental institutions in capacities involving at least 1,500 occupations and more than 15,000 of the 25,000 or so job titles found in American enterprise of all types. The central direction of this political and administrative edifice, at the national level, has been the principal function of the men whose composite portrait is the subject of the pages to follow.

Profiles of the Civilian Executives

Before going into a comprehensive analysis of the characteristics of each of the civilian services, we will present brief factual profiles of the men in the military and civilian services. To equip the reader with relevant evidence, a summary of the social characteristics of business leaders is given. The intention is to give an over-all view of the central tendencies of the more important social and economic characteristics of these executives.

For all civilian federal executives, the percentage differences between the maternal and paternal grandfathers' occupations

9. These various figures are derived from Leonard D. White, *The Federalists* (New York, Macmillan, 1948), p. 146; Solomon Fabricant, *The Trend of Government Activity in the United States since 1900* (New York, National Bureau of Economic Research, 1952), pp. 180–81; and Statistical Services Center, Office of the Secretary of Defense, "Military Personnel on Active Duty by Grade in Which Serving, 31 May, 1959," Table P26.0, August 4, 1959.

are not great, indicating that the two sides of the family come from similar origins. These men were born in all major regions of the country, with the South Central region (see map, p. 42) somewhat lower and the Mountain states and the West North Central somewhat higher than would be expected from the representation of these areas in the general population. They come from big cities in disproportionately high percentages, with a ratio of 182 for every 100 expected by chance; the ratio for small towns is 64 for every 100.

Fewer than one out of twenty were foreign born; and about one in five had foreign-born fathers.

Education was the principal preparation for advancement: nine out of ten have at least some college training, and eight of ten are college graduates. Less than one-half of one per cent have less than high-school education. Moreover, college education did not terminate with the A.B. degree: one-fourth have the M.A., one-tenth the Ph.D., and one-tenth a degree in law. Areas of specialization cover every field, from the humanities (9 per cent) and the behavioral sciences (16 per cent) to business administration (12 per cent) and engineering (33 per cent). As they advance from the A.B. to the Ph.D. the emphasis tends to be toward the behavioral, physical, and biological sciences.

Ten universities granted one-fifth of all the B.A. degrees: five are in the Big Ten (Minnesota, Illinois, Michigan, Wisconsin, Ohio State); two are West Coast (California at Berkeley and Washington); the one that led all others is in Washington, D.C. (George Washington University); one in New York City (City College of New York); and one in New England (Harvard). At the doctoral level, many of these colleges and universities drop out, and Harvard, Chicago, and Wisconsin lead.

Women executives are conspicuous by the small percentage of their representation in the civilian federal executive. Among the approximately 11,000 civilian federal executives in our sample, there are only 145 women. Among all full-time employees under the General Schedule salary system, 1959, there were 476,448 women, representing about half the total, yet only approximately 459 were at the top level of executive command. There are no women in our military sample; only a handful are in actual military service at the level of colonel or naval captain, with none at higher ranks.

Over a third of the fathers of women executives were professional men (34 per cent), 18 per cent were business executives, 14 per cent farmers, and 13 per cent skilled and unskilled workers.

Almost all the women federal executives had some college education, 88 per cent being graduates. Proportionately speaking, 978 out of every 100 that might be expected are college graduates and only 5 for every 100 are graduates of high school only. The women are not particularly different from male civilian federal executives in the amount of education that they acquired to compete for high positions in the federal government.

The fathers of the *career civil service executives* were well distributed among the several types present in the work force of the country. The highest percentage, almost 25 per cent, were laborers, most of them skilled workers or mechanics, then business executives and farmers, each with 15 per cent. The ratio between these percentages and those for the general population are significant. (If sheer chance were operating and each occupation were represented in the executives' background to the same degree as in the general population, the ratio, of course, would be 100.) Several of the nine types of occupation considered are over-represented among the career civil service executives. For instance, business executives are five times what might be expected, professional men four times, and skilled workers only slightly above. On the other hand, unskilled workers, white-collar workers, farm laborers, and farm tenants and owners are below expected representation.

For the latter occupations, in this and the other services, mobility often takes more than one generation. These occupations may have appeared among the grandfathers, whereas the fathers entered such urban occupations as laborer, small business owner, or white-collar worker.

The civil service executive entered his career when he was twenty-seven years of age; it took him seventeen years to achieve the position he held when studied by this research.

Among all civilian federal executives, there are more similarities than differences. The average age of the *politically appointed executive* is forty-nine; he began his career when he was thirty; and it took him fifteen years to arrive at his present position.

Almost one-fourth of the political executives had fathers who were professional men, followed by business owners and executives with over a third, combined; these are followed by laborers and farmers with 15 and 13 per cent.

Interpreting these figures as ratios gives somewhat different emphasis; business executives and large business owners rank first, followed by professional men, foremen, and owners of small business with ratios over expectancy, while all other occupations are below.

In geographic origin, these executives come first from the Middle Atlantic states, with New York leading; then from the East North Central, with Illinois first, followed by the West North Central, the South Atlantic, and the Mountain and Pacific states. The proportions of political executives seem to follow those of the general population, geographically.

Native, foreign born, and native with foreign-born fathers or grandfathers, among this group, closely approximate the pattern for the general population: about 59 per cent are native with fathers and paternal grandfathers also native, and about 16 per cent are native and with native fathers but foreign-born grandfathers. About 17 per cent are native with foreign-born fathers, and some 5 per cent of these executives are of foreign birth. In ratios, foreign-born executives are underrepresented, in terms of the general population, and the others are slightly over.

All of the federal executives are highly educated, and a very high percentage of each service are college graduates; but among all the services the politically appointed executives lead —90 per cent are college graduates and 7 per cent have some college. In ratios there are 1,121 college men for every 100 expected and only 9 with high-school education for every 100. About three-fourths of these men have the A.B. degree; a fifth, the M.A.; about 13 per cent the Ph.D.; and 40 per cent a degree in law. Only a very few have M.D. degrees. In advanced degrees these executives far surpass the general population. About half went to private colleges and universities, about 43 per cent attended public colleges and universities, and the rest went to technical or foreign institutions.

Foreign-service officers are always a special target of people opposed to the American public servant. The foreign-service officer is repeatedly represented as an Ivy League boy who inherited wealth; a man without imagination or ability who was sent to the best schools and ultimately got the best job. Although foreign-service executives do come in greater than expected proportions from high prestige occupational groups, it is certainly not true that the foreign service is exclusively the domain of people of such origin.

Twenty-five per cent of the fathers of foreign-service executives were professional men, leading all others, followed by business executives and owners, with 20 and 19 per cent, and laborers, farmers, and white-collar workers. Only 2 per cent had fathers in some kind of federal service.

A different story is told by the ratios of these figures to the general population, for business executives and owners lead with 800 for every 100 that might be expected, professional men come next with 625 for every 100, followed by small business with 171, and foremen with 150. All other occupations are below expectancy.

Since professional background appears to be important, we will consider each profession: fathers who were professors lead all others—2,750 for every 100 that might be expected; then ministers, 1,190; lawyers, 1,000; engineers, 492; and last, teachers, 190.

In regional origins, the Middle Atlantic states come first (New York leading), followed by the East North Central (Illinois first), West North Central (Missouri), and—trailing

—the South Atlantic (with Virginia first). The South Central region is in last place, following the Pacific and Mountain states. This pattern of regional background is rather similar to that of the career civil service and political executives and follows closely the rank-order percentages for all civilian federal executives.

Sixty-three per cent of all executives in the foreign service and their fathers and grandfathers are native; 15 per cent and their fathers are native born, and slightly more are native of foreign-born fathers. Only 5 per cent of these executives are foreign born. The ratios show close correspondence with the general population.

Eighty-eight per cent of foreign-service executives have college degrees and another 10 per cent had at least some college. Only 2 per cent are high-school graduates. For every 100 that would be expected from proportions in the general population, 613 of these executives are college graduates. Eighty-one per cent have A.B. degrees, 33 per cent M.A.'s, 13 per cent Ph.D.'s, 8 per cent degrees in law, and slightly over 1 per cent have degrees in medicine. Over half attended private colleges and universities; two-fifths, public institutions; the remainder went to technical institutions or one of the academies of the United States Government.

The average age of the executive of the foreign service when he was studied was forty-eight. He had taken some eighteen years to reach his position. Prior to entering the service he had, typically, worked in many private and public activities. Rather than being a parochial domain of a handful of men from the Atlantic seaboard, the foreign service has representation from all over the United States.

Profiles of the Military Executives

Closely coupled to the foreign-service officer as a target of attack is the military officer. The notion that through the generations a military dynasty has developed in the United States is often expressed. It is felt that high command may be increasingly handed down from father to son. Our data show that a sizable but still small minority had military fathers. Military men, like foreign service and political and career civil service executives, are drawn from the whole country. They are highly professionalized, although often in a much narrower sense than other federal executives.

The occupations of the fathers of the military executives are similar to those of the civilian federal executives. Business executives outrank all others with 20 per cent but are almost tied by business owners, with 19 per cent, and professional men, 18 per cent. Laborers are not far behind with 14 per cent, followed by white-collar workers, 9 per cent. The point of marked difference from other federal executives is that, whereas they did not have fathers in government occupation, 9 per cent of the military had fathers in the uniformed services. The continuity between generations that is lacking in the other federal services is revealed to at least some degree in the military, which in this respect, indeed, has established some kind of tradition.

Five general occupations are over-represented in the backgrounds of military executives: business executives and owners of large business, uniformed and other government occupations, professional men, and foremen and owners of small business.

Within the important professional category, military executives show some variations from the other services: lawyers lead all others with 1,133 for every 100; followed by doctors with over 900; professors, 750; engineers, 431; and ministers, 405. Sons of professors drop noticeably for military leaders—especially from the ratio in the foreign service.

There is some but not great variation in the geographical origins of military executives. The Middle Atlantic and East North Central regions tie with 16 per cent each, closely followed by East North Central (14 per cent), South Atlantic (12 per cent), and West South Central (11 per cent). Last are the Mountain and Pacific states with 7 per cent each.

The military lead all others for having at least three generations of native ancestry: over 71 per cent are native born of

Image of the Bureaucrat

native fathers and paternal grandfathers and less than 2 per cent are foreign born, the lowest for any service. The ratios to the general population are 116 to 100 for native born with father and father's father native born and 21 to 100 for foreign born.

The percentage of college graduates among the military leaders is very high: about nine out of ten have at least an A.B. degree, and only 2 per cent are high-school graduates. Twenty-four per cent have Master's degrees, only 1 per cent (the lowest of any service) have the Ph.D., 4 per cent a law degree, and a few have an M.D. degree. As to the institutions they attended, 62 per cent went to technical institutes or a United States academy, 26 per cent to public colleges or universities, and 12 per cent to private colleges and universities.

The officers of the Army, Navy, and Air Force who were part of this study (see elsewhere for the levels included) were on the average fifty years of age at the time studied; they had been in the service for twenty-five years; and had started their careers at the age of twenty-three.

Comparison of the Civilian and Military Services

In comparing the civilian with the military federal executives, we find that the occupational backgrounds of the former tend to be spread more through the general population. The ratios for these two categories of service confirm this. For every 100 sons of business executives or of owners of a large business that might be expected, there are 570 in the civilian federal executive and 700 in the military; for every 100 sons of professional men, 480 in the civilian executive and 450 in the military; foremen, 250 in the civilian and also 250 in the military; owners of small business, 200 for civilian and 185 for the military. Sons of skilled laborers have a ratio of 113 for the civilian and only 80 for the military; farm tenants or owners, 88 for the civilian and only 56 for the military; white-collar, 75 for the civilian and the same for the military; unskilled and semiskilled workers, a low ratio of 12 for the civilian executives but an even lower ratio, 6, for the military.

Within the professions as occupational background, there is considerable difference between the civilian and military executives: professors lead all others in the civilian group with a ratio of 1,400 for every 100 that might be expected, compared with 750 for the military. On the other hand, lawyers have a much higher proportion among the military—1,100 for every 100—than among the civilian—850 for every 100. The clergy have a higher ratio among the civilians—670 compared with 400; doctors reverse this with 930 among the military and 600 among the civilian executives. Differences between the two services for engineers and for teachers are not very great.

Broadly speaking, the backgrounds of the military and civilian executives are similar whether we are considering occupation, region, or state of origin. They are also similar in level of education; but military executives had often attended the United States academies, where, with their specific purposes, higher education differs as a variety.

The Executives of American Big Business and Big Government

American big business executives differ in many respects from American federal executives, but in broad outline they are far more alike than different in social and economic characteristics, including family and occupation as well as educational attainments. A brief summary of these characteristics of big business leaders will establish a comparative base for the discussion which follows. (What is said here is a paraphrase from a summary in Warner and Abegglen, *Occupational Mobility in American Business and Industry*, pp. 23–36.)

There are four categories of occupation over-represented in the backgrounds of big business and four under-represented. For every 100 that might be expected from their proportion in the general population, there are approximately 800 sons of business leaders, 400 sons of small business men, about 400 sons of professional men, and slightly over 100 sons of foremen. For every 100 expected there are only 80 sons of clerks and salesmen, 60 sons of skilled laborers, and 40 or 50 sons of farm tenants and owners. Fewer than 20 of the expected

100 turn up for the semiskilled or unskilled and almost none for sons of farm laborers.

The geographical regions of the United States contributed unevenly to the group of business leaders. (The following figures are corrected for the size of the population in each of the regions.) The Middle Atlantic states rank first (a ratio of 147), the New England states second (143), and the Pacific Coast states third (133). The southern states, including the East South Central, West South Central, and South Atlantic regions, produced a disproportionately smaller share. These regional differences seem to be related to differences in standards of living and education. A comparison of the present distribution of business leaders with place of birth shows that a sizable number left New England and the West North Central states and that a considerable proportion moved into the Middle Atlantic and Pacific regions. The movement to and from regions is not random but likely to take place in a fairly definite pattern.

The size of a man's birthplace, like the region in which he is born, plays a part in occupational mobility. Most of the men of the business elite were born in big cities. When the proportions of the business leaders born in the several sizes of community are compared with the proportions for the total population, it is found that relatively few are from small town or rural backgrounds. When the occupation of father, the region of birth, and the size of birthplace are considered together, the very small number of men from the small town and rural South in business leadership is sharply revealed.

Most of the business leaders were college men and well over half were college graduates. Seventy-six per cent of the men studied had gone to college; 57 per cent had graduated, 19 per cent had not. One-fifth of the whole group not only had graduated but had gone on to advanced graduate study. Comparatively, the American businessman tends to be highly educated: whereas 76 of every 100 had gone to college, only 13 of every 100 adult males (30 years and over) in the general population had some college training; 57 of every 100 business leaders had graduated, as compared with 7 of every 100 in the general population.

More than half the adult males in the general population had not attended high school, compared with only 4 of 100 business leaders. Nine per cent of the leaders had some high school but did not graduate, and 11 per cent graduated but did not go on to college, compared with 16 per cent in each of these two categories in the general population.

In general, business leaders originating from all levels went to college, and those from higher levels attended and graduated from college in higher proportions. Another moderately accurate measure of the effect of occupational rank on education is obtained from a comparison of the percentages of men of diverse origins who did not graduate from high school. Whereas only 3 per cent of the sons of professional men and 3 per cent of the sons of business leaders left school before graduating from high school, one-third of the sons of unskilled and semi-skilled laborers and one-fourth of the sons of skilled laborers failed to go on. The other levels fell between the two extremes.

Education is now one of the principal avenues to business leadership. The mobile men use it in greatly increased numbers in their drive to places of leadership and power. Education clearly helps many from all levels to reach the top, yet financial and other restrictions on access to higher education are also important factors in the maintenance of occupational inheritance by the elite.

The average business leader in our study had almost reached his fifty-fourth birthday (53.7 years). He entered business a few months after reaching his majority (21.4 years). It took him almost twenty-four years to reach his present business position. Occupational origin has an effect on the age of entering business: sons of laborers became self-supporting earlier (before reaching nineteen) than those of any other occupational category. The sons of professional men and businessmen did not enter business until they were nearly twenty-two.

The length of time it took to reach a top business position was shortest for the sons of major executives (20.6 years) and longest for the sons of laborers (26 years). The sons of farmers took about a year less than those of laborers (25.1 years). On the whole, territorial mobility, while an integral part of the mobility process, seems to be related to retarding the career, although some men would probably not have advanced so far if they had not been territorially mobile. Men who move about a lot tend to achieve business leadership later than those who stay closer to home.

Approximately half of the wives of the business leaders studied (51 per cent) were the daughters of business or professional men, and about one-sixth were from the laboring class. Men born to high station married women from similar backgrounds in greater proportion than did any other class: but in general the men married women from their own occupational level more than from any other group of women. The men whose fathers were white-collar workers married out of their occupational origins more than any others; men with laboring, farming, and big business backgrounds were more likely than others to marry within their occupational origins. In general, both endogamic and exogamic factors—marriage within and outside one's group—seem to be operating in the choice of mates. Flexibility, individual choice, freedom to go beyond the confines of the occupational level—all are exhibited in the marriages made by the business leaders.

The question arises as to the effect of in- and out-marriage on the careers of these men. The sons of the elite who married the daughters of laborers took 23 years to achieve positions at the executive level; those who married at their own level took 2 years longer. The laborer who "married the boss's daughter" took almost exactly the amount of time for achievement as the one who married someone from his own level of origin (25.9 years for the first, 26.1 for the latter). The general effect of marriage on the career is quite similar for all categories; there is only a limited range of difference in time for the careers of men who marry above or below their occupational origins. The status of the wife generally does not have a direct effect on accelerating the career of the business leader.

In broad review big business and government executives, insofar as their social and economic characteristics are concerned, are more alike than not, yet differences are present and significant. Both derive more often and significantly from the higher occupations, but the range of occupations of their fathers runs from the top to the lowest levels. The proportions of federal executives are somewhat more evenly spread through all occupational levels. Variations in regional origins for the two are present, yet in general their territorial origins are more alike than different. Their birthplaces tend to be similar; for example, the big cities are disproportionately high for both business and government men. The business leaders take longer to reach high position, and they are correspondingly older than the federal executives. Both groups are highly educated, far above the average citizen, but the government men are significantly more often college graduates and holders of higher degrees. Moreover, higher education for both groups is not just for the sons of the highly placed fathers but is available to, and increasingly used by, the talented who come from the lower levels of society to occupy high position in government and business.

In the broadest sense, the research on business and government executives indicates that at the levels studied American society is not becoming more caste-like; the recruitment of business leaders from the bottom is taking place now and has been slowly increasing for the last quarter century. In spite of the pessimistic predictions about an immobilized society, this evidence shows that our society, although much like what it has been in past generations, is more flexible than it was; more men and their families are in social motion.

Despite these facts, there is strong evidence of the operation of rank and the effects of high birth in the selection of the American business and government elites. Men born to the top have more advantages and are more likely to succeed than those born farther down. There is not full freedom of competition; the system is still sufficiently status-bound to work to the considerable advantage of men born to higher position.

Fathers at the elite levels still find it possible to endow their sons with greater opportunity, but, in business and in all probability in government, they do so now in decreased numbers.[10] The sons of men from the wrong side of the tracks are finding their way increasingly to the places of power and prestige. The values of competitive and open status are higher today than yesterday and those of inherited position and fixed position, while still powerful, are less potent now than they were a generation ago.

10. Earlier study of business executives (1928) allows precise comparison between today and yesterday; precise measurements of federal leaders of previous periods are not available, but incomplete evidence indicates more mobility to higher places today.

PART II

Social Origins: How Representative of America Are They?

CHAPTER 2

Fathers and Sons: Occupational Origins

One of the basic questions about the nature and representative character of the federal executives is whether they come from all occupational levels in the American society. Do their fathers occupy only the elite positions in business, government, and the professions? Or do the sons of laborers and white-collar workers, of farmers and small business men, move into the higher levels of the federal services? This is the critical nexus of occupational succession and biological continuity, broadly speaking—that between the continuity of the social structure and the generational processes of the species.

We want to know the similarities and differences in occupational origin among the executives in the several services—whether, for example, the men in the career civil service more often come from lower occupational levels than those with political appointments or in the foreign service. We can then compare the civilian with the military, and all federal executives in our study, including the military, with the general population to discover which groups are over- or under-represented as measured by their percentages in the total work force.

We do not have as accurate and precise information about the previous generations of federal leaders as we did in the Taussig-Joslyn study of 1928 for big business leaders,[1] and

Author of this chapter: W. Lloyd Warner.
1. F. W. Taussig and C. S. Joslyn, *American Business Leaders* (New York, Macmillan, 1932).

thus we cannot determine whether or not the trends from the previous generation are toward more mobility from the lower occupational levels into the higher rungs of the governmental hierarchy. But since the methodology for the study of the federal leaders of 1959 is precisely the same as for the big business leaders of the 1952 study, we can ask this question: Do federal executives proportionately come from all levels of society more often than the leaders of big business? Are men in certain services more like business leaders in occupational origin than others? Comparison of the father's occupation between men from the two most powerful kinds of hierarchies, government and business, can tell us how much mobility there is from the several occupational levels for these two generations.

The Origins of Civilian Federal Executives

Table 1 presents a general list of seven occupations with a breakdown into twenty-two groups. The occupation of the father is given as of the time when the federal executive left home to begin his own occupational career. The largest group of civilian federal executives is from the laborer class; and business owners, professional men, business executives, and farmers follow closely, in that order.

The sons of professional men rank high; the principal professions include doctors, engineers, lawyers, and ministers. The category, "Other professional," is composed primarily of teachers and professors.

Farmers, present in fairly substantial numbers, are most frequently from the owner and manager group with paid help, the most highly placed among the four varieties listed. Finally, in "Other occupations," a very small percentage come from the uniformed service and from government service, composing no more than 1 per cent of the total. It seems clear that the men whose fathers were in government make up a very unsubstantial number, that there is little tendency to succeed fathers who have been in either higher or lower positions of civilian or military government service.

More accurate understanding of the meaning of the occupa-

Table 1

Occupation of Fathers of 1959 Civilian Federal Executives

Occupation of Father

Laborer		21%
Unskilled or semiskilled	3.5%	
Skilled worker or mechanic	17.0	
White-collar worker		9
Clerk or retail salesman	3.8	
Salesman	5.3	
Business executive		15
Foreman	4.9	
Minor executive	5.9	
Major executive	4.6	
Business owner		20
Small business	14.3	
Medium business	4.3	
Large business	1.9	
Professional man		19
Doctor	2.5	
Engineer	3.1	
Lawyer	3.8	
Minister	2.8	
Other profession*	6.3	
Farmer		15
Farm tenant or farm worker	0.4	
Tenant with paid help	0.7	
Farm owner without paid help	6.5	
Owner or manager with paid help	7.1	
Other occupations		1
Uniformed service	0.7	
Government service	0.2	
Other occupation	0.4	
Total per cent	100.0	100
Total number 10,851		

*Composed primarily of professors and teachers.

tional background of these civilian federal executives can be derived by comparing the proportions here with those for the general population. Since the average age of our federal executives was approximately fifty years in 1960 and we want the occupations of their fathers at the time these men started supporting themselves, to compare with the general population, the census of 1930 is used.

Some 21 per cent of the fathers of civilian federal executives were skilled or unskilled laborers, but 48 per cent of the U.S. adult male population of 1930 were in this class. Only 4 per cent of the U.S. male population was in the professional class, yet 19 per cent of the fathers of federal executives were in this category. Less than 0.5 per cent of farm laborers' sons were in the federal executive, yet some 6 per cent, more than composed the class of professional men, were in the general population. A higher percentage of sons of foremen were in the federal executive than in the work force of the United States, and clerks and salesmen tended to be somewhat under-represented, whereas the sons of owners of small business were approximately double what might have been expected from the percentage in the general population. Perhaps significantly, and most importantly for our present purposes, we should note that skilled laborers were somewhat more represented in the civilian federal executive than in the general adult population for 1930.

A simple measurement makes possible exact comparisons among the several occupations to learn how well each fared in the civilian federal executive. We have already demonstrated that all occupational levels are represented, some more than others; in varying degrees there is occupational mobility from fathers to sons for most occupations. We must now ask what the exact comparisons are between the proportions of each occupation in the federal executive and of each in the general population.

By using a simple ratio of the proportion of each occupational group in the federal executive to that in the general male adult population of 1930, we can measure which groups are over- and under-represented. The principal sources of the 1959 civilian federal executives are disproportionately high for the business executive or owner of large business, which ranks above all others with 5.67; and for the sons of professional men, who follow with 4.75. Foremen follow with 2.5 and small business men with 2.0, both double or ·more what would be expected from their proportions in the general population. Perhaps the most significant ratio is for skilled laborers, which shows this class slightly over-represented with 1.13, or 113 for every 100 that might be expected if only chance were operating. Farm laborers, tenants and owners, clerks or salesmen, and semiskilled and unskilled laborers are under-represented.

Thus we can say that, compared with the general population, most of these men, with a notable exception, come from the more highly placed occupational levels; that their fathers tended to be in disproportionately high numbers from the executive or owner of large business class or from the comparably high position of professional men, including doctors, lawyers, ministers, and engineers. However, there are indications that some of the more lowly placed positions are also well represented, including skilled laborer and the somewhat underrepresented white-collar worker. Farmers are below what might be expected. The ratio of movement tends to be not so much up as across from the high positions of the professions into government. Still, there is definite movement from all classes of occupations and from all levels of society.

The Origins of Military Leaders

The officers in this group include 2,078 men in the Army, Navy, Air Force, and Marine Corps. They rank from admirals to Navy captains and from generals to full colonels. It is impossible to assess the comparability of all the levels in the civilian federal executive with those in the military group, or all the levels in the civilian and military with business leaders. We have attempted to examine men who occupy powerful positions in each of these hierarchies. All efforts to equate the positions (both by field work and by inquiry among men who had occupied positions in both the civilian and the military hierarchies as well as in business) failed to provide satisfactory operative answers. We therefore decided to use the comparative methods of anthropology and simply say that these were the highest positions, with the most power and prestige, in each type of hierarchy, and that consequently they had many elements of comparability.

Among the fathers of military leaders, the laboring group is no longer first, this rank being occupied by business execuives; business owners and professional men, with 19 and 18 per cent respectively, are a very close second and third. The laboring class comes fourth, followed by farmers and white-collar workers. Some 9 per cent of the military leaders, at the time they took up their own careers, had fathers who were in the military force.

Again, the higher of the subcategories are more likely to have sons in the military executive. For example, the officers whose fathers were skilled workers or mechanics compose some 12 per cent, while unskilled or semiskilled workers have only 1.9 per cent of the total, and sons of salesmen outrank clerks. However, among businessmen, minor executives far outrank major executives who are followed by foremen; and, among business owners, small business is more often represented than large business.

The sons of lawyers are more frequent than those of any other profession, followed by doctors, engineers, and ministers in that order. Later, since other professionals rank high, we shall reinspect this problem of representation from the professions.

Among those men whose fathers were farmers, the owners who had paid help or who were managers of large farms outrank all others, indicating that in the farming class those who go into military life are more likely to be from the superior groups.

From inspection of the broad occupational backgrounds of these men, the military leaders are more likely to come from more highly placed positions. Over half are sons of men who were in business or in the professional class. They are more likely to be urban than rural. Also, they come in some numbers from their own nuclear professional group.

In their ratios to the general population the sons of executives or owners of large business rank first, with seven times greater than chance expectation. The uniformed services rank second, the professions third, and foremen fourth with 2.5, meaning that for every 100 that might be expected there are 250 whose fathers were foremen. The owners of small business follow closely with 1.86.

All other categories of occupation are under-represented, beginning with skilled laborers, with 80 out of every 100 that might be expected, followed by clerks and salesmen with 75, farmers with only 56, and sons of unskilled laborers with only 6 for every 100 (0.06).

Generally speaking, leaders in the civilian federal services tend to represent the proportions of occupations in the general population more closely than do the military. For example, among military leaders the sons of big business leaders are present seven times more than expected from their proportions in the population, whereas this drops to 5.67 among civilian federal executives. On the other hand, the sons of professional men among civilians are in higher proportions than among military leaders. However, most significantly, the sons of civilian federal leaders, or for that matter any kind of government worker, are barely present among civilian leaders, whereas among the military leaders the uniformed services are represented five times more than would be expected from their proportions in the general population. This latter figure means, as we shall see later, that there is a solid core of continuing representation and perhaps "inherited" position from father to son among the leaders of the Army, Navy, Air Force, and Marine Corps.

The Professions as Sources of Federal Executives

Throughout our discussion of the sources of federal leadership, it is apparent that the professions contribute a disproportionately high percentage of federal leaders, not only for the civilian but also for each of the military services. Nineteen per cent of the civilian federal executives and 18 per cent of the military are sons of professional men. Among the civilian leaders, the largest percentage, 25, is in the foreign service, closely followed by the political leaders, with 24 per cent, and the career civil service with 16 per cent.

When these figures for professional backgrounds of the fathers are compared with those for the business leaders, a considerable difference is apparent. Since 25 per cent of the foreign service and 24 per cent of the political leaders had fathers who were professional men, compared with only 14 per cent of the business leaders, it seems probable that certain influences are operating to direct the sons of professional men into these two services. This possibility seems particularly true when one finds that only 16 per cent of the career civil service had fathers from the professional class, closely approximating the percentage for business leaders. What professions lead all others and what professions are more prominent for certain services than for others?

The ratios of the fathers of federal and business executives in the various professions to fathers in the professions in the adult male population give a measurement of significant similarities and differences among the services and among the professions. When one compares these ratios between all big business leaders and the civilian federal executives (the combined civilian federal services) in many respects they look very much alike. The proportions for the sons of lawyers are almost identical. Ministers are second for the big business leaders and for civilian federal executives, but the latter ratio is larger. Engineers are almost exactly the same: 4.8 for business leaders and 4.77 for civilian federal executives. Doctors, however, rank third for civilian federal executives (almost 600 for every 100 that might be expected by sheer chance) and fourth for business leaders (478 for every 100). The other professions, including teachers and professors, have a ratio of 1.89 for business leaders and 2.74 for civilian federal execu-

Fathers and Sons: Occupational Origins 35

tives. We have no separate ratios for teachers and professors for the business leaders.

The sons of professors are present in the civilian federal executive approximately fourteen times more than might be expected, outranking all other professional groups. On the other hand, among all the professions, teachers rank last.

Comparison between the civilian federal executives and military leaders brings out a number of rather significant differences. The sons of lawyers rather than those of professors outrank all others as sources of military leaders. Their representation is eleven times greater than would be expected from their proportions in the general population. These are followed by the sons of doctors with nine times more than might be expected, and by professors, with 7.5. Teachers, again, are last.

As a point of generalization, teachers rank last for all the professions for all the services. Among the separate civilian services, including career civil service, foreign service, and political, the sons of professors outrank all others; the foreign service ranks first with 27.5; political appointees, second with 14.17; career civil service, third with 11.67. All of them rank above the military.

Lawyers outrank all others among political leaders with a ratio of 20.44, professors are second with 14.17, and doctors third with 7.14.

The sons of ministers are disproportionately high among all the civilian services, 6.67; among business leaders, 5.48; and among military leaders, 4.05. They are highest for the foreign service with a ratio of 11.9, or over twice the figure for business leaders and almost three times the figure for military leaders.

Comparative Analysis of the Origins of the Several Services

To provide the base for all other comparisons in relation to occupational origin that will be made between government and business executives, the percentages of the different occupations that contributed to big business leadership are given in Table 2. (The figures for all the characteristics of the busi-

Table 2

Occupations of Fathers of 1952 Business Leaders*

Occupation of Father

Laborer		15%
Unskilled or semiskilled	4.5%	
Skilled worker or mechanic	10.3	
White-collar worker		8
Clerk or retail salesman	2.5	
Salesman	5.9	
Business executive		26
Foreman	3.1	
Minor executive	7.4	
Major executive	14.6	
Business owner		26
Small business	17.7	
Medium business	6.4	
Large business	2.4	
Professional man		14
Doctor	2.2	
Engineer	2.2	
Lawyer	2.2	
Minister	2.3	
Other profession	4.2	
Farmer		9
Farm tenant or farm worker	0.3	
Tenant with paid help	0.4	
Farm owner without paid help	3.7	
Owner or manager with paid help	4.2	
Other occupations		2
Uniformed service	0.3	
Government service	1.8	
Other occupation	0.4	
Total per cent	100.0	100
Total number	7,500	

*Warner and Abbegglen, *Occupational Mobility*, p. 38, Table 1.

Fathers and Sons: Occupational Origins

ness leaders should be examined in the two books that report on this research.) When these percentages are compared with those for the civilian federal executive, one sees that, as would be expected, the sons of business executives and the sons of business owners are much more highly represented among business leaders and that the sons of professional men are more highly represented among civilian federal executives. Moreover, the sons of laborers and farmers are also higher among the civilian federal executives. In brief, one can say broadly that civilian federal executives are more representative of the occupational structure of the United States than are the leaders of big business. It must be added, however, that the differences are not so great as many might expect from their assumptions that political leadership is more likely than the aristocratic structure of business enterprise to yield to equalitarian principles.

The ratios of fathers in occupational groups to the proportions of occupational groups in the adult male population summarize all the basic differences and similarities between the two major hierarchies, business and government, and among the several services within the government. The business leaders and the civilian federal executives are disproportionately high in executives and owners of large business, ranking first for both. The category of professional men ranks second for all the services, except the military, and third for business leaders. Skilled laborers rank fifth for all civilian federal executives and for the career civil service executives, sixth for political and military leaders, and seventh both for business leaders and the foreign service. Unskilled and semiskilled laborers rank ninth, and farm laborers tenth and last for all categories of the government and business elites.

Except for the fact that the professions rank disproportionately high as a source for the foreign service, this category of federal leadership looks more like business leaders than does any of the other services. The career civil service executives are least like the business leaders. For example, among them a disproportionate number, more than would be expected, comes from the skilled laborer group, whereas among business leaders this category is disproportionately low.

Although the ratio of executives and owners of large business is first for the career civil service, 4.67, it is lower than the ratios of this category for all civilian and military leaders and ranks well below the ratio for business leaders, 7.75. All the government services, including the military, have a higher ratio from the farming class, tenant or owner, than have big business leaders. The career civil service executives have the highest ratio of farmers, but it is only slightly less than would be expected from the proportion of farmers in the total population, 0.94, whereas the business leaders' ratio is 0.45. The military leaders are nearest the businessmen, and they are followed in turn by the foreign service, the political leaders, and all civilian federal executives. Speaking generally, the similarities between the executives of big business and those who occupy the top ranks of the federal government are more evident than the differences.

On the whole, through the father's occupation, the general cultural values that rank occupations and are common to American society seem to exercise their influence on business and government leaders. Occupations that are highly regarded and have most prestige and power are most likely to be represented by the largest proportion of both business and government leaders; occupations with the least prestige in the total society tend to be low as sources of leaders for both government and industry.

CHAPTER 3

The States and Regions That Produce Executives

The sentiments and values attached to locality and region have always been powerful in American life. They are felt deeply within the mores of our culture; their principles were deliberately and wisely made integral parts of the moral and conceptual structure of the Constitution. The principles of just representation in our governing bodies include the firm belief that all sections of our country should have their needs, sentiments, and political convictions expressed at the national level.

Regional and territorial differences from the beginning have played vital and crucial parts in national political events. The territories of the sovereign states are sharply and often artificially bounded, yet people's values and sentiments are often strongly held to the state in which they were born and reside. Legislators in the national Senate act as Americans, yet they do so as men deeply responsible to their states; the men and women in the House of Representatives serve not only their country and their states but the peculiarities and special interests of their own congressional districts. In the United States, unlike England, local representation is emphasized to the point that Senators and Congressmen must be residents of the states and districts which elect them. There are feelings of collective

Author of this chapter: W. Lloyd Warner.

identity that, vaguely or not, unite and combine some of the meanings of a federal representative with the people and voters he represents and they with the states and localities where they live. Americans assume that a man who lives in a territory can better represent its interests at the national level. Colloquial place names that arouse feelings and refer to the economic and geographic meanings of their peoples have significance and find expression not only locally and regionally but at the national level.

The informal and formal values operating in the selection of the men and women of the federal services express many of these same locality values. We know this is true for both military and civilian executives, but we want to know the degree and the manner. What states and major regions produce our federal leaders and what states and regions get them? If some supply more and others get more than their proportionate share we want to know which states and the kinds and numbers of leaders involved. Or possibly, and more invidiously, are some states so situated that they operate to the disadvantage of other states in placing their own sons as national leaders in the federal government? More specifically, there may be differences of nativity among those federal leaders located at the centers of power in Washington and those outside the nation's capital in the field and in the fifty states. Do the regions and states contiguous to Washington produce and receive more leaders than the more distant regions of the Pacific Coast and the Mountain states? Are locality factors operating, other than propinquity, that give certain states advantages in the promotion of their sons to national leadership and put other states at a disadvantage?

Finally, are there regional differences among the several services, between the military and civilian, the political and civil, or between all civilian federal executives and big business leaders? Perhaps some regions produce government leaders but not leaders of business and industry, or neither or both. If so, what regions are they, and what appear to be the factors respon-

The States and Regions That Produce Executives

sible for the differences or possibly the similarities that occur?

State and Regional Representation

The same exposition will be used in this chapter as in the preceding one. The leaders of both government and industry were asked in the two researches to tell whether they were born in the United States and, if so, which state. Nativity of the father and his father was also learned. These can be related to significant questions about how far being an "old" or a "new" American affects a man's opportunities for federal leadership.

The map used by the federal census divides the United States into nine regions.[1] Table 3 gives the percentages and ratios of productivity for each area of all civilian federal executives in our sample (10,851). The percentages and ratios for all civilian federal executives, and for those working in Washington and away from Washington, "in the field," are separated to answer questions that often arise about the nativity of Washington and field executives.

States stretching from the Hudson River to the Mississippi down as far as the Ohio River—the Middle Atlantic (22 per cent) and the East North Central regions (19 per cent)— produced the highest percentage of all civilian federal executives. Their productivity ratios are not much more or less than the proportions of the population living in the region. The Mountain States (see map) gave but 5 per cent of the government leaders, but this area's productivity ratio is the highest of all regions (1.67). The West North Central, an area bordering on the Mountain States and starting with the tier of states beginning on the north with the two Dakotas, is also high (1.23). The East and West South Central regions, broadly the western and central southern states, are low (0.67).

1. It should be said here, as it was for the study of business leaders, that the problem of regional classification of the states has never been satisfactorily resolved. Because the census classification of states into regions gives a meaningful division of the states for the most part, and because much of the analysis of this study must be made in terms of census data, the census categories are employed throughout.

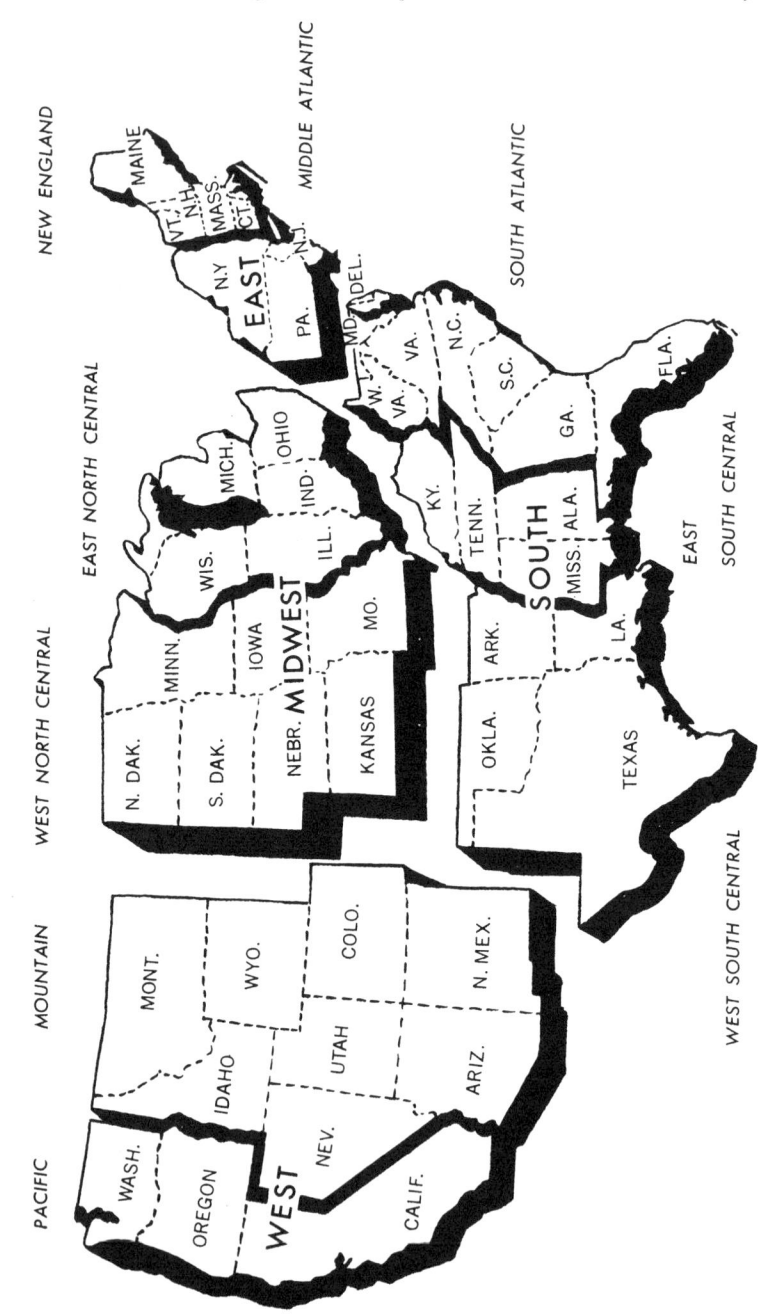

Map 1. The United States divided into the nine Federal Census regions

Table 3

Distribution of 1959 Civilian Federal Executives by Region of Birth and
1910 Adult Population by Region of Residence*

Region	1910 U.S. population living in region	All Civilian Federal Executives Born in region	All Civilian Federal Executives Productivity ratio of region	Washington Civilian Federal Executives Born in region	Washington Civilian Federal Executives Productivity ratio of region	Field Civilian Federal Executives Born in region	Field Civilian Federal Executives Productivity ratio of region
New England	7%	8%	1.14	8%	1.14	7%	1.00
Middle Atlantic	21	22	1.05	24	1.14	20	0.95
East North Central	20	19	0.95	18	0.90	20	1.00
West North Central	13	16	1.23	16	1.23	17	1.31
South Atlantic	13	13	1.00	16	1.23	9	0.69
East South Central	9	6	0.67	5	0.56	8	0.89
West South Central	9	6	0.67	5	0.56	7	0.78
Mountain	3	5	1.67	4	1.33	7	2.33
Pacific	5	5	1.00	4	0.80	5	1.00
Total per cent	100	100		100		100	
Total number	10,851						

*Bureau of the Census, 1910, Vol. I.

The comparison of the regions producing Washington and field executives brings out internal differences in the civilian federal executive. Whereas the South Atlantic region including the states of Delaware, Maryland, Virginia, the Carolinas, and others, for the civilian federal executives has a ratio of 1.00, for those in Washington the proportion goes up to 1.23 and for those in the field, down to 0.69. The Pacific drops from 1.00 for all executives to 0.80 in Washington; the Mountain drops from 1.67 to 1.33 but leads all regions for the proportion of civilian federal executives in the field (2.33). Propinquity to Washington, D.C. seems to give the South Atlantic states certain advantages. Those far removed seem disadvantaged, yet New England—considerably to the northeast of Washington—has a high proportion, above expectancy, of Washington leaders.

Only eight states, led by New York with 12 per cent, each produced 3 per cent or more of civilian federal executives. The city of Washington itself (3 per cent) outranks forty-one states in the number of federal leaders born within its boundaries. Most of the states it outranks have a larger population to draw from than this city. Five major regions, including the Pacific Coast with California, the Mountain states with Colorado and Denver, the West South Central with the great state of Texas, the East South Central and the South Atlantic that surround Washington with such states as Virginia, Georgia, and the two Carolinas, have no state that outranks or ties Washington, D.C., in the percentage of civilian federal executives born there.

Eight states exceeded 3 per cent in production of military leaders, with New York far outranking the others. Washington, D.C. ranks well below them (2.2 per cent). Six states are in both civilian and military upper ranks: New York, Pennsylvania, Illinois, Massachusetts, Ohio, and Missouri. Texas moves into second place (6.1) to New York State (8.8) for military leaders; California also rises into this top ranking group for military leaders (3.9).

Six regions produced a higher percentage of military leaders than civilian, not only the high West South Central (civilian,

The States and Regions That Produce Executives 45

6 per cent, military, 11.2 per cent), but others including the South Atlantic (civilian, 9.5 per cent, military, 11.9 per cent) and the Pacific Coast.

Reinspection of individual states shows that Texas more than doubled its contribution to the military (2.8, civilian, 6.1, military) over the civilian; and Oklahoma doubled its military leaders over civilian (2.7 to 1.4). There was little or no difference between the two services in Louisiana. In the South Atlantic states, Georgia alone among the nine localities, including Washington, D.C., doubled her contribution of military over civilian leaders (2.5, military, 1.4, civilian).

Washington, D.C. produced more civilian than military leaders (civilian, 3.1, military, 2.2) and leads all the eight states in the area for political appointments: 4.7 per cent. Maryland and Virginia are second with 2 per cent each. Furthermore, in political appointments no state in the Northeast exceeds or ties Washington, D.C.—in fact, no state west of the Mississippi River and only a few among the entire forty-eight states[2]: New York (12.6 per cent), Pennsylvania (7.4), and Illinois (6.2); Ohio ties Washington (4.7). Washington is decidedly a convenient location for political lightning to strike if a man is moving toward federal advancement through political position.

Among the three civilian services, civil, political, and foreign, in all the regions, similarities are more frequent than differences. New England is slightly higher for foreign-service executives than for the other two, as are the West South Central, the Mountain, and the Pacific regions: Massachusetts' percentage in New England (6.4) and California's in the West (3.9 per cent) for foreign service rise over the domestic and home services. Washington, D.C. (2.0), East South Central (3.9), and the West North Central (13.7) tend to be low in foreign-service executives as compared with the other civilian services. Kentucky, Tennessee, Alabama, Mississippi—the East South Central region—stand high for their contribution of career civil service executives.

2. Hawaii and Alaska were not yet states at the time the field research was conducted.

More exact measurements of the productivity of leaders by each region are given by the comparative ratios for all services, and we can also compare them with business leaders. Seen in broader perspective, the proportionate contributions of the several regions in themselves become more significant. In the conclusions about the regional productivity for business leaders, it was said that, "It is quite clear . . . that the only areas of the United States in which relatively few business leaders are born are the southern states—the East South Central, West South Central, and South Atlantic regions. We will not discuss this finding in detail . . . but the basis for this result is not hard to establish. In general, the regions' productivity in business leaders parallels closely their industrial development, and until recent years the South has lagged tremendously in this respect; moreover, its relatively meager industrial plant is often absentee-owned. Further, the low standard of living and level of education in the area are relevant to this outcome."

The similarities and differences of the regions of low productivity for business leaders can be compared with those for government executives. The East South Central is low for all government leaders; the West South Central is low for all except military leaders; the South Atlantic is below expectancy for career civil service executives and the foreign service, but it is slightly above for political and military leaders. This region produced exactly its proportionate share (1.00) of all civilian federal executives.

The Mountain states which score high, well above average for all government services, contributed only their proportionate share of business leaders. The two leading producers of business leaders were New England and the Middle Atlantic regions, which also generally score high for the executives of the several services of the government. The Pacific Coast, ranking high for business leaders, scores still higher for foreign service and military leaders but contributed no more than its proportionate share to political appointments and career civil service.

As to the territorial movement of these successful men, a

The States and Regions That Produce Executives

very high number of the civilian federal executives, approximately 50 per cent, is now in the South Atlantic region, many of course in Washington, D.C., and 11 per cent are in the East North Central. All of the remaining regions have less than 10 per cent. The residence ratios, except for the South Atlantic and the Mountain states, are below statistical expectancy.

As to regional stability for civilian federal executives, in three regions approximately two-thirds of the executives born in the region now have their legal residence there: the Middle Atlantic, West North Central, and New England. Three regions lost two-thirds or more of the leaders born there: the Mountain, Pacific, and South Atlantic.

There is an enormous increase of 294 per cent for the South Atlantic due, of course, in large part to the fact that Washington is the headquarters of the United States Government and the legal residence of many of those in the foreign and political service who are abroad. The Pacific Coast also ranks high for regional gains. The West North Central had the greatest loss (71 per cent), followed by the Middle Atlantic (59 per cent), and New England (58 per cent).

With a ratio of 1.0 for random movement in or out of a region the average ratio of mobility out of the West North Central (0.83) and the Mountain states (0.75) is high; New England, for example, is 0.52. The highest movement out is from the West North Central (0.83), and the lowest, the South Atlantic (0.43).

The big business leaders moved in clearly defined directions from birthplace to leadership in the high places of great business enterprise. To learn whether government men, including those who go to Washington, follow certain routes upward that take them away from their native regions, we used the same methods as those for occupational mobility. The extent to which civilian federal executives, born in one region, move to others can be expressed in ratios showing the amount of movement from the place of birth to other regions.

Since Washington is the head of most government hierarchies, it would be supposed that the region in which it is located, the South Atlantic, would rank above all others for the reception of mobile civilian federal executives. The movement from New England into the South Atlantic (and Washington) is 1.00, well over the mobility ratio out of New England and higher than all other regions. However, movement into the Middle Atlantic (0.88) is also above the New England mean.

The South Atlantic (with Washington) as the region of present legal address for those born in other regions ranks high and above the mean for all regions, but despite the great importance of Washington for our federal government, it ranks first for movement into it from only two major regions, New England and the Middle Atlantic (1.09).

The ratios of reception for the Pacific states are higher than those of the South Atlantic for movement from the East North Central, West North Central, and Mountain states, and tie for movement from the West South Central. The executives who chose the West are from the Middle West and from those states bounding those of the West Coast. The ratios of the West North Central (the Dakotas to Kansas and across to the Mississippi River) are higher than those for the South Atlantic, Mountain, and West South Central states. The Mountain states are proportionately higher than the South Atlantic or tie with it for the present residence of leaders from the West North Central, East South Central, West South Central, and Pacific Coast.

The states of the West North Central have a higher mobility rate than any other region. They are followed by those in the Mountain and the East North Central regions, the whole forming a vast block from the Rocky Mountains across the northern prairies to the Ohio River on the south and the Great Lakes and the Alleghenies on the north and east. Where did the men from this vast region go? Did the men of the several regions tend to go in the same direction or not? The Mountain men went to the West Coast (2.00), to Texas and the other states of the West South Central region, and to Washington, D.C. and the South Atlantic. The men of Illinois and the eastern prairies went to the West as well as to the South Atlantic and

Mountain states. Those from the western prairies—the Dakotas, Minnesota, and on down to Kansas and Missouri—went to the West Coast, the Mountain states, West South Central, and the South Atlantic. The Pacific Coast beats Washington for the proportion of men from the northern states from the Mississippi River to the Rockies who migrated there. The movement west by government leaders is a significant and important one. When they start upward Washington is not their only destination.

From the previous analysis of the birth and present residence of federal executives, the nine regions can be usefully classified into broad categories that are informative summaries about the significance of locality for the origin and development of government leadership. The Mountain states and the West North Central regions are disproportionately high producers of government leaders but lose more than other regions.

The South Atlantic and the Pacific Coast contributed their proportionate share, but the East North Central, East South Central, and West South Central contributed less than their share.

Four regions produced above expectancy: New England, Middle Atlantic, West North Central, and Mountain regions all contributed more than their share.

State and Regional Mobility

The 1952 research on the origins and mobility of big business leaders not only inquired into their regional movements as they advanced to leadership but also examined movements between and among states and kinds of communities. Since the evidence was based on state of birth, this part of the analysis was limited to the native born. The present research has followed a similar procedure concerning the amount and kind of geographical mobility generally among civilian federal executives[3]: the size of community involved, rural to urban move-

---

3. See Chapter 10 for career lines that were entirely in government and others that were partly outside it.

ment, and movement within the states of birth and between the major regions.

What occupations moved most interregionally, in and between states, and from rural to urban communities?

We shall group the government leaders, as the business leaders, into five categories:

1. Government leaders "whose state of birth and state of residence are the same and who were born in communities of over 25,000 population." This group is identified in subsequent analysis by the term "intrastate" mobility.

2. Government leaders "whose state of birth and state of residence are the same, but who were born in communities of less than 2,500 population." This group is termed "intrastate, rural to urban."

3. Government leaders "whose state of birth and state of residence are different but within the same region." This group is termed "interstate, intraregion."

4. Government leaders "whose region of birth and region of residence are different." This group is termed "interregion."

5. One other category for government leaders is added for those whose careers and positions took them beyond the United States. This group is identified as "abroad" and is primarily necessary, of course, for the foreign-service people.

The five categories of territorial mobility are rough measurements of the extent of movement from birth to the present time, the first category being most limited, the last two most extended. At best these are no more than approximations; they are likely to underestimate the amount of territorial movement that actually occurred. A man might have been born in Los Angeles, gone to school in the East, returned to California to reside in a small community, and finally settled in San Francisco as a high-level government executive; but still he is classified as category 1, having the least amount of movement. The five mobility classifications supply approximate groupings which aid in drawing conclusions about some of the functions of territorial mobility in the careers of the federal executive. Generally speaking, the men in the interregional category and those who are classed as being abroad are most likely to have been territorially mobile.

From the corresponding analysis among business leaders, the 1952 study concluded that "a very high rate of territorial mobility characterizes this group of men." Almost half (45 per cent) of the business leaders had moved interregionally, the most extended form; a third was categorized as intrastate, the most limited type.

Of the civilian federal executives, 67 per cent had moved interregionally, 10 per cent had worked abroad, and only 9 per cent had confined their movements within the state of birth. The geographical movement of federal civilian executives far exceeds that of businessmen.

Forty per cent of the business leaders and only 12 per cent of the government civilian leaders were in the state in which they were born. In a country noted for migrations and movements of its people back and forth these status-mobile men lead all others.

The movement of business leaders and their families during their advance in the big business hierarchies takes them from community to community and from one region to another, from local installations to regional headquarters on to the central home office. The size of big business enterprise in the United States increases the kind and amount of territorial movement in the great hierarchies of these organizations by mobile men. The national and international structure of the U.S. Government, a great monolith divided into services and other smaller units, takes more men and their families over even greater distances.

Increasingly, the primary locality for many mobile big business leaders is not the local community but the whole country. This statement seems to apply even more to civilian government leaders.[4]

Further inspection of the separate civilian services amplifies

---

4. Later publications on military men are likely to show even greater movement. They are not included here since, with legally enforced mobility, they are not comparable to other groups except—to some extent—the foreign service.

and intensifies previous discussion about the civilian federal executives. Seventy-five per cent of the career civil service executives and 73 per cent of the political executives had been interregionally mobile, and some 70 per cent of the foreign-service executives had served in foreign countries.

The territorial mobility of big business leaders was related to their movement to large cities. It was believed that "the extent of mobility of the business leader" would support the sociological assumption "that movement through social space and the implied break with the family and the class of orientation requires sheer physical distance." The authors went on to say, "in following this argument, it may be held that the relatively low territorial mobility rate of the city-born person (cities of over 100,000 population) is a function of the fact that within the confines of the complex, modern, large community a relatively short geographic distance will place an enormous social distance between the mobile individual and his social and physical antecedents."[5]

Table 4 gives comparative evidence about geographic mobility and size of birthplace for federal executives in 1959 in the civilian services and business leaders in 1952. Whereas 58 per cent of the business leaders born in big cities stayed in the state of birth, only 14 per cent of the federal executives from great cities remained where they were born. A third of business leaders born in smaller places (2,500–25,000) remained in the state of birth compared with an even smaller proportion (9 per cent) of the federal executives. Regardless of size of community, more business leaders than federal executives remained in the state of their birth. From the earlier research it was inferred that, "A major force in the territorial mobility is a function of a need to move to larger cities to conduct a business career."

Interregional mobility of business leaders rose from 30 per cent for communities of 400,000 to 54 per cent for those under 2,500—over half the men born in smaller towns not only

5. See pp. 82–84 of *Occupational Mobility* for full analysis of the evidence and statement of the inferences drawn from it.

Table 4

*Comparison of Geographical Mobility and Size of Birthplace of 1952 Business Leaders and 1959 Federal Executives**

	Type of Mobility				
Size of birthplace	Career civil service executives	Political executives	Foreign-service executives	Civilian federal executives	Business leaders
			Intrastate		
400,000 and over	15%	15%	3%	14%	58%
100,000–400,000	24	32	2	23	49
25,000–100,000	12	12	0	11	39
2,500–25,000	10	11	0†	9	32
Under 2,500	0	0	0	0	0
		Intrastate, Rural to Urban			
400,000 and over	0	0	0	0	0
100,000–400,000	0	0	0	0	0
25,000–100,000	0	0	0	0	0
2,500–25,000	0	0	0	0	0
Under 2,500	10	9	0†	9	28
			Interstate		
400,000 and over	9	8	1	8	12
100,000–400,000	11	6	2	9	12
25,000–100,000	13	12	5	12	15
2,500–25,000	12	11	2	11	17
Under 2,500	14	12	4	13	18
			Interregion		
400,000 and over	76	75	27	67	30
100,000–400,000	65	62	34	59	39
25,000–100,000	75	74	25	66	46
2,500–25,000	78	63	23	69	51
Under 2,500	76	76	25	68	54
			Abroad		
400,000 and over	0	2	69	11	
100,000–400,000	0	0†	62	9	
25,000–100,000	0	2	70	11	
2,500–25,000	0	5	75	11	
Under 2,500	0	3	71	10	

*Size of birthplace is given, at the left, for each of the five categories of degree of movement, from intrastate to interregional and abroad. The four categories of occupation are listed with the percentages for each type of community and type of territorial mobility. The sum of the frequencies may be obtained by adding the percentages for each type of career in each vertical column. For example, in the column for career civil service executives for men born in communities of 400,000, intrastate mobility is 15 per cent, intrastate rural to urban, 0; interstate, 9 per cent; interregional, 76 per cent; jobs abroad, 0; total, 100 per cent.

†Less than 0.5 per cent.

moved away but moved to other regions. It was from this evidence that inferences were made about staying in large cities and leaving small towns.

The evidence from the research on civilian federal executives permits further sharpening of the inferences and certain delimitations and expansions of the earlier hypotheses about social and territorial space as related to community heterogeneity and complexity. We have noted that the federal executives born in great cities stayed in their birth states in smaller percentages than business leaders. The percentages for interregional mobility do not increase as the size of the community decreases as they did for the business leaders, but remain very similar. Since the differences here hardly exist, some other factors seem to be involved. What are they?

The answer, it would seem, lies in the nature of the status and social structures of public and private enterprise. The business organizations in which the big business leaders held their positions were very large indeed. Some hierarchies extended throughout the United States and far beyond to other countries. Many men as they moved up to business leadership also moved from place to place. However, hundreds of companies and their hierarchies were involved and, in all, careers to high position were possible. Headquarters were in the large cities of every region and many states of the Union. Men could rise to the top in many of these great companies without ever leaving their state and region. Moreover, given acquaintanceship with others and participation in the business and social life of a large city in a state and given the presence of other large companies' headquarters there, upward mobility could be out from one company and up in other corporations should a man wish to change his company to achieve more rapid mobility. Despite the increasing tendency of business executives to move from community to community as they climb, many can and do conduct successful advance to business leadership in the same community or in communities in the same state (see the high percentages for intrastate mobility of business leaders previously referred to).

The government executive belongs to a monolithic organization which, despite certain successful efforts at decentralization, has its headquarters in Washington. From there the hierarchy of a given service, all departments, and most agencies spread out to the country and, for the State Department particularly and certain other organizations, to many other countries. The careers of the men are likely to flow through these great integrated social structures. Big city men and small town men in California, Illinois, or New York, regardless of their community's size, move interregionally in national and international bureaucracies. For example, 76 per cent of the career civil service and 75 per cent of the men politically appointed from cities of 400,000 and over moved interregionally, compared with only 30 per cent of the business leaders.

Regardless of the size of their city of birth, federal executives moved interregionally in about equal proportions. By contrast, business leaders show greater interregional movement (from 30 to 54 per cent) as size of city of birth decreases. The multiple and autonomous social structures of business enterprise still permit shorter-span territorial movements for many men on the advance for business leadership. Careers in government may not be confined to one service; some have been in the foreign and domestic services, the career civil service, and have been politically appointed, but all of them are centered in one organization where status mobility for the ambitious and successful federal executive is often accompanied by extended territorial movement.

CHAPTER 4

The Urban, Rural, and Foreign-born Executives

The Contribution of Big Cities, Small Towns, and Rural Villages

The legal and other formal records of an American's place of birth usually include not only the state but city and county. The affiliations of Americans to their region of birth, particularly in New England and the South, although meaningful and often powerful, tend to be unofficial and personal. The city and state of birth, formally and explicitly stated, are important categories of significant placement for every native-born American. The effects of the cultures of towns and rural communities on personality and behavior are deeply embedded in our assumptions about ourselves. The country boy and his city cousin are popular topics of folklore; dirty stories are told about them with knowing understanding; and, at another level of discourse, they are the heroes and villains of some of our greatest novels. In each generation their respective environments have been attacked and defended by some of our most thoughtful leaders, Thomas Jefferson among them.

The study of federal executives was concerned with possible differences in the contribution to this leadership from the various types of communities by region. A corresponding phase of the study of business leaders concluded that, "there is a marked

Author of this chapter: W. Lloyd Warner.

size gradient. The larger communities are the primary source of future business leaders, while the small communities decline in importance with the size of the community." Does this pertain to the production of business leaders as integral parts of our industrial life or does it extend beyond to the American culture itself to the point that government leaders also originate disproportionately from the great cities?

In the questionnaire about size of birthplace, five categories were used: rural areas under 2,500; 2,500 to 25,000; 25,000 to 100,000; 100,000 to 400,000; and over 400,000.[1] Twenty-one per cent of all civilian federal executives were born in the largest communities and 34 per cent in the smallest; but compared with the general population for place of birth in 1910, the ratio for largest communities was 1.91 and for the smallest, only 0.59. All towns and cities above 2,500 produce more leaders than would be expected and would be more likely places from which to launch a successful career into the federal elites.

A comparison of the Washington and field representatives, within the civilian executive, shows that a higher proportion of Washington leaders are big city people whereas field executives, still men from big cities, have proportionately more leaders from the smaller communities.

Table 5 compares the ratios of all services with each other and with those of business leaders, permitting us to draw certain broader generalizations from this evidence. In all cases, including the military, the rural areas and villages fall below expectancy, with the career civil service executives highest and business leaders lowest. In all but the military, the proportions of leaders are highest from the great cities.

Region, Community, and Occupational Background

The information that we have on occupational origins, relative size of community, and territorial and regional variations is, of course, all related to the cultural and structural factors

---

1. See pp. 85-86 of *Occupational Mobility* for a full discussion of the use of these categories and the reliability of the responses.

Table 5

*Ratio of Size of Birthplace of 1952 Business Leaders and 1959 Federal Executives and Size of Community of Residence of U.S. Population**

Size of community	Career civil service executives	Political executives	Foreign-service executives	Civilian federal executives	Business leaders	Military executives
400,000 and over	1.82	2.09	2.18	1.91	2.36	1.27
100,000–400,000	1.38	1.63	1.50	1.50	1.75	1.25
25,000–100,000	1.38	1.50	1.63	1.50	1.71	1.88
2,500–25,000	1.40	1.33	1.53	1.40	1.57	1.87
Under 2,500	0.64	0.55	0.48	0.59	0.43	0.57

*1952 business leaders/1900 U.S. population = ratio; 1959 federal executives/1910 U.S. population = ratio.

implicit in our study of government and business leaders. By asking what happens to widen or close the routes of mobility in federal leadership when locality sources are combined with occupational levels and by noting which combinations increase the appearance of certain kinds of people in Washington or field positions and reduce the percentage of others, we come nearer to understanding how regional culture, community complexity, and occupational structure combine to produce leaders.

This more complex analysis shows, for example, that there is a slight tendency for sons of lower-status fathers (laborer and white-collar) from northern and southern large cities to move into the civilian federal executive in higher proportions than the national average; they are below average in the Far West. Sons of high-status men (business leaders and the higher professions) from the Middle West and West are above average; from the North slightly below the national average.

A higher percentage from the big cities of three regions, the North, Middle West, and Far West, is in Washington than in the field; and more men of higher status from smaller communities in the North, South, and West are in Washington than in the field.

Those born to lower status in northern, middle western, and far western cities are represented in the field in higher percentages than in Washington. This is also true for smaller cities, towns, and rural areas in the Far West, Middle West, and the South.

In the civilian federal executive, big city men who were laborers' sons are over the national percentage in the North and lower in the West. Small city men of laboring origins for the North are also high. The percentages for big city men who were sons of laborers decrease for Washington and increase for the field.

Percentages for middle western sons of laborers from big cities also decrease below the national average for Washington and increase for the field. Those from small cities are down slightly in Washington and up in the field, as are those from small towns.

In brief, laboring men's sons from big and small places from all regions do somewhat better in the field than in Washington, possibly indicating that for these men who have farther to go in their mobility Washington is a more difficult place to reach.

At the other occupational pole, sons of big business leaders, the opposite could be true. Big city men, nationally, are slightly higher in percentage in Washington than in the field. The percentages for big city men who are the sons of big business men rise in Washington and fall in the field for the North, the South, the Middle West, and the Far West. For those from smaller places nationally, about 8 per cent are in the field, and for all regions they remain more or less the same except for the West where they rise about two and one-half times.

The percentages of sons of professional men coming from big and small cities nationally slightly favor the former (19 as compared with 17 per cent). In Washington the percentages for each are exactly the same (19), and in the field they both drop slightly. The percentages for professional men coming from big cities of the North, South, and West are above the national average. The West's percentages for professional men from big cities and from smaller places rise in Washington and fall in the field. Only in the South do the percentages for field men from big cities whose fathers were professional men exceed those for Washington and the national average for southern large cities.

Government Leaders Who Are Foreign Born

Substantial numbers of the federal executives are foreign born. We will now examine the meaning and effects of foreign birth on their careers. It is often asserted that being ethnic and carrying some of the traces of foreign birth act to the disadvantage of the ambitious and those attempting to gain higher position, that discriminations are made which work to the advantage of the native born and the disadvantage of those born elsewhere or whose families originated in other countries. On the other hand, foreign ancestry has often been viewed as an advantage in our political life, and the rapid rise of representatives of various ethnic groups in American politics often commented on. Does the fact of foreign birth help or hinder the careers of federal executives? Are the occupational origins of the foreign born in the federal leadership different from those of the native born? The study of big business leaders indicated that the foreign born of lower position tended to do better climbing to top industrial positions than native Americans.

As in the 1952 study of business leaders, the 1959 research on government leaders asked if a man's father and his father's father were born in this or some other country. The replies, classified into four categories for each of the several services, are presented in Table 6. The percentages of the U.S. white population for 1940 are given for the businessmen and 1950 census figures for the government leaders.

Well over half of the civilian government sample, 58 per cent, are "old American." Only 3.8 are foreign born (7.5 per cent in the U.S. white population),[2] but a fifth of the fathers were born outside this country, making about one-fourth who were foreign born or the sons of foreign born.

Comparisons with the military leaders show a considerable difference: 71 per cent were old American, and 87 per cent had fathers who were born here, whereas 75 per cent of the general population were old American or had fathers born in the United States. Only 1.6 per cent of the military leaders were foreign born, and 11.2 per cent had foreign-born fathers—about *half* the proportions for civilian executives.

The proportion of foreign-born civilian federal executives is about half that of the foreign born in the adult population, yet the percentage for the first generation (executives, U.S. born) is higher than that for the population generally (20 per cent as to 17.5 per cent). The foreign service tends to be high

2. There are a few Negro civilian federal executives. How many, since such an inquiry seemed to be unwise, we were unable to learn. Neither could we ask about religion or political affiliation. Preliminary investigation in a pilot study indicated such questions might reduce the return or raise questions which would endanger the size of the response.

Table 6

Comparison of Nativity of 1959 Federal Executives and U.S. Population in 1950 with 1952 Business Leaders and U.S. Population in 1940*

Nativity	Civilian federal executives	Military executives	Career civil service executives	Political executives	Foreign-service executives	U.S. white population in 1950	Business leaders	U.S. white population in 1940
Paternal grandfather, father, and executive U.S. born	58.3%	71.2%	57.3%	58.9%	63.2% }	75.0%	54.8% }	70.9%
Father and executive U.S. born	17.7	16.0	18.4	16.4	15.4		20.2	
Executive U.S. born	20.2	11.2	20.8	20.2	16.7	17.5	19.7	19.5
Executive foreign born	3.8	1.6	3.5	4.5	4.7	7.5	5.3	9.6
Total	100.0	100.0	100.0	100.0	100.0	100.0	100.0	100.0

*Bureau of the Census, 1950, Special Report, PE no. 3A, Table 3.

for old Americans (63 per cent) and the career civil service low (57 per cent).

Comparative ratios were established for all the executive categories using the 1940 U.S. population for business leaders and 1950 for federal executives. The military men are low in foreign born (0.21); foreign-service men are highest (0.63). Military leaders are also lowest (0.64) for the native-born of foreign parentage, civilian federal executives are somewhat above chance (1.15), and the business leaders at expectancy (1.01). The military lead all others including the business leaders for native-born executives of American parentage (1.16). The others are at or above what chance might indicate.

The Occupational Origins of the Foreign Born

We can begin our inquiry into the occupational background of the foreign-born executives by quoting from the research on big business leaders.[3] "Occupational rigidity," it was said at the conclusion of the study of ethnic influence on career success in business, "is greater in those groups established in American society for longer periods of time." The longer the family had been here, the less likely its sons were to leave their place of origin and to push upward into the higher positions of the business elite. The executive who was native born with a foreign-born father had at least the time of his own generation to prepare himself to compete for higher positions with all others, particularly with those who had the advantage of native parents. As noted elsewhere in our comments about business leaders, the native American of foreign-born parents is a good test of the melting pot theory and a further test of how well American cultural processes operate to utilize these fresh sources of leadership. Do men of lowly occupational and ethnic derivation rise to the top?

Thirty-two per cent of all civilian federal executives whose fathers were foreign born had fathers who were laborers; 23 per cent of those whose fathers were born here and only 16

3. The same procedures and the same data used in that study will be used here.

per cent whose fathers' fathers were native Americans had fathers who were laborers. Small businesses vary in size and importance in America, yet most are comparatively small and inconsequential; 25 per cent of the first generation executives had fathers who were small business men, only 11 per cent had fathers born here, and 12 per cent were of the old Americans. The other categories, with certain exceptions, are inclined to reverse this tendency.

A breakdown was made for Washington and field executives, but the differences for the two areas are not significant as is true for many, but not all, of the other breakdowns between Washington and field. The same general tendencies for military leaders as for civilian federal executives are apparent.

Since over half the executives who are first generation Americans are sons of laborers or small business men and only 28 per cent of the old Americans are from these occupational classes, it seems possible that "the American dream" and the myth of the melting pot do have some validity for the sons of immigrant fathers. This seems a more likely hypothesis when we remember that a similar mobility pattern exists for the same generation among business leaders. There 48 per cent of those who were U.S. born with immigrant fathers were sons of laborers and sons of small business men, and only 25 per cent of the old Americans had such fathers. Before examining the separate services, let us complete the task of finding more exact answers about the effect of ethnic and foreign background on mobility and career aspirations for Americans in the civilian federal executive by comparing the distribution by nativity and occupation of the executives' fathers with those of the general population, using U.S. census figures for 1930. About two-thirds of the foreign-born adult males in 1930 were laborers; 32 per cent of the foreign-born fathers of the civilian executives were laborers. The percentage of native males in the laborer group drops to 42 per cent, but the native fathers of civilian federal executives in this group drop to 17 per cent. Similar parallels between the government and business leaders' fathers' occupations appear for the foreign and native born for such occupations as professionals and farmers. In broad outline, the similarities of mobility between the two, government and business, are large, particularly the percentages of long-distance mobility of the executives who are native with foreign-born fathers.

A further test of the hypothesis about ethnic mobility was made by taking the percentages of American- and foreign-born fathers of business leaders and of the males in the adult working force of 1920 as computed by the U.S. census (1920 being the time when the business leaders began their occupational career) and comparing them with the percentages for the executives in the various federal services and those for the general male population as in the 1930 census. Only nonsignificant differences appeared.

Table 7 completes the answer to the question of mobility for the sons of foreign and native born in the civilian federal executive by using percentages for all the separate services including the military.

The ratios for fathers who were unskilled laborers and foreign born (0.18) for the civilian federal executive and for business leaders (0.17) are almost identical. For U.S.-born fathers the ratio for business leaders (0.13) is higher than for civilian federal executives (0.08). Both are *lower* than for foreign born. The sons of foreign-born fathers who were skilled laborers rank higher for civilian federal executives (1.20) than for business leaders (0.84). But both are higher (see U.S.-born in the table) than for the native-born father. In brief, *there is more long-distance mobility for both big business leaders and high government officials for the foreign born than for those native-born men whose fathers were in this occupational category.* This is also true for the categories of skilled laborer, white-collar worker, and farmer.

Such diverse occupations as the military and the career civil service, the foreign service, and big business show more mobility than might be expected for the sons of the foreign born for the four levels of occupation that are often thought to be most disadvantaged. In many instances the differences are slight, in

Table 7

Place of Birth as a Factor in Occupational Mobility: Ratio of Proportion of U.S. Adult Males* in Occupation to Proportion of Fathers of 1952 and 1959 Executives in Occupation, by Two Nativity Groups

	Foreign Born								U.S. Born					
Occupation	Career civil service executives	Political executives	Foreign-service executives	Civilian federal executives	Business leaders	Military executives		Career civil service executives	Political executives	Foreign-service executives	Civilian federal executives	Business leaders	Military executives
Unskilled and semi-skilled laborer	0.18	0.09	0.16	0.18	0.17	0.09		0.12	0.08	0.08	0.08	0.13	0.08
Skilled laborer	1.30	0.95	1.10	1.20	0.84	1.15		1.06	0.69	0.56	0.94	0.53	0.63
Clerk or salesman	0.75	0.75	0.88	0.75	1.60	0.63		0.73	0.67	0.47	0.67	0.75	0.67
Business owner or executive	2.93	3.29	2.93	3.00	4.25	2.93		2.67	2.92	3.17	2.92	4.73	3.25
Professional man	3.00	4.33	4.67	3.33	3.33	4.00		3.60	5.20	5.20	4.00	3.20	3.80
Farmer	0.90	1.10	0.70	0.90	0.42	1.00		0.62	0.56	0.56	0.68	0.30	0.40
Uniformed service	0.00	0.00	0.00	0.00	0.00	5.00		0.00	0.00	0.00	0.00	0.00	10.00

*1952 business leaders/1920 U.S. adult males = ratio; 1959 federal executives/1930 U.S. adult males = ratio.

The Urban, Rural, and Foreign-born Executives 67

others they are considerable, but all move in the same direction —more long-distance mobility for the first generation of Americans, the immigrant fathers' sons over those of the native born.

The two high level categories are different from those just analyzed. The foreign-born fathers who were professional men rank lower than native for the civilian federal executive and for the three civilian services but higher for business leaders and for military leaders.

On a much broader base, now including mobility in all the military hierarchies, in the foreign services, in services subject to the examinations and practices of the Civil Service, in the field of political appointments, and in big business in such diverse industries as manufacturing, transportation, finance, and other types of big business enterprise, we can now further substantiate the statement for big business leaders at the conclusion of that research: "Occupational rigidity is greater and vertical occupational mobility less in those groups in the population that have been established in American society for longer periods of time." But, contrary to many popular and academic views, the federal government does not provide a special or unusually good avenue of opportunity for the foreign born in comparison to business.

PART III

The Influence of Family

CHAPTER 5

Three Generations: Marriage, Descent, and Occupation

The Father's Father's Influence on the Movement of Men into the Federal Executive

The movement of sons from their fathers' occupations, presented earlier, was concerned with a sequence of only two generations. Since occupational mobility may take longer than two generations and since, in all societies, alternate generations, father's father and the son, are close and influential upon each other, the research on the careers of military and civilian federal executives was extended to the third generation, to the father's father in the male line and bilaterally through the mother to her father.

The previous study of big business leaders demonstrated that the third generation was an important determinant in how the second, the fathers, selected occupations; we know that the father himself is significant. Therefore, we hypothesized that (1) the occupation of the father's father was influential on his son's son (namely, the executive himself); (2) that being true, well-traveled routes of mobility through certain occupations are present and meaningful for understanding who gets into the federal executive in all services—the movements up were not merely random; and (3) that the mother's side of the family

Author of this chapter: W. Lloyd Warner.

would exercise its own kind of influence on the occupational succession leading to the federal elites.[1]

Since stability and continuity of succession are integral parts of an open system of occupational rank, it may be supposed that certain occupations would hold the fathers of the executives to the same place as their own fathers, and that this occupational continuity could be measured. Factors involved would be the status of these occupations, their flexibility at intermediate levels in yielding the sons to others, and which occupations were favored or avoided by the executives' fathers in moving from one occupation to another. For example, through the years and a generation did occupations which are low as immediate sources of executives increase in importance, just as others, in the third generation of the grandfathers, decreased?

Among civilian federal executives, the most outstanding difference between the father's father's occupation and the father's is the large decrease among all classes of farmers, from 44 to 15 per cent. Moreover, all four subcategories, from large farmers to farm tenants, decreased—farm owners without paid help from 25 to 7 per cent across the two generations. The percentages of fathers' fathers who were farmers who contributed sons to other occupations are very high, to the point of outranking all other occupations.

Some of the sons of farmers go to the city and into the laboring class, for this occupation increases slightly, from 18 to 21 per cent from the father's father to the father's generation. The unskilled worker group is somewhat smaller in the younger generation than in the older, but the skilled class increases considerably to help account for more workers in the father's generation than in the father's father's. Farmers' sons seem to have helped build this occupational rank.

Since there was little or no movement from other occupations into the farmer category, it is the highest group for occupational continuity from the third to the second generation, although in all groups occupational continuity is sizable (35 per cent of the

1. See pp. 51–68 of *Occupational Mobility*.

unskilled workers and 34 per cent of the skilled workers had fathers of their own class). The mobility from farm families to other positions spreads widely enough across the occupational structure to be significant in all.

The white-collar group is tripled in size from 3 to 9 per cent; the minor executives increase from 4 to 11 per cent; major executives from 2 to 4 per cent; business owners from 18 to 20 per cent; and professional men from 10 to 19 per cent.

The civilian federal executive's occupational history through the generations shows a strong movement away from rural areas to towns and cities. Moreover, although there is a steady advance upward to positions such as the professions and major executives, which rank at least equal to many executives in the federal government, there is another movement into the lower urban levels that for some may be downward.

The Occupational Routes through the Generations to the Federal Executive

In general, there was a considerable exodus from the position of the earlier generation to the one that staged locations from which the executives later moved to their own high governmental position. The degree of movement and immobility for each and for all occupations tells us much not only about the origins of federal executives but about the open and closed nature of our social system.

The broad routes of mobility through three generations to civilian executive position in the federal government can be more firmly grasped from the general categories of Table 8, in using the ratios of the father's occupation to the father's father's. This table presents the patterns or routes of mobility of the two preceding generations in the paternal line. At the bottom of the table the mean interoccupational movement for all can be used to determine the comparative place of any occupation's movement with the others. The general mobility mean is 0.77. The mean for stability for all occupations is 2.74 (see diagonal ratios, underlined).

Table 8

Patterns of Occupational Mobility for 1959 Civilian Federal Executives: Mobility Ratios of Six Occupational Groups*

Occupation of father's father	Fathers' fathers in occupation†	Occupation of Father						Mean mobility out of occupation
		Major business executive	Professional man	White-collar worker	Business owner	Laborer	Farmer	
Major business executive	2%	5.72	1.22	0.94	0.56	0.44	0.06	0.64
Professional man	10	1.57	2.50	0.81	0.66	0.42	0.34	0.76
White-collar worker	7	2.18	0.94	2.00	0.78	0.54	0.24	0.94
Business owner	18	1.16	0.96	1.16	1.94	0.50	0.23	0.80
Laborer	18	0.70	0.56	1.05	0.75	2.31	0.23	0.66
Farmer	44	0.56	0.83	0.81	0.86	0.89	1.96	0.79

*Mean = 0.77; diagonal mean = 2.74.
†Miscellaneous occupation (1%) not included.

Three occupations are below the general intergenerational mean: major business executives (0.64), laborers (0.66), and professional men (0.76)—two at the highest position and one, the most disadvantaged for movement. The three that are high are the white-collar (0.94), business owners (0.80), and farmers (0.79). Farmers' and professional men's scores approach the general mean.

The average amount of mobility out of each occupation shows that to a very high degree fathers from all categories moved from occupation to occupation; fluidity was a marked characteristic of occupational succession in the earlier as in the later generations. Yet many also continue in the father's occupation.

A more detailed analysis of these data shows that unskilled laborers for continuity (and closure) outrank all other occupations, followed closely by the other occupational extreme, major business executives and owners of large business. The two lowest are farmers and the owners of small business, the former largely an expression of the movement from farm to city occupations, and the latter possibly the well-known instability of small business enterprises. The high ranking of unskilled laborer is related to the social distance of this class from the other types of occupation and the disadvantages in motivation and opportunity from which its children suffer; the high stability of the big business men is an expression of their sons' and families' unwillingness to move from highly advantaged positions.

All but three occupations, farmers and skilled and unskilled workers, show strong movement into the major business executive class; the three highest are minor executives, owners of large business, and professional men; the lowest is unskilled worker.

The mobile men in the father's generation whose own fathers were major business executives often moved into the professions and white-collar classes. Those fathers whose own fathers were professional men were likely to move to major business executive or white-collar positions. Paternal grandfathers who were white-collar workers were likely to have sons who became major business executives or professional men.

The fathers whose own fathers were business owners moved into the white-collar, professional, and major business executive positions. For all these four categories, there is great similarity. The offspring of professional men become major business executives, the sons of the latter go into professional positions, and both move into white-collar positions. The same pattern of exchange holds true for the sons of the white-collar class. Although the sons of business owners move into these same classes, there is low reciprocity from these occupations into this class. Mobility is likely to be only in the opposite direction.

For the fathers of executives whose own fathers were laborers other variations appear. The sons of laborers move into the white-collar class and into the business-owner group, but there is no reciprocity from these groups into the laboring class. This is a clear case of one-way mobility from lower to higher levels that occurred with the fathers and, as it were, laid preparations for the further movement of the third generation, that of the executive, into the federal government.

The fathers of executives whose own fathers were farmers are most deviant. They came into two classes, laborers and business owners, well above the mean; for one, the major business executives, far below; and for the other two, white-collar and professional classes, slightly above. That they were most likely to move into the laboring class, and that the laboring class was least likely to move into the farming level, is a clear indication of the farmer's position in this movement of people through the generations up to and into the federal executive.

Among fathers who were mobile from other occupations into the farm group, all scores are lower than for all mobile fathers into all other occupations. Mobile men take the long trip up to the federal executive by other routes; very few enter the farming class before preparing the way for their sons' movement into the federal executive.

The Military: Three Generations of Mobility

In broad perspective, the civilian and military appear much alike. For the military, the farming category also drops quite sharply, from 41 per cent in the grandparental generation to 10 per cent in the father's. The white-collar workers triple their percentage; both minor and major executives more than double theirs; and the professional class also expands. All of these transitions bear close resemblance to the civilian federal executives.

There are also interesting variations, however. The worker group moves down very slightly in the military, whereas in the civilian it increases somewhat. The farmer group is cut to three-fourths its size in the military and to one-third in the civilian executive group. Among the military there is only 5 as compared with 9 per cent advance in the civilian services for the professional group.

The uniformed executive increases from 2 to 9 per cent for all military leaders, with no increase indicated among those in the civilian federal executive. The evidence from our research shows clearly that the military regards itself and behaves in such a manner that there seems to be a solid, inherited, core of meaning, feeling, and values about this service that is passed on from father to son to the point that many continue in the profession of their fathers. Moreover, this feeling is definitely connected with professional standards so that the kind of advanced training the military receives at such great schools as West Point and Annapolis clearly prepares them not only with the skills necessary for their profession but also with a code of conduct and honor that places this group in a high and distinct profession. The evidence, as we shall see later, is less clear about the civilian federal executives. However, the claims to professional status for the various services in the federal executive cannot be idly dismissed; they deserve very serious consideration.

In general, the differences between the civilian and military in the third and second generations indicate broad advancement in the father's generation toward the present position of military leaders that is greater than among the generations preceding the civilian federal executives. The movement away from the rural life of the farming occupation is greatly advanced during the father's generation. The movement from lower to higher positions for many has been staged, and an actual final advancement of considerable size into the military leadership itself has been achieved by the father's generation. All these separate tendencies combine to make a considerable difference between the career lines of the military and civilian executives.

In Table 9, on the ratios of stability and movement for the military, to the six broad categories of occupation, used with the civilian executive, uniformed service is added. The mean of total mobility out of all occupations into all occupations, it will be noticed, is 0.74. The "diagonal" mean, for stability and continuity, is 3.17. Four major categories contributed directly to military leadership, well above average, in the father's generation. They were the military itself, the professions, white-collar worker, and business owners.

The fathers of military leaders who were major business executives were most likely to have fathers in this same category (4.35). The principal moves from major business executives in the grandfather's generation to the father's were to the white-collar class, to the professions, and business owners, and slightly to the uniformed services but only very slightly to the farming class.

Professional men's sons (father's father to father) went directly to the uniformed service (2.06) at a higher ratio than stayed in the grandparental occupation (1.95). White-collar men (fathers) stayed in the grandparental occupation (2.07) and then moved to the military above all others (1.37), and to major business executive positions and into the professions. Business owners were mobile into the white-collar class (1.95), into major business executives, and into the military (1.03). The uniformed service entirely avoided the laboring and farm-

Table 9

Patterns of Occupational Mobility for 1959 Military Executives: Mobility Ratios of Seven Occupational Groups*

Occupation of father's father	Fathers' fathers in occupation	Major business executive	Professional man	White-collar worker	Business owner	Laborer	Farmer	Uniformed service	Mean mobility out of occupation†
Major business executive	2%	4.35	0.77	1.35	0.77	0.46	0.19	0.73	0.71
Professional man	13	1.39	1.95	0.57	0.64	0.52	0.42	2.06	0.93
White-collar worker	9	0.99	0.94	2.07	0.55	0.29	0.12	1.37	0.71
Business owner	18	1.56	0.68	1.95	1.94	0.47	0.31	1.03	1.00
Laborer	15	0.90	0.66	1.17	0.74	2.63	0.26	0.31	0.67
Farmer	41	0.51	0.98	0.84	0.95	1.04	2.06	0.53	0.81
Uniformed service	2	0.00	1.05	0.47	0.47	0.00	0.00	7.16	0.33

†Uniformed service being an extra occupational category, 6 was used as the divider instead of 5.
*Mean = 0.74; diagonal mean = 3.17.

ing and the major business executive classes. Only the business owners and the professional classes were strongly attractive to the sons of this small category of paternal grandfathers.

The sons of laborers, as in the civilian group, entered the white-collar level (1.17); the major business executives and business owner groups are above the mobility mean for this occupation. The large group of farmers (41 per cent in the father's father's generation) moved mostly into the laboring group (1.04), then into the professions (0.98) and into the business owners group (0.95). With only a ratio of 0.53, farmers and laborers (0.31) at the father's generation are lower than all other occupations as direct sources for the uniformed services.

The striking differences between the military and civilian services are that *in the father's generation* many of the military made a direct and final advance into the service where the leaders under study now are. Several major occupations also directly contributed in moves from the generation of the fathers before their military sons (the present military command) took these positions: the professions, the white-collar class, and business owners as well as the sons of major business executives. Only the laboring and farming classes did not.

The civilian federal executives do not have a substantial reservoir of fathers who are in the federal civilian elite. It has remained for the present generation of leaders to accomplish this. What the next generation, the civilian federal executives' sons, will do is not, of course, known. With the government becoming increasingly important and much more visible to young men and women as a place for a career, the civilian federal executive today may produce children who will possibly continue in the father's occupation (and, for a few, the mother's). Moreover, there seems to be a developing concept of the occupation that makes it more and more attractive as a profession with its own high standards, its own code and values, and its own sense of importance and significance.

The General Routes of Mobility: A Comparative Analysis

A comparison of occupations for continuity (and stability) for father's father to father of the executive, the big business leaders with the entire civilian federal executive with the military and individual civilian services, as presented in Table 10, is informative about the nature of opportunity and motivation in the two kinds of mobility structures. For example, at the table's far right the vertical column gives the ratios of continuity of occupation for the preceding generations of big business leaders. The occupations for business leaders' backgrounds are listed in exact rank order for this group. It will be noted that the ratio for unskilled workers is 6.86 (for business), rises to 7.59 for all civilian government leaders, and still higher to 9.31 for political executives, and up to 11.76 for military executives to reach the highest point of 14.96 for foreign-service executives, whose fathers stayed in their own fathers' occupations and did not move on. Only the career civil service is below, but slightly below, the ratio for big business leaders.

The ratios for owners of large business and major business executives of fathers who stayed in their fathers' occupations are higher in all cases, including military and civilian leaders, than for the fathers of big business leaders. For the sons of owners of small business, the ratio is lower than for any others. The ratios of business leaders for clerks and salesmen are lower than for all the separate services except for the career civil service. The score for farmers and, generally, for minor executives, professional men, and skilled laborers is slightly higher for business leaders than for government services.

Several major considerations must be recalled in examining the significance of these findings. We must repeat that, for civilian federal executives, all but a tiny percentage had to make the move from the father's occupation into the government structure. On the other hand, the business leaders not only could remain in the elite position of their fathers, such as owner of large business or major business executive, as did some of their fathers, but they and their fathers were born to

Table 10

Ratios* of Stability and Occupational Continuity for the Several Services
(from the Executive's Paternal Grandfather to His Father)

Occupation of Paternal Grandfather	Military Executives	Civilian federal executives	Career civil service executives	Political executives	Foreign-service executives	Business leaders
Unskilled laborer	11.76	7.59	6.60	9.31	14.96	6.86
Owner of large business	4.90	5.83	5.94	5.47	4.39	3.71
Major business executive	4.35	6.06	6.83	4.83	3.79	3.60
Clerk or salesman	4.03	2.93	2.54	3.91	4.46	3.50
Skilled laborer	2.40	2.43	2.28	2.79	3.12	2.92
Professional man	1.95	2.53	2.71	2.15	2.08	2.70
Minor business executive	2.53	2.59	2.72	2.36	2.30	2.67
Owner of small business	2.06	1.95	1.88	2.15	2.15	2.37
Farmer	2.38	2.13	2.14	2.14	1.96	1.76
Uniformed service	7.16	0.00	0.00	0.00	0.00	0.00

*Ratio derived by dividing the proportion of fathers in each occupation by the proportion of paternal grandfathers in the same occupation.

fathers in several occupations that are part of the structure of business and industrial enterprise. Such occupations include skilled and unskilled laboring groups, most clerks and salesmen, owners of small business, and minor executives.

Most of the professions are useful and socially near to both business and government enterprise. Farmers are not within the realm of either hierarchy. The loci of government and business tend to be the urban agglomerates and their subcultures where the values, beliefs, and behavior tend to vary from those of rural communities.

On the other hand, with increasing city life and decreasing farm populations, the economic and social "forces" operating to drive men from farms to cities reduce the proportions of farmers staying in the father's occupation and increase the likelihood of their going into urban occupations.

The earlier analysis of the occupation of the father's father, showing that farmers were high for mobility by the executives' fathers into all occupations, tells a story of rural to urban movement which resulted for some in the mobility of the present generation into federal leadership.

In general the routes of mobility for business and government leaders, no matter what the service—military or civilian, foreign or domestic—have a broad resemblance. They therefore seem to fit into the larger occupational pattern of America and, no doubt, into the larger values, behavior, and social structure of this country. The factors operating are not only within the separate hierarchies themselves but, beyond, within the American culture. The fact that until this generation there were no men in the paternal lines of the federal executive in any significant numbers who were themselves members of government civilian services is one of the more significant aspects of this occupational elite and one of the more significant differences between the two great hierarchies, business and government. It seems most likely that the next generation of government leaders, civilian and military, will have a sizable proportion of fathers who were members of the federal services.

CHAPTER 6

Mothers and Sons

The Mother's Lineage: Kinship Certainty and Occupational Ambiguity

The interstructural connections of the family and occupation through the generations are among the most powerful foundations of our economic and social life. On the male side of the executive's family each generation's occupation is firmly related to a lineage of fathers and sons, a principal status for any American male being his occupational location. Occupational succession, mobility, and continuity, from one generation of males to the next can be easily and securely traced.

This is not true for women in our society. Only infrequently are women directly part of occupational succession and the structural interconnections of family and occupational status. Through marriage they ordinarily assume the husband's status, much of it derived from his occupation. Previously, as daughters of their fathers, their families of orientation gave them social place in American society. As mothers, wives, and daughters they are directly in the kinship generational structure; only indirectly, through their fathers and husbands, do they derive occupational position. The first is a birthright; the second, a derivation dependent on the status of males.

In their status and persons as mothers, they exercise a powerful influence on their sons' development and later careers, but their occupational backgrounds are traced not to their own

Author of this chapter: W. Lloyd Warner.

mothers but to their fathers. Accordingly, on the mother's side to trace occupational background one must go back from the executive to his mother's father.

In order to study occupational succession through the mother's line, several operations and several different kinds of inquiry are necessary. The occupation of the mother's father and the comparison in status with the father's father give the positions of the parents at the time of marriage. (It does not give us information about the position of the mother at the time the executive left home, since the mother's position at this later date might have increased or decreased according to what had happened to the occupational position of her husband.)

The occupational origin of the man the mother married is not only directly related to occupational succession but to in-and-out-marriages or, in anthropological terms, endogamy and exogamy. If the fathers of the executives married women from their own occupational groups, the marriages were endogamous; if they married women from other occupations they were exogamous, in terms of occupation. This does not mean that a man and woman who came from different occupations might not be of relatively the same social class position—for example, owners of small business and white-collar workers. This is a kinship question; importantly, it tells us whether, and to what degree, marriage is controlled by socioeconomic factors of rank and whether our society rigidly or flexibly controls the selection of mates. Particularly for this study, it informs us of the extent occupational factors operated in the parental generation in the selection of mates and the kinds of families in which the federal executives developed and became adults.

If the controls were absolute and men and women at the parental generation, the one with which we are now concerned, could marry only at the levels of their occupational origin, then there would be complete endogamy. The sons and daughters of professional men would marry only each other, and sons and daughters of farmers would intermarry, as would those of all other occupations. There would be no exogamy. This rule of marriage, characteristic of a caste society, might eliminate another possibility (mobility by marriage) which complicates the study of bilateral occupational succession. Since occupational mobility is a prominent characteristic of government and business hierarchies, and men might be mobile occupationally and women (particularly from the previous generation) could not be, we can ask whether women marry men who are mobile from lower positions.

The Status Relations of the Mother's and Father's Lineages

Generational comparisons of marriages provide firm knowledge about stability and continuity of marriage at the same levels. Do government leaders who are the sons of fathers who married women of lower status marry wives who are lower, or do they marry women higher than they are? Do government leaders whose fathers and mothers were of the same status continue these endogamic marriages? In brief, we can view structurally the degrees of stability and continuity in marriage, degrees of out-marriage and mobility at the parents' and executives' generation, and the possible trends toward a more open or closed system of marriage.

Table 11 states succinctly a number of descriptive propositions. Generally speaking, there are few differences between the mothers' and fathers' lines in occupational background.

There is a somewhat lower percentage of families in the maternal than paternal lines for those who came from the farming class. The same close parallels between the occupations of the two sets of grandparents hold true for all the services, except for the white-collar category in the career civil service where the percentage for the mother's father doubles that of the father's father.

The percentages in each service who were major business executives for all but one service are identical. Significantly, as the percentages move from 1 per cent for the father's father in the career civil service, through 3 per cent for the political appointments, on up to 4 per cent for the father's father in the

Table 11

Comparison of Occupation of Father's Father and Mother's Father for All Services

Occupation	Civilian Federal Executives Father's father	Civilian Federal Executives Mother's father	Military Executives Father's father	Military Executives Mother's father	Career Civil Service Executives Father's father	Career Civil Service Executives Mother's father	Political Executives Father's father	Political Executives Mother's father	Foreign-Service Executives Father's father	Foreign-Service Executives Mother's father
Laborer	18%	19%	15%	14%	20%	20%	16%	16%	13%	14%
Farmer	44	39	41	38	46	41	39	35	39	32
White-collar worker	3	4	3	3	2	4	4	4	3	3
Minor business executive	4	5	6	7	4	5	5	5	5	7
Major business executive	2	2	2	3	1	1	3	3	4	4
Business owner	18	20	18	18	17	19	20	24	20	24
Professional man	10	10	13	13	9	9	12	12	14	14
Other occupation	0*	0*	0*	1	1	1	1	1	0	1
Uniformed service	1	1	2	3	0	0*	0*	0*	2	1
Total	100	100	100	100	100	100	100	100	100	100

*Less than 0.5 per cent.

foreign service, the same percentage rise takes place for the fathers of the mothers. *The differences are among the services, not between the two lines of descent.*

Among owners of business there is a slightly larger percentage for mother's father than for father's father. The percentages for the professions for all services are identical. "Government service" for both is less than 1 per cent; however, the father's father for political leaders is about twice that of the mother's father (0.9 to 0.5).

The military executives and foreign service score above 1 per cent: for the uniformed service, 2 per cent for the father's father and 3 per cent for the mother's father; for the foreign service, 1.3 per cent for the father's father and 1.1 per cent for the mother's. All other services score less than 1 per cent for grandparents in the military.

This evidence for the two sources for the leader's occupation in the third generation demonstrates the remarkable similarity between the mother's and father's lines of descent. The variations are among occupations, farming being very high and white-collar very low; among the services themselves, the career civil service is high for fathers who were laborers, and the foreign and military services low. Although there are smaller variations among the services and larger differences among the several occupations for the different services, the two lines of descent remain extraordinarily similar and constant. As the percentages for the occupation rise and fall for one paternal grandparent they do so for the other; as the smaller changes take place for any given occupation among the services, the percentages for the mother's father usually change with those of the father's father. In brief, the sources of federal leadership in the third generation bilaterally are most similar.

Why is this true? The evidence would suggest that strong influences are felt by men and women to marry those of the same or similar occupational levels of origin and family backgrounds. Although the processes leading to marriage must be diverse and multiple, central tendencies are evidently strongly

Mothers and Sons 89

felt. The men and women of the several generations were powerfully influenced by pervasively similar socioeconomic values, beliefs, and customary behavior surrounding the structural nexus of occupational succession, marriage, and status continuity.

Still we know that the fathers of the executives were often mobile men and that high proportions of them moved away from the grandparental generation into new occupations. What do their movements mean for the mobility and stability in status of the women whose own occupational origins were so similar to those of the men they married? Before answering these questions, we need to reconsider our problem.

At the time of marriage, when the mothers left their families of birth to enter their families of procreation (which produced the future government leaders), they were at the occupational levels of their own fathers. Their husbands, usually young, with careers not yet established, were like their own fathers occupationally. In the research we asked for the father's occupation at the time the leader began his own career. This meant a minimum of some twenty or twenty-five years *after* the marriage of his father and mother. Consequently, the father would have had ample time to advance his own career or, more strictly speaking, to be occupationally mobile.

If he had moved up or down or not at all before he married and if he moved up, down, or not at all after marriage, both parts of his career would be reflected in the evidence we have about his occupation. Consequently, if mobility took place for a woman from marriage, it might have been at the time of marriage, later in team with her husband, or both. She might have been ambitious and aspired to marry a man who had achieved higher status or had been born to higher status. On the other hand, she might have married a man of her own status and the two of them together achieved higher occupational position, or the two might have combined both—achievement on the part of the man before marriage and achievement of the two after marriage.

CHAPTER 7

The Wives of Government Leaders

Wives and Husbands

Many of the values and beliefs Americans share about marriage bear a close resemblance to those held about occupation: an ambitious young man can aspire to a position of highest prestige and power; and an ambitious young lady can not only dream about her prince but marry him. Sometimes dreams about marriage and job become realities; more often, reality does not easily fit such pleasant fantasies. Still everyone knows, and facts support him, that in the lives of most Americans jobs, career, and marriage are closely intertwined.[1]

At the time of the research, 96 per cent of the federal executives and 93 per cent of the business leaders were married. Our inquiries about the leaders' wives and husbands were designed to answer several important questions about the relation of occupational succession and mobility to the family structure. Briefly, we wanted to know the kinds of women the future leaders married: social and economic backgrounds; who their fathers were and their occupations. Did these men (and women) tend to emphasize the values of endogamy and marry spouses from their own occupational levels?[2]

Author of this chapter: W. Lloyd Warner.

1. See pp. 177–211 of *Occupational Mobility* and pp. 108–119 of *Big Business Leaders in America*.
2. Chapter 11, "The Careers of Women in the Federal Executive," reports that only 145 of the 10,851 civilian federal executives in this study were

The Wives of Government Leaders

Among the civilian federal executives there is an extraordinary similarity between the proportions of the occupations of the fathers and of the wives' fathers. The five occupations—laborer, white-collar worker, minor and major executive, and farmer—show exactly the same percentages for each side of the family. A slightly higher proportion of wives' fathers are business owners; a slightly higher percentage of fathers are professional men.

It will be recalled that, except in certain instances, there were no striking differences among the services in the percentages for occupational origin—the fathers were distributed rather alike among the eight occupations. But it might be supposed that the separate civilian services or the military would reveal sharp or significant differences between the percentages for the origin of the spouse. For those differences that do obtain, do the percentages for the executive's and spouse's fathers' occupations synchronize, indicating possible closely related status and endogamic values about marriage and occupation?

The foreign and military services both show a low percentage (14) of fathers who were laborers, compared with those of the career civil service, and a low percentage (12) of spouses' fathers who were laborers. The fathers of the career civil service executives who were laborers were correspondingly high (23 per cent) as were the wives' fathers (24 per cent). The percentages for father and wife's father who were white-collar men were about the same for all services.

The fathers of the foreign-service men who were major executives rise to 9 per cent and the wives' fathers who were major executives also rise to 9 per cent; for the career civil service this occupation of father drops to only 4 per cent and for the wife's father, 3 per cent. The political leaders' fathers

---

women, and only 50 were married. In other words, at the time they filled in their questionnaires approximately two-thirds were unmarried. Since our statistics about federal executives' spouses are overwhelmingly about wives, not husbands, in this chapter we shall largely refer to the spouse by the term "wife."

who were major executives held at 6 per cent, the wives' fathers at 5 per cent. The other occupations of the fathers of leaders and wives indicated similar interrelated regularity and constancy. It might be noticed that in all the services the percentages of leaders' fathers who were business owners were slightly lower than for spouses' fathers.

The military leaders, the only service having a small nucleus of fathers in their own profession (9 per cent), married wives (11 per cent) who were daughters of military men. There seem to be twin tendencies present—a solid core of military men marry endogamically and a sizable percentage continue the military life of their fathers.

The marriages of the business leaders do not always show such a close correspondence between the occupation of the executive's father and that of his wife; those for minor and major executives and for farmers vary considerably, yet in broad outline they resemble the alignments previously spoken of for the consanguine and affinal parental occupations of government executives.

The comparative frequency of marriage to persons of the same occupational background, we must add, does not actually tell us whether in fact laborers' children largely marry each other or if the daughters and sons of white-collar men intermarry and rarely marry those of other groups. Further perspective can be gained by comparing the origins of wives and mothers. Given mobile tendencies, perhaps wives were more often high born than mothers. Also, changes in American culture during this time must have affected the choice of spouses.

Table 12 shows a massive drop in all services from the percentages of mothers to wives who were farmers' daughters. Among the services there are from 2.5 to approximately 5 times the percentage of mothers who were farmers' daughters over wives. On the high side are the military leaders; the career civil services are on the low side.

The second major change between the two generations is a covariant of the first. The percentages for wives' fathers for

Table 12

The Occupational Origins of the Executives' Wives and Mothers (for the Several Services)

Occupation of spouse's father	Civilian federal executives Mother	Civilian federal executives Wife	Career civil service executives Mother	Career civil service executives Wife	Political executives Mother	Political executives Wife	Foreign-service executives Mother	Foreign-service executives Wife	Military executives Mother	Military executives Wife
Laborer	(21)* 19%	21%	(23) 20%	24%	(15) 16%	17%	(14) 14%	12%	(14) 14%	12%
White-collar worker	(9) 4	9	(10) 4	9	(9) 4	10	(7) 3	7	(9) 3	8
Minor executive	(11) 5	11	(11) 5	10	(10) 5	10	(11) 7	11	(15) 7	12
Major executive	(4) 2	4	(4) 1	3	(6) 3	5	(9) 4	9	(5) 3	7
Business owner	(20) 20	23	(20) 19	22	(21) 24	25	(19) 24	24	(19) 18	22
Professional	(19) 10	16	(16) 9	15	(24) 12	19	(25) 14	23	(18) 13	19
Farmer	(15) 39	15	(15) 41	16	(13) 35	12	(12) 32	11	(10) 38	8
Military	(0) 0	0	(0) 0	0	(0) 0	0	(0) 0	0	(9) 3	11
Other	(1) 1	1	(1) 1	1	(2) 1	2	(3) 2	3	(1) 1	1
Total	100	100	100	100	100	100	100	100	100	100

*The figures in parentheses between the percentages for the seven occupations in the four separate services are for the father.

all occupations other than farmers, and for all services, increase over those for mothers' fathers; for professional men the percentage for wife's father for each service is about half again as much as for the mother's father. In the career civil service the increase is from 9 to 15 per cent, for the political from 12 to 19 per cent, for the military from 13 to 19 per cent, and for the foreign service from 14 to 23 per cent. For all civilian federal executives the increase is from 10 to 16 per cent from the mother's father to the wife's father.

For major executives the increase for each service is approximately doubled for wife's father over mother's father, for minor executives from 0.5 to 2, and for white-collar workers from 2 to 2.5 times. For business owners there is a small but general increase for all but the foreign service. For laborers, percentages increase in the political and career civil services and decrease in the foreign service and military.

The figures in parentheses, for the father, tell a significant story about the processes of occupational succession, the bilateral family's influence on the executive's choice of his mate. They raise significant questions that later must be answered. If an executive selected a wife more in the occupational image of the mother's background it might be supposed that the cultural values within the structural influences of the mother's side were more powerful than the father's. On the other hand, if he were more likely to select a wife whose background was like the father's it might be supposed that for these purposes the influence on the executive flowed from his (own) father's position and more generally and culturally from the influence of the socially defined power in this position which helps place the family in the American economic and social structures.

It will be remembered that the percentages of farmers two generations ago all ran very high, and those for the wives, one generation ago, dropped from 2.5 to 5 times from those for the mothers of the executives. The percentages for the executives' fathers for all services are quite close to those of the wives. *The wives' percentages for all services are like the fathers of executives, not like the mothers.*

The percentages of wives with professional origins for all services are all near those of the executives' fathers (Table 12). For all services the percentages for wives' fathers who were professional men rise considerably; those with fathers who were farmers fall. Yet despite the opposing directions of the percentages for the two occupations the executives married women more like the father's side than the mother's.

A very similar story is true for the wives chosen by sons of major and minor executives and for those with fathers in the white-collar class. Given four separate governmental services (political, military, foreign, and civil) and four urban occupations (professional, white-collar, and major and minor executives), out of the sixteen possible chances that the percentages of wives' fathers' occupations would be nearer the mothers' than the fathers', it is remarkable that in no case was this true. All, with one tie, favored the father's side.

The two other occupations, laborers and business owners (the latter mostly small business men), are quite different from the others. Several of the services' percentages of the wives' occupational backgrounds for these two were nearer those of the mother; a few, however, were closer to the father's origin. Many of the small businesses are very insubstantial, ephemeral, and the owners rank relatively low occupationally, some below skilled workers.[3] The differences between these two occupations and the other four occupations *may be* that the sons of laborers and small business owners could have had less mobility drive and fewer opportunities in the generations that preceded the executive.

We must notice again that the mother's ascribed occupational origin goes back two generations to her father; the executive's father's occupational origin to only one, the parental generation. The fathers' positions tend to be nearer the ones where the executives found their mates, partly because of the direct influence of the father's position generationally, and partly because the time since the parents' marriage has

3. See pp. 131-138, Warner, Meeker and Eells, *Social Class in America* (New York, Harper, 1960).

made the mother's status more like her husband's (the executive's father), since their status as a married couple is socially defined as one. This closeness to the father also seems present partly because the influence of his whole family of birth on the executive has given him *social* place, economic position, and cultural values that more often turn him toward the father's socioeconomic position. Through the generations the exclusion of women from the line of occupational succession works for status assignment to the father's side; moreover, the values learned often move the executive's choice of mate toward the social and occupational location of the male rather than to that of the female side of the family in the placement of the next generation.

The greater transmission of social and economic place by the family and the emphasis on the father's side rather than the mother's seems in all probability to be a product of the family's reflection of change within the total world of American culture. The influences here are not confined to the structure of government or to economic and occupational matters but are much more extended. They spread throughout the value systems of this society. Historical change over a longer period of time, from a rural to an urban culture, is also heavily reflected in the lowering of the percentage of farmers from mother's father to wife's father. A greater resemblance between the occupational origins of the wife's father and the executive's father is related to their being in the same generation.

Education, Marriage, and Occupational Mobility

Higher education is the most popular and most used route for social achievement and occupational advancement. The study of the big business leaders in the United States brought out that a very high percentage was college-trained and many had higher degrees. It was also learned from this study that "higher education, particularly college, tends to lift the level of marriage from lower occupational levels and to increase the likelihood of those of higher levels marrying within their own class. Therefore, college education has, paradoxically, a double effect, the two tendencies opposing each other. On the one hand, it increases the likelihood of the complete social acceptance (marriage) of those from lower levels, but for those born to high position it tends to strengthen status discriminations in the choice of a mate."

The federal executives were also queried about their educational achievements; this and other matters about education are fully treated in Chapter 8. Here the concern is with the relation of the kinds of marriages made by the federal executives to differing educational attainments, by type of service. For example, is it possible that the men of the foreign service who are highly educated are more likely to marry at higher levels than men with the same educational achievement in some of the other services such as career civil service? Table 13 gives the percentages for all services of college graduates and those with some college or with high-school training who married wives from different occupational levels. Those with less education were too few in this context to treat statistically.[4]

The effect of a college degree on marriage is not so substantial for the civilian federal executives as for business leaders. On the whole, those with less education marry in larger proportions women of lower status than those who have at least an A.B. The column at the far left of Table 13 shows that a higher percentage of civilian federal executives who did not complete college (27 per cent) married the daughters of laborers than those who did (20 per cent). On the other hand, there is only a slight rise in the percentage of college graduates (13 per cent) over nongraduates (11 per cent) who married daughters of big businessmen; but a considerable one for college graduates (18 per cent) over those who did not go on (10 per cent) among men who married the daughters of professional men. A considerably lower percentage of college graduates (14 per cent) married farmers' daughters than those with lower educational attainments (19 per cent).

4. See Ch. 8 for the percentages of those who have college degrees; the percentage of men with little education is exceedingly small for federal executives.

Table 13

Education and Marriage by the Occupation of the Spouse's Father

Occupation of spouse's father	Civilian Federal Executives Col. grad.	Civilian Federal Executives Some col. or H.S. grad.	Military Executives Col. grad.	Military Executives Some col. or H.S. grad.	Career Civil Executives Col. grad.	Career Civil Executives Some col. or H.S. grad.	Political Executives Col. grad.	Political Executives Some col. or H.S. grad.	Foreign-Service Executives Col. grad.	Foreign-Service Executives Some col. or H.S. grad.
Laborer	20%	27%	11%	22%	23%	28%	17%	20%	12%	17%
White-collar worker	20	20	19	21	20	20	22	17	18	19
Owner of small business	15	13	12	16	15	13	14	15	11	14
Major executive or owner of large business	13	11	18	11	11	10	16	20	22	19
Professional man	18	10	20	16	16	10	20	9	26	14
Farmer	14	19	8	11	15	19	11	19	11	17
Uniformed service	0	0	12	3	0	0	0	0	0	0
Total per cent	100	100	100	100	100	100	100	100	100	100
Total number	8,131	1,774	1,803	233	5,537	1,459	1,505	162	1,033	140

This same broad configuration holds for the separate services, the status differences in marriage being somewhat accentuated by military leaders. The other services individually do not vary much from the general civilian federal executives for marriage to daughters of laborers, big business leaders, professional men, and farmers. Marriage to daughters of owners of small business and of white-collar men shows slight variation among the services; college achievement or less seems to make little difference.

Briefly, higher education has a similar effect on the marriage of federal executives and business leaders: those of lower occupational origins with a college degree are more likely to marry out and up; those of higher origin are more likely to marry at their own level and less likely to marry women of lower occupational rank. The principal differences in education and marriage between the elites are two: (1) higher education among the big business leaders seems to accent endogamy more for those of high origin and emphasize exogamy more for those of lower origin than among government leaders; and (2) higher education, since it occurs more often among federal executives than among business leaders, is possibly less remarkable, and therefore may not enter into their values so strongly in choosing a wife.

The spread of business leaders runs from the extreme of the very highly educated with several higher degrees to those with no more, and sometimes less, than a grade-school diploma. The poorly educated business leader from a laboring background is less likely to be able to marry a woman of higher status, who is usually college trained. Moreover, a laborer's son who is college trained is less likely to choose an "uneducated" woman. An educated man who is an up-and-coming son of a laborer may have more to recommend him as a mate to an educated daughter of a big business leader than a man of higher origins with low educational attainment.

However, the values of marriage, occupation, career, and higher education mesh and motivate all these American men and women. Paradoxically, the greater emphasis on higher education and its achievement among federal executives seems to have partly reduced the discriminatory effects that it seems to have exerted among business leaders. Nevertheless, the effect of higher education on federal executives is more like that exerted on business leaders than not.

Further demonstration of these several propositions about education and marriage in the two elites was carried out by combining the aristocratic principles of occupational succession with higher and lower educational achievement. Two generations of business leaders and professional men were examined plus the current generation of civilian federal executives and big business leaders; four occupations are present and two levels of educational achievement. (Less than highschool graduation is cut because of too few cases.)

We found that daughters of higher-status occupations— major business executives and high professions—are more often chosen by the college graduates of both elites: about two-thirds of the business leaders who were college graduates married women of this level and approximately half of the college-trained civilian federal executives.

Only 2 per cent of the college graduates among business leaders married laborers' daughters compared with 9 per cent of the civilian federal executives (over four times higher). Slightly more of the latter, percentagewise, also married daughters of farmers and white-collar men. Higher education is related to the endogamic values of this birth elite, and exogamic values are reduced among the more highly educated in both; yet education is less likely to keep men bound to their own kind among federal executives than among business leaders.

In the lowest categories of education, the federal executives without college degrees have a higher percentage than business leaders who married laborers' daughters (17 and 9 per cent), farmers' daughters (16 and 11 per cent), and daughters of white-collar workers (32 and 27 per cent). A much smaller percentage (35 per cent) married women of higher status than did business leaders (53 per cent).

The less educated government leaders more often marry women from less highly valued occupations than do business leaders; moreover, business leaders who are college graduates are more status conscious in choosing a wife than are the highly educated federal executives.

Marriage and Achievement

Since it is often asserted that marrying the boss's daughter is a quick and easy way to get ahead we wanted to know if men of high and low status who marry women of high rank achieve higher position in less time than those who marry women of lower status. In brief, what is the relation of marriage to achievement time (the period from the time the executive became self-supporting until he held the first high position in the government elite)?

The mean number of years to reach the top was determined for each kind of occupation and for each type of marriage. For example, it took the sons of laborers who married the daughters of laborers 18 years (17.8) to get to the top and a year more (19.2) when they married daughters of farmers; but when they married big business leaders' daughters it took them only 16 years (15.7). From all occupational backgrounds except the professions a man who married the daughter of a farmer took longer than the average for his occupational background to reach the position of high federal executive.

There is a span of over three years, from 16 to 19, among the means of the time taken to reach the top for the civilian federal executives. The span of time for each service, for the business leaders, and for the six occupations varies, but not greatly: for the business leader the span ranged from 21 to 26 years; for the military leader, from 24 to 28 years; for the career civil service from 16 to 19 years; for the political leaders from 12 to 19 years; and for the foreign service from 17 to 20 years, or a period of some three years' time difference for marriages to women from different backgrounds.

Nativity, Geographic Origins, and Marriage

Since there is a significant and important relation between family background and occupational career, both for big business leaders and for federal executives, the kinds of women the executives marry (i.e. of high or low origin) can be a crucial test of the aristocratic and equalitarian values of the American society. Ethnic status and other cultural differences between those of ethnic background and those classed as "old Americans" can provide further barriers to marriage and test further how other extraneous factors may operate in the careers of the men in the different services. Since rank and ethnic status are closely interrelated it would be supposed that the old American would be advantaged, and the foreign born disadvantaged, in obtaining mates. This should be the hypothesis, given the more general one that status and rank do have an influence on the careers of the men in federal service.

The study of executives in business and industry indicated that, "in general those men whose grandfathers and fathers were American born tend more to marry women from the higher levels and less to marry those from the lower levels than the men who were foreign born or first generation American." Moreover, the study also concluded that "a comparison with the percentage for the total showed that while old Americans are advantaged, the differences are not drastic and do not indicate that ethnic status is necessarily a deterrent to marriage at any higher levels."

The results of the study of the federal executives tell a somewhat different story. The nativity of the civilian federal executive (from father's father U.S. born to the executive himself being foreign born) was charted against the occupation of the spouse's father. For all civilian executives, 13 per cent of the marriages were to daughters of big business men; for those who were foreign born, 18 per cent of the marriages were to women of this high position; and for those who had been in America at least three generations, only 13 per cent.

The marriage of business leaders whose fathers were old Americans to women who came from a background of the professional classes ranks over those of the foreign-born business leaders, the former with 18 per cent, the latter with 11 per cent; among the federal executives who married the daughters of professional men the foreign born have a slight advantage over old Americans (20 and 18 per cent). Moreover, the percentage of foreign-born federal executives who married daughters of laborers was lower than for any other category of nativity—16 per cent as compared with 26 per cent of those executives who were American born but of foreign parentage, 25 per cent of those whose fathers were U.S. born, and 18 per cent of those whose families had been here for at least three generations. The foreign born were much less likely to marry among the disadvantaged farmers—only 9 per cent, compared with 18 per cent of those executives whose families had been here for at least three generations.

The foreign-born executive is not disadvantaged in his ability to acquire a mate; rather, he seems to be at a slight advantage. In both these powerful and prestigeful hierarchies, business and government, ethnic origin does not generally create insuperable barriers for marriage into the occupational classes that are evaluated as superior nor does being born in America make it likely that an executive will not marry women who come from modest backgrounds.

The percentages for the military are rather similar to those of the civilian federal executives. For example, the same percentages of foreign born marry the daughters of big business leaders (18 per cent), and more of the foreign born marry the daughters of professional men (25 per cent) than those whose fathers' fathers were born in the United States (19 per cent).

PART IV

Education

CHAPTER 8

The Education of Federal Executives

That formal education is the key to occupational mobility in American life has long been understood; many studies underscore and reaffirm that almost every area of the higher occupations in America is staffed by men with college educations. In this chapter we will find that the high-level public administrators, with few exceptions, have at least been to college, and that the great majority are college graduates. We will examine the function of education as the instrument in American society most closely linked to occupational succession—the tendency for some men to continue at the same occupational levels as their fathers—and to occupational mobility for others out of their fathers' lower occupations into higher occupational status.

College training is a basic step in the careers of the overwhelming proportion of federal executives, regardless of occupational and geographic origins. Higher education is crucial in that failure to achieve it bars all but a few men from entrance into the federal elites.

The relation of the kind of college training to success is important, as are, also, type of degree, area of specialization, and the differences in college training as related to differences in backgrounds derived from the family of origin.

College Training and the Federal Elites

Ninety-five per cent of all civilian federal executives in 1959 had at least some college training, and 81 per cent were college

Author of this chapter: Orvis F. Collins.

graduates. Even a larger proportion, 88 per cent, of military executives were college graduates, and 98 per cent had attended college. Among each of the three separate civilian elites there were only minor differences in the proportions who went to college. Smaller proportions of career civil service executives than of foreign service and political executives were college graduates, but with few exceptions men in all the civilian elites had some college training.

Failure to attend high school, the other extreme in the educational ladder, is disqualifying. In each of the federal elites, less than one-half of one per cent terminated education before attending high school. The proportions for those who left the educational ladder at the high-school level are only slightly larger.

How higher education functions to sort men who are qualified for entrance into the federal elites from those who are not is forcefully underscored by Table 14, showing the ratios between proportions of federal executives at three levels of education and proportions of males in the U.S. adult population at these levels. For every person in the national adult male population who has been to college, 5.94 civilian and 6.13 military federal executives have been to college. Men with high-school education are as heavily under-represented as those with college are over-represented. For every hundred men in the adult male population who finished education with high school, there were only thirteen civilian and five military federal executives. Men in the federal elites with less than high-school education are not, in terms of these ratios, represented at all.

The three broad, traditional American educational strata of grade school, high school, and college obscure the important fact that, although men who merely attended college are over-represented, they are not nearly so over-represented as college graduates. For every man in the adult male population who is a college graduate, nine civilian and almost ten military executives are college graduates. Only 2 civilian and 1.43 military leaders merely attended college for each person in the

Table 14

*Ratios of Educational Levels of Men in the Elites to Educational Levels of U.S. Adult Males**

Education of executive	Civilian federal executives	Career civil service executives	Foreign-service executives	Political executives	Military executives	Business leaders
Less than high school	0.00	0.00	0.00	0.00	0.00	0.07
High school	0.13	0.18	0.05	0.08	0.05	0.63
College	5.94	5.81	6.13	6.06	6.13	5.85

*1952 business leaders/1950 U.S. adult males = ratio; 1959 federal executives/1957 U.S. adult males = ratio.

adult male population in this category. It is clear that, while merely attending college improves a man's chances of becoming a federal executive, college graduation is the really crucial qualifying step.

Since the decision to go to college and the line of action leading to college graduation are of decisive importance, we need to know the social and economic factors involved. This is a social process of basic importance for a society subscribing to Jeffersonian principles of equal opportunity.

Father's Occupation and College Education

Table 15 shows how college education acts as a selector among men with different occupational backgrounds, at the same time transforming those with unequal occupational backgrounds into men with more or less equal chances to become federal executives. The data in this table have been arranged to give the reader an immediate and over-all view of the crucial role of college graduation in preparation for government executive status. Percentages of men from each occupational origin have been distributed through four educational levels. For example, of the sons of unskilled workers who became federal executives, 4 per cent did not graduate from high school, 7 per cent graduated from high school, 11 per cent attended college but dropped out, and 78 per cent graduated (a total of 100 per cent of sons of unskilled workers).

In the four educational levels, the reader will see immediately the function of college graduation as a preparatory step for entering the administrative elites. In each instance over 70 per cent of executives are college graduates, regardless of the occupations of their fathers, but there are differences in the percentages of college graduates by occupational origin. For example, among all civilian federal executives 89 per cent of sons of professional men are college graduates and only 73 per cent of the sons of skilled laborers are college graduates. Ninety-one per cent of sons of professional men who are foreign-service executives are college graduates compared to only 77 per cent of sons of skilled laborers in this elite. These per-

Table 15

Percentages, by Father's Occupation, of Men in the Elites at Four Levels of Education

Occupation of Father	Civilian federal executives	Career civil service executives	Foreign-service executives	Political executives	Military executives	Business leaders
Executives Who Did not Graduate from High School							
Unskilled laborer	4%	5%	0%	3%	3%	32%
Skilled laborer	3	4	2	1	1	25
Owner of small business	1	1	0	1	0*	13
White-collar worker	1	2	0*	1	0	16
Major business executive	0*	0*	1	0	0*	5
Professional man	0*	0*	0	0*	0*	5
Farmer	1	2	0	1	1	15
Uniformed service	0	0	0	0	1	0
Executives Who Graduated from High School							
Unskilled laborer	7	8	3	5	0	16
Skilled laborer	7	8	2	2	5	20
Owner of small business	4	4	3	3	1	12
White-collar worker	5	6	2	2	2	14
Major business executive	2	3	1	2	1	7
Professional man	2	2	2	2	1	6
Farmer	5	6	1	3	1	15
Uniformed service	0	0	0	0	1	0
Executives Who Had Some College							
Unskilled laborer	11	12	6	3	18	16
Skilled laborer	17	17	19	13	13	21
Owner of small business	12	14	11	4	11	18
White-collar worker	15	16	14	9	11	20
Major business executive	15	19	8	8	11	18
Professional man	9	12	7	4	7	17
Farmer	14	15	9	9	12	20
Uniformed service	0	0	0	0	5	0
Executives Who Graduated from College							
Unskilled laborer	78	75	91	89	79	36
Skilled laborer	73	71	77	84	81	34
Owner of small business	83	81	86	92	88	57
White-collar worker	79	76	84	88	87	50
Major business executive	83	78	90	90	88	70
Professional man	89	86	91	94	92	72
Farmer	80	77	90	87	86	50
Uniformed service	0	0	0	0	93	0

*Less than 0.5 per cent.

centage differences are in themselves important, but they are of small consequence when compared with the fact that federal executives from all occupational levels are selected primarily from the population of college graduates.

When we recall[1] the great differences in percentage of men from these various groups in the federal elites, we can see how higher education has functioned as a selective device. There are more men of higher occupational backgrounds in the federal elites precisely because more men from these prestigeful groups are able to attend college. In this manner higher education functions to maintain occupational succession. Sons of men in high occupational status have more than equal opportunity to secure the educational qualifications necessary to maintain or enhance high status in their own lifetime.

Higher education has, however, a second and opposite function since it acts as a transforming agent to qualify men from all occupational backgrounds for entrance into elite positions. Where it operates in this fashion, it functions as a leveling device. Once a man, regardless of occupational origins, enters college, he begins a process that qualifies him for entrance into the elites. A worker's son who decides to go to college and carries out his decision to the point of graduation has made the crucial step in placing himself on an equal opportunity footing with sons of professional men and major executives.

The awareness on the part of men from higher occupational backgrounds that college is a necessary step, and their possession of resources with which to implement this awareness, is their crucial advantage over men from less favored economic origins. In this perception, and execution of the line of action devolving from it, they are supported by the adults around them, both attitudinally and economically.

This dual function of higher education clearly fits the fundamental principles of American life, in (1) receiving in greater than equal representation sons of men from higher occupational status, accounting for its importance for occupational stability between the generations, and (2) transforming men

1. See Ch. 2, "Fathers and Sons: Occupational Origins."

from lower occupational levels, making it important in the process of occupational mobility.

Education Levels of Executives and Their Fathers

Education as a method of both occupational stability and mobility is also seen in the fact that federal executives went to college regardless of the educational level achieved by their fathers. Ninety-one per cent of civilian and 98 per cent of military executives whose fathers had less than high-school education went to college; and 94 per cent of civilian and 97 per cent of military executives whose father had only high-school education went to college. These figures on educational mobility are in part a reflection of the general increase in education levels in the United States but, more importantly, they show the overwhelming importance of college training as qualification for movement into these administrative elites. Each of the separate civilian elites shows variation, but this is not important in comparison with the over-all pattern of educational mobility. Of the small percentage of executives who did not go beyond high school a very small percentage had fathers who went to college—i.e. almost no educational mobility downward. Fathers who went to college produced sons who went to college, with exceptions to this generalization occurring only two or three times out of every hundred. Men whose fathers had not achieved higher education showed in almost all cases an upward mobility in education which foreshadowed and laid the groundwork for later occupational mobility. The federal executives went to college, regardless of occupational or educational levels attained by their fathers.

Education Levels of Federal and Business Executives

To this point we have discussed only the educational levels of federal elites, although tables presented include figures for the 1952 business leaders. (This procedure has been followed to reduce the number of tables and at the same time to simplify delineation.) A brief comparison of federal executives with business leaders will aid primarily in examining one problem.

Federal executives are, on the whole, much more highly educated than business leaders: 95 per cent of all civilian executives and 98 of military executives had some college education, compared with only 76 per cent of the business leaders; 81 per cent of the civilian executives and 88 per cent of the military leaders are college graduates, compared with only 57 per cent of the business leaders.

But how many of these differences in proportions result from the fact that the data for federal executives were collected seven years after those for the business leader—seven years during which the GI bill and generally high levels of prosperity greatly increased the percentage of college-trained men in the total population? For every 100 men in the adult male population in 1950 who were college graduates, 814 business leaders were college graduates. This figure is less than, but not much less than, the 1 to 9 ratio for all civilian executives and the 1 to 9.78 ratio for military leaders. We see that shifts in the national adult male percentages of college-educated men result in much smaller differences in ratios of federal executives and business leaders than is shown by the percentages alone. If one compares business leaders and federal executives against the mediating fact of national educational levels, the differences are not so pronounced as they appear at first sight.

The fact does remain, however, that the 1959 executives are more often college trained than the business leaders of 1952. While it is likely that a similar sample of business leaders taken in 1959 would show a much higher proportion college-trained than in 1952 (for example, recent studies by Fortune Magazine), it is not likely that the entire 24 per cent of the business leaders who had not been to college would have—in the seven-year interval—been replaced by college-trained men. Would they have been replaced in sufficient numbers to bring the figures down to equal the 5 per cent for all civilian and 2 per cent for military executives?

From the discussion so far in this chapter, higher education emerges as a very basic process which transforms men from all walks of life into candidates for eventual movement into the business and federal elites. Men from the more prestigeful occupations may be over-represented in the federal elites largely because they are the men who more often attend and graduate from college; but the main route for men from all occupational, educational, and regional backgrounds into the federal elites is higher education.

What Kind of Higher Education Do They Get?

Since civilian and military executives in overwhelming proportions graduated from college, a bachelor's degree at the four-year level has become almost a minimal requirement. We must therefore shift our interest from college graduation to levels of college education: How many men received degrees beyond the four-year level and what is the influence of the father's occupation upon securing advanced degrees?

We divided the number of advanced degrees reported in each of the four elites and then repeated this operation by occupational background. Relatively large proportions of these executives went beyond the four-year degree. Almost one-fourth of all civilian and an only slightly smaller proportion of military executives obtained a master's degree. Among the civilian elites, almost one-third of the foreign-service officers reported the master's degree, slightly less than one-fourth of the career civil service executives, and about one-fifth of the political executives. Almost 40 per cent, however, of the political executives hold law degrees.[2] The four-year degree, which only a decade ago was thought of as the terminal degree for the majority of college people, is becoming increasingly only a step toward achievement of full educational qualification for movement into the administrative elites.

As education increases at the master's level, men tend to go on to the doctoral degree. There is at present one doctoral degree among every ten civilian executives, and only about one for every hundred military executives.

2. The political executive group has a sizable number of lawyers in legal positions; there are almost no legal positions in the career civil service.

After receiving the bachelor's degree, education may continue up the academic ladder to the doctorate, or it may follow an alternative route of securing the formal academic requisites for entering one of the established and prestigeful professions. For political executives a law degree is the alternative to a master's degree. A smaller proportion of political executives than any other elite took a master's degree, but well over one-third of all political executives report holding a law degree, a proportion much greater than for any of the other elites, reflecting the fact that political executives are characteristically men who come into the federal executive through careers anchored in law. Slightly less than one in ten of the career civil service executives holds a law degree, and the proportion is even less (8 per cent) for foreign-service executives. The 3.5 per cent of military executives who hold the law degree indicates that law is not a main route into this group. Doctors of medicine, whose profession is one of great prestige, are not present in great numbers in any of these elites. This may in part result from the fact that the uniformed Public Health Service is not represented in the present sample and in part from the fact that the unique requirements of the medical profession do not prepare or motivate men to administrative leadership.

Advanced Degrees and Father's Occupation

With increasing numbers of men taking advanced academic and professional degrees, a question of great import for the functioning of our society is: Do the sons of men in occupations of power and prestige dominate in this area and thus maintain an advantage over men from occupations of less prestige? If such is the case, the functioning of higher education as a mechanism of upward occupational mobility may be an illusion and securing the A.B. degree not really a passport into the administrative elites.

Rather decisive evidence indicates that the more advanced degrees are not monopolized by sons of high-status men; on the contrary, men from lower status compete quite successfully.

Master's degrees were taken by 24.1 per cent of civilian and 23.6 per cent of military executives. Within the civilian elites, however, considerable variation exists. Almost a third of the foreign-service men and only one in five of the political executives took master's degrees. But in law degrees these proportions are reversed, with well over a third of the political and only one out of ten of the foreign-service executives taking these degrees. Political executives, then, took law as an alternative to the master's degree.

Among those men who did take the master's degree, several economic, cultural, and psychological forces appear to operate differentially for men from the various occupational groups. For example, master's degrees are held by sons of professional men among civilian executives (29.3 per cent) and among military executives (24.2 per cent)—percentages placing them near the upper extreme. This is in keeping with the cultural traditions of professional families. We could dismiss this group if it were not for the fact that sons of farm tenants or owners do about as well as sons of professional men; also, among military leaders, sons of unskilled laborers and clerical workers have higher proportions with master's degrees.

These contradictions are partly resolved by regrouping selected professions. For example, we arranged seven selected occupations by scalar values within one status hierarchy. The percentages for unskilled laborers, skilled laborers, and foremen show that the assumption that men from higher occupations tend to go on for the master's degree is not true—in fact for this subhierarchy within the occupational groups quite the opposite is true. Among all civilian and among military executives larger proportions of sons of unskilled workers have their master's, then skilled workers, then foremen. The same pattern holds for each of the three civilian elites viewed separately. Although the differences between percentages are quite small, when we compare owners of small with owners of large business, or when we compare clerical people with executives, the same pattern emerges.

Within these subhierarchies are operating factors differing

from the cultural one to which may be ascribed the high proportions of sons of professional men who took master's degrees. We can speculate that two influences are present. Sons of men in the lower statuses may be men of unusual motivation toward higher education. They are the men who had the imagination and purpose to break away from their backgrounds and push on through the first four years of college. Having achieved the first four years, they chose to use even further the route of education to overcome initial handicaps.

A second factor may also operate; there may be no alternative to the master's degree among a group not having opportunities open for employment. While sons of foremen, executives, and owners of large business may have had opportunities thrust upon them, men from lower occupational status may have continued with their education in lieu of such opportunities. As we shall see, one opportunity they may not have had was to move into the profession of law. This theory that higher-status men may be drained out of the educational process by intervening opportunity is reinforced by the strong showing of sons of farmers at the master's level. Coming from rural areas, they may simply not have had strong enough contacts in the urban world of bureaucracy into which they were moving.

One method for testing these ideas is to apply them to the percentages of men from the various occupations who took Ph.D. degrees. Sons of professional men have the highest percentage among all civilian executives with doctoral degrees, and this is also true among career civil service executives. Among political executives, however, sons of farm tenants or owners have a slightly higher (17.3 to 14.8) percentage than do sons of professional men. Among foreign-service men, sons of clerks or salesmen, farm tenants or owners, owners of small business, and unskilled or semiskilled laborers all have greater percentages with the doctoral degree than do sons of professional men. So few military leaders reported having the Ph.D. that they were not considered.

When the selected occupations are arranged by scalar value,

The Education of Federal Executives

as for the master's degree, the percentages of men holding the doctoral degree are smaller than those holding the master's degree, but the same pattern of higher percentages from lower statuses holds for all civilian and for each of the individual civilian services.

The cultural and social forces that function to select greater proportions for colleges and universities from higher occupational status have even been reversed. The forces that prevent sons of men in less privileged occupations from entering college may have the opposite effect of holding these same men in college to secure the advanced master's and doctoral degrees. It should be borne in mind that the selective process which prevented the bulk of men of lower status from entering college has insured that the men from these statuses who did take four-year degrees were unusually motivated toward securing higher education. Once they achieved the four-year degree, they pushed on to higher degrees. In part this results, as we postulated earlier, from a lack of suitable alternatives.

One alternative to continuing for the strictly academic master's and doctoral degrees is to choose one of the two great professions—law or medicine. We do not have enough cases to examine the occupational origins of men who took the alternative route of medicine. However, the higher proportions of men who took law degrees are not from occupational groups with either more or less prestige.

As we saw earlier, law is the main occupational route leading to the status of political executive. The 40 per cent of all political appointees having degrees in law show no pattern of either high or low occupational origin: the highest percentage (45) is for sons of professional men, but the next highest is for sons of small business owners (43.6), and third for sons of unskilled laborers (43.2). The percentages for all occupational origin groups, except foremen and farm tenants or owners, are remarkably similar.

The relationship between the occupational origins of these executives and advanced degrees is more complex than might be expected. We have suggested in this chapter a notion that going on toward advanced work is, in part, an alternative to more immediate opportunities. The strong showing of sons of professional men holding all types of advanced degrees suggests that family traditions of scholarship deterred these men from accepting more immediate employment before they completed what they believe to be their proper educational goals. Sons of unskilled workers and farmers, on the other hand, may continue on to advanced degrees not so much because of family tradition but because in their early years stable, continuous employment may not be open to them. Sons of owners of large business and of executives seem not to value advanced degrees over beginning their careers, but do go into the profession of law as a step in their career line. Men coming from supervisory and white-collar families lack the traditions of men from professional families, have more job opportunities than sons of unskilled workers and farmers, but do not have the career lines open to them as do sons of executives and business owners. They move into jobs when these are available, but not so large a number of good opportunities is available to them.

Academic Areas in Which They Took Degrees

For these predominantly college-educated men, the first of a series of steps leading to their present occupational status was choice of an area of specialization in college.[3] This choice may be regarded as the first of a long series of moves, each of which opens up certain career perspectives and closes others. For men who go beyond the four-year degree, not one but several choices of areas of specialization may be made, each at a succeeding level. For men who were to become federal executives,

3. The humanities were defined in this research as including languages (except where studied "scientifically" as linguistics) and literature, the fine arts and music, classical studies, philosophy, and history. The behavioral sciences include psychology, economics, political science, anthropology, sociology, and other aspects of human behavior in which the study was not conceived of as directly applicable to solution of "practical problems." The physical sciences were conceived of as those studies (physics, chemistry,

these decisions were of crucial importance and had great influence on which of the federal elites they entered. The initial choice was specialization for the four-year degree. Table 16 shows that career civil service executives concentrated heavily in the applied fields of engineering and administration, or in the physical or biological sciences. This is in sharp contrast to foreign-service leaders, who concentrated in the hu-

Table 16

Areas of Specialization by Type of Service

at the Four-Year Level

Executive	The humanities	Behavioral sciences	Physical and Biological sciences	Applied Fields
Career civil service executives	9.3%	15.7%	23.4%	47.6%
Political executives	21.5	24.0	16.9	33.1
Foreign-service executives	32.1	30.1	12.2	19.6
Military executives	5.5	5.0	7.9	78.8

mathematics, and so on) of physical phenomena not directly addressed to solution of "practical" problems. Fields of applied knowledge in the physical sciences were considered engineering. Biological sciences as a field exclude those specializations intended to prepare for careers in such occupations as teaching, agriculture, and so on.

Law degrees leading to professional status were grouped together as one class whether at the bachelor, master, or doctoral level. The rationale for this was to group together all men with professional degrees in law. A small number of men reported degrees in law (and in medicine) not leading to professional standing. These have not been included as law degrees but have been treated separately at the bachelor's, master's, and doctoral levels.

The term "medical degree" includes all those fields which apply the biological sciences to the arts of healing. It includes medical doctor, veterinarian, nursing, and dentistry, as well as other categories of medicine. The point is to manities and in the behavioral sciences. Political executives were spread fairly evenly through the four areas, occupying something of a middle ground between career and foreign-service executives. Military executives were concentrated in the applied fields; this is partly accounted for by the fact that we have included military science in this field.

At this early point in their careers the proportions of men in these four federal elites already differed greatly in the areas of study and work that appealed to them. Relatively large proportions of career civil service and military executives chose fields of applied knowledge, in contrast to the foreign-service leaders who chose the humanities.

As the men advanced to higher academic and professional degrees they increasingly concentrated in a few areas, but these fields of specialization differ from one elite to another. Civilian executives concentrated in the sciences, with almost three-fourths of all their doctoral degrees taken within these areas: about one-half in the physical and biological sciences, and about one-fourth in the behavioral sciences. The tendency for federal executives to seek formal education appropriate to their careers is shown by the fact that 465 of these men took a second degree at the same level as their first one. Over one-third of the second degrees at the same level were taken in law.

The alternative route into law was also followed by a large number of the civilian executives—men who were to become civilian federal executives and who first attained professional and doctoral degrees, concentrated in the behavioral, physical, and biological sciences and in the profession of law.

For career civil service executives, the pattern is much the

---

bring all these specializations together, and the decision to do this was taken partly because of the number (less than 300) of the civilian executives who reported holding various kinds of medical degrees.

The categories for types of degrees received will be understandable to the reader, except for the category of "second degree—all levels." These include 452 degrees listed by civilian and 82 degrees listed by military executives in addition to a first degree taken earlier at one or another academic level. For example, an executive who reported he had taken a master's degree in public administration and had then taken a master's level law degree had his law degree recorded as a "second" degree.

The Education of Federal Executives

same as for all civilian executives. At the four-year level a third of these men took work in engineering. Otherwise, the proportions are spread through the other areas of specialization. Here again, however, the movement into the sciences takes place. As in the case of civilian executives, career civil service executives are drawn at the doctoral level from the three science areas, with law probably less important than for all civilian executives.

Political executives at the bachelor's level come from the liberal arts more than do career civil service leaders. At the bachelor's level higher proportions are trained in the humanities and in the behavioral sciences. The physical and biological sciences and engineering are relatively of less importance at the four-year level.

Political executives resemble both civilian executives and career civil service executives in their movement at the master's and doctoral levels into the sciences. At the master's level, the percentage in the humanities drops from 21.5 to 4.8, and the percentage in the physical sciences increases from 11.9 to 23.8. At the doctoral level, 46.4 per cent of the degrees are in the physical sciences and 25.7 per cent in the behavioral sciences, with these two areas accounting for 72.1 per cent of all doctoral degrees. The important characteristic of political executives is, however, their concentration in the area of law. Of the 134 second degrees at all levels taken by these men, almost two-thirds were in law. They received 751 law degrees compared with only 361 master and 229 doctoral degrees. The heaviest proportion of political executives built their careers primarily on the practice of law.

In sharp contrast to both career and political executives, the greater proportions of foreign-service officers did not receive training in the physical sciences, in engineering, or in law. At the four-year level they concentrated most heavily in the humanities and in the behavioral sciences. Almost two-thirds of the bachelor's degrees received by foreign-service officers were in these two areas, with the remainder scattered over the other areas. We have seen that in the other civilian elites men, who as undergraduates were in the humanities, moved out of this field upon taking the bachelor's degree. Although the proportions in the humanities drop slightly, almost a fourth of the foreign-service executives took doctoral degrees in the humanities, and over a third took doctorals in the behavioral sciences. The sharpest contrast between foreign-service executives and career and political executives is that relatively few foreign-service officers take advanced degrees in the physical or biological sciences. Law is unimportant as a preparatory step for entrance into the foreign-service elite, with only 102 of 1,773 total degrees being held in this field.

About 60 per cent of the men holding high position in the military elites laid the groundwork for their careers by securing military science educations. This figure heavily underscores the importance of military science as the first step toward a military career. However, 40 per cent in these high positions did not take military science at the four-year level, contradicting the popular conception that the upper reaches of military rank are the exclusive preserve of men who went through Annapolis or West Point. The concentration in military science and in engineering at the four-year level is, however, quite high: if we add to the 59.8 per cent who took military science the 11.7 per cent who took engineering, we find that over 70 per cent of all four-year degrees reported were in these two areas.

At the master's level, the majority of military leaders shift into engineering. At this level engineering and business administration combined account for 72.6 per cent of all degrees reported. Although a heavy shift out of military science into engineering takes place, the educational backgrounds of the majority of military executives are confined to these two areas, and to the closely allied area of business administration. Only 23 military executives went on to their doctorates, and only 74 specialized in law.

Military executives are trained in military science, in engineering, and to a much lesser extent in business administration. Only two out of ten military executives were trained in the aggregate of all other areas at the A.B. level, and only one out of four at the M.A. level.

The process of specialization, which was to channel the careers of federal executives into the four different federal elites, began to take shape at the undergraduate level. A third of the career civil service executives took four-year degrees in engineering, compared with only about 20 per cent of political and about 7 per cent of foreign-service executives. Military leaders in 60 per cent of the instances began their careers with training in the military sciences. At the doctoral level career civil service executives concentrated in the physical and biological sciences, with a lesser concentration in the behavioral sciences. In sharp contrast, foreign-service leaders began their college careers in about equal proportions in the humanities and the social sciences and stayed in these or closely allied fields, on the whole through the doctoral programs. Political executives showed a strong tendency to move out of the strictly academic fields into the profession of law. The military executives have military science and engineering backgrounds. Although few of these men could have known while they were in college that they were to become executives in government, by their choice of area of specialization they were enhancing the possibility that they would move eventually into one of the federal elites.

CHAPTER 9

The Colleges and Universities That Produce Executives

The routes into the federal elites have many different beginnings. In greater or lesser proportions, men come from affluent families and from families of low economic and social standing. They come from great cities and from isolated farms, and from every region of the country. Regardless, however, of place of birth and occupation of father, for the vast majority the route led through higher education.

The overwhelming importance of higher education and advanced degrees in the careers of federal executives focuses our attention on the institutions that produced them. There are over two thousand institutions of higher learning in the United States, but thirty of them granted 40 per cent of all the civilian federal executives' A.B. degrees and thirty granted 75 per cent of all the Ph.D.'s.

Although each elite is different from the others in the proportions who attended different types of institutions, and a relatively small number of schools produced the majority of federal executives, all types of colleges and universities are represented.[1]

Author of this chapter: Orvis F. Collins.

1. There is an extremely complex variety of colleges and universities in this country. They can be classified in many different ways. We have chosen to use only four categories: (1) those financed by state and municipal governments, (2) those sponsored and financed by private, religious, and philan-

Career civil service, political, foreign-service, and military executives began their careers by choosing—in varying proportions—different areas of specialization in college. They also attended in varying proportions different types of colleges (Table 17). Career civil service executives more often attended public institutions than did political, foreign-service, or military executives. Foreign-service officers more than others attended private institutions. Almost two-thirds of the military executives attended technical institutions (including 17 per cent at the U.S. Naval Academy and 32 per cent at West Point) which sets this elite sharply apart from the others.

When we consider that the simple classification of institutions employed here throws together within each category widely differing schools, the proportional differences are quite distinct. At the M.A. degree level these differences continue among civilian elites, but military executives have moved in large proportions out of the technical schools into the private colleges and universities. At the doctoral level, career civil service executives are still more highly represented in the public institutions than are political and career executives. Thus, at all three levels of advanced degrees the foreign-service and political executives more often received their degrees at private institutions than did career civil service executives.

At the same time, the career civil service executives tended to take each advanced level of degree more often in the private universities (see Table 18). While attendance in private schools by foreign-service and political executives increased slightly at the three levels, the proportions of career civil service executives increased by over 10 per cent. Political and foreign-service executives who took their four-year degrees in public institutions did not in large numbers shift to private institutions,

---

thropic agencies, (3) those, including the United States Academies, which are primarily technological schools, and (4) all foreign schools. This simple system of classification, obscuring important distinctions, prevents our examining many important educational-background characteristics of executives. On the other hand, it brings out in bold relief important facts about educational backgrounds of the four elites.

Table 17

Types of Institutions from Which Four-Year Degrees Were Received

Type of institution	Civilian federal executives	Career civil service executives	Political executives	Foreign-service executives	Military executives
Private colleges and universities	42.4%	37.8%	49.6%	56.1%	12.0%
Public colleges and universities	47.9	50.9	42.9	39.0	26.2
Technical institutions and U.S. academies	6.7†	7.7	5.7	3.2	61.5†
Miscellaneous U.S. institutions	2.2	2.7	1.1	1.0	0.2
Foreign institutions	0.8	0.9	0.7	0.7	0.1
Total degrees reported with name of institution*	7,417	5,070	1,304	992	1,727

*Fifty-one degrees reported by men not classifiable into one of the three services.
†These percentages break down for all civilian executives to 5.7 per cent to technical institutions and 1.0 per cent to U.S. and other military and naval academies; for all military executives, 2.3 per cent to the former and 59.2 per cent to the latter.

Table 18

Summary of Men at Each of the Education Levels Who Reported Degrees from Public and Private Institutions

Degrees	Career civil service executives	Political executives	Foreign-service executives	Military executives
Private Institutions				
Four-year	37.8%	49.6%	56.1%	12.0%
Master's	41.4	47.0	58.5	45.2
Doctoral	49.2	51.4	60.2	68.3
Public Institutions				
Doctoral	50.9	42.9	39.0	26.2
Four-year	47.8	38.0	37.7	23.8
Master's	42.8	29.8	28.5	22.7

but a relatively large number shifted into foreign institutions: 10 per cent of political and 8.2 per cent of foreign-service executives who reported the doctorate earned it at a foreign institution.

The law schools play an important role in preparing men for executive careers. Among the 10,851 civilian federal executives in this study 1,865, or about 18 per cent, are political appointees. They hold one-half of all the law degrees reported by civilian executives. Among all civilian executives, law degrees were overwhelmingly from private institutions: 71.1 per cent, with only 24.1 from public institutions—a difference of 47.0 per cent. The difference between the two percentages for political executives is 40.1, and for foreign-service executives, 58.7. Among the military executives the difference is less but is still a considerable 22.4 per cent.

Almost equal proportions of all civilian executives took medical degrees from private and public institutions. A greater proportion of career civil service executives took medical degrees at public institutions (51.7 per cent) than at private institutions (44.1 per cent). The relationship is sharply reversed for political and foreign-service executives. Only thirty-six political executives reported having taken medical degrees, but of these exactly two-thirds took their degrees at private and less than one-third (30.6 per cent) at public institutions. For foreign-service executives, the difference is 35.4 per cent. Political and foreign-service executives received their medical degrees more often in private institutions than did career civil service executives.

Among civilian and military executives, 415 men reported the names of schools from which they received a degree at a level on which they already had one. These second degrees involved switching major areas, schools, or both, and these "second-thought" degrees represent a change in, and focusing of, career perspectives and plans. Men who decided to take a second degree at the level at which they held one chose in overwhelming proportions private institutions. For all civilian executives the difference is 32.2 per cent, for career civil service executives 19.0 per cent, for political executives 54.4 per cent, and for foreign-service executives 42.5 per cent. Among military executives the difference is only 7.3 per cent, but over a third (37 per cent) of military executives took second degrees at technical schools.

Both prestige and proximity appear to be factors in choice of private institutions for a second degree. First, many political and foreign-service executives were already in a private institution, and so taking a second degree may have involved only a shift in area of specialization. Second, most of the institutions in and around Washington, D.C., are private and are chosen primarily because of their geographic proximity by men already in the government. Finally, it must not be overlooked that many men who had the opportunity to take a second degree at the same level probably chose a private institution for the increased prestige. That 22.5 per cent of foreign service executives took second degrees in foreign schools may have been due

The Colleges and Universities That Produce Executives 131

to overseas assignment, but fewer than ten men are involved here.

The Colleges and Universities Where They Were Trained

Analysis of degrees received by *type* of institution is important for understanding general patterns, but such categories at times obscure important facts about the role of colleges and universities in producing federal executives.

No two institutions of higher learning are alike; indeed, considering the elements of history, geography, endowment, type of sponsorship, academic standards, and the welter of other characteristics which can be combined and recombined, no two institutions of higher learning are, when compared along more than one or two dimensions, even approximately alike. Consequently, categorizing institutions as we have done so far results in rather featureless groupings. In this section we will look directly at thirty institutions which produced the most degrees held by federal executives at the four-year, the master's, and the doctoral levels, and in law. Our purpose will be to discover whether colleges that produced the largest numbers of federal executives have characteristics in common.

The thirty institutions in rank order in Table 19 produced the largest numbers of executives holding four-year degrees. The accumulated percentages are obtained by dividing the accumulated number by the total number of degrees held by civilian executives.

These thirty colleges and universities produced 41.7 per cent of all civilian executives reporting four-year degrees; the first twenty produced a third of these executives; and the first ten, a fifth. Of the more than 2,000 institutions of higher learning listed in such publications as *Lovejoy's College Guide,* only thirty produce 40 per cent of all civilian federal executives reporting four-year degrees. Does this mean that one type of college tends to monopolize the training of such men?

There is no one set of characteristics shared by all these colleges and universities. Sheer size seems to be important, but not all are large. C.C.N.Y., California (at Berkeley), Minne-

Table 19

Thirty Institutions Which Produced the Largest Number of Four-Year Degrees Reported by Civilian Federal Executives

Number of degrees granted	Accumulative number	Accumulative percentage	Institution
260	260	3.4	George Washington
180	440	5.8	City College of New York
173	613	8.0	California (Berkeley)
156	769	10.1	Harvard
138	907	11.9	Minnesota
135	1,042	13.7	Illinois
134	1,176	15.4	Michigan
130	1,306	17.1	Wisconsin
128	1,434	18.8	Ohio State
123	1,557	20.4	Washington
120	1,677	22.0	Mass. Inst. of Tech.
115	1,792	23.5	Princeton
110	1,902	24.9	Yale
107	2,009	26.3	New York
107	2,116	27.7	Cornell
87	2,203	28.9	Benjamin Franklin
86	2,289	30.0	Pennsylvania
81	2,370	31.1	Missouri
79	2,450	32.1	Purdue
77	2,527	33.1	Georgetown
76	2,603	34.1	Nebraska
76	2,679	35.1	Chicago
76	2,755	36.1	Stanford
71	2,826	37.0	Pennsylvania State
63	2,889	37.9	Colorado
60	2,949	38.7	Iowa
60	3,009	39.4	Iowa State
59	3,068	40.2	Columbia
59	3,127	41.0	Kansas
55	3,182	41.7	Syracuse

Total four-year level degrees 7,628.

sota, Illinois, and other large universities rank high on the list. Benjamin Franklin University with less than a thousand students in 1956–57, on the other hand, is in the top group. The criterion of public as against private control and sponsorship does not appear critical. Fifteen of the thirty are state universities, and City College of New York is a municipal institution. Fourteen are privately, or in part privately, sponsored. There is in consequence a balance between private and public institutions. All geographic regions are represented among the state universities but, with the exception of Chicago and Stanford, the private institutions are on the more northerly Atlantic seaboard. There is, then, no one characteristic that makes these colleges and universities distinctive.

Different groups of colleges are, for quite different reasons, among the first thirty. George Washington, Benjamin Franklin, and Georgetown are in the District of Columbia, where about half of all civilian federal executives are stationed. These schools are represented in the top thirty, in all probability, because men employed by the federal government either attended them with federal employment in mind or, after such employment, attended the schools to finish their bachelor's degrees. There is also the interesting possibility that because of geographic proximity relatively larger proportions of graduates of these schools are drawn into federal service. Chapter 3, which reports that men born in the District of Columbia are highly over-represented in the federal elites, partly supports this idea.

Six of the prestigeful Ivy League schools appear. In rank order they are Harvard, Princeton, Yale, Cornell, Pennsylvania, and Columbia. Two other "prestige" schools, Chicago and Stanford, bring the total for this group of schools to eight. Did the men who attended these schools tend to come from families of high occupational status? We will examine the question later in this section.

A third major grouping is the great state universities. These schools are located in every region of the country except the Deep South and the Southwest. Sheer size is without question partially responsible for their appearing among the first thirty. Seven among the first ten schools are state universities: California, Minnesota, Illinois, Michigan, Wisconsin, Ohio State, and Washington, in rank order. These are among the largest universities in the country. Five of the enormous Midwestern state universities are among the first ten. Simply because of numbers of men graduated at the bachelor level, these schools have a greater than equal chance of producing men who will become federal executives.

We must not, however, overlook three other characteristics of state universities. First, through low tuition rates they offer opportunities to intelligent young men who otherwise find the door to higher education closed. Men who lack family sponsorship or other contacts with which to enter business also are more likely than their more fortunate peers to attend them. Do such men go to state universities and then, because business careers are not immediately open to them, enter the federal service? Second, many of these state universities have strong undergraduate and graduate programs in fields highly represented in the federal elites, including engineering, business administration, and the several sciences. Third, these universities in different regions of the country train men who may enter the federal service first in local and regional offices and later, through promotion, move to Washington, D.C.

But when we have said all these things, we have said little about why certain colleges appear on the list. For instance, Massachusetts Institute of Technology is present, but not the other great technical schools. Why? To answer this question would involve all the subtle complex problems of weighing Massachusetts Institute of Technology against the other technical schools, which cannot be done within the present volume. Nor can we more than touch on the complex of academic excellence, sponsorship of younger by older alumni already in government, experiences of faculty members in federal service, and the interweaving of all the elements involved in these schools contributing so strongly to the federal elites.

As we said earlier, one in five of all executives comes from one of the top ten schools, and one in three comes from one of

The Colleges and Universities That Produce Executives

the first twenty; yet the three civilian elites show important variations.

Of the fifteen schools, colleges, and universities among the top thirty for all executive elites, eight are state and seven are private:

State			Private		
California	Illinois	Michigan	Geo. Washington	Harvard	Stanford
Ohio State	Washington	Missouri	Georgetown	Penn.	M.I.T.
Minnesota	Wisconsin		Cornell		

Five of the state universities are in the Midwest; three of the private colleges are Ivy League, and two are within the District of Columbia.

Ten of the first thirty colleges and universities from which career civil service executives received four-year degrees appeared only for this career service. They are all public institutions:

Nebraska
Pennsylvania State
Colorado
Kansas State
Iowa State

Tennessee
Maryland
Alabama Polytechnic
Cincinnati
Oregon State

Political and foreign-service executives did not take four-year degrees at these colleges. The four at which only political executives took four-year degrees are all public: Iowa, Kansas, Alabama, and Texas. Colleges from which only foreign-service executives took four-year degrees are Dartmouth, Utah, Oberlin, U. S. Naval Academy, and Oklahoma State.

Career civil service and political executives have three universities in common which do not appear for foreign-service executives; City College of New York, New York University, and Purdue. Political and foreign-service executives have, among their first thirty, eight colleges which do not appear on the list for career civil service executives:

Public

South Dakota State
North Carolina

Private

Princeton
Yale
Chicago

Columbia
Northwestern
Brown

In rank order of attendance there is considerable variation among the three civilian services. The first ten for career civil service executives include none of the Ivy League schools, but the Harvard-Yale-Princeton group is present among the first ten for both political and foreign-service executives. Taken as a whole, we see more "prestige" schools among the political and the foreign-service than among the career civil service executives.

This does not mean, however, that the foreign-service—or, for that matter, the political—elite is the exclusive preserve of the Ivy League and other prestige schools. It is true that Harvard, Princeton, and Yale produced 14 per cent of all foreign-service executives, which is much more than proportional representation for these schools. California, Illinois, and Wisconsin, however, are also among the top ten in producing foreign-service executives. A fair conclusion seems to be that the Ivy League (eight among the first thirty) has an advantage in supplying executives to the State Department, but that other private schools such as George Washington, New York University, Georgetown, Stanford, Chicago, Columbia and Syracuse are also represented; and that men graduated from state universities are far from excluded.

The tendency for a few schools to produce a large proportion of degrees is sharply increased at the master's level. Thirty institutions produced about 40 per cent of the bachelor's degrees of civilian executives; thirty institutions produced 60 per cent of the master's degrees of civilian executives—an increase of 20 per cent. Twenty institutions produced a third of the four-year degrees, but twenty institutions produced half of the master's degrees. Ten schools produced a fifth of the four-year degrees, but ten schools produced a third of the master's degrees. There is a marked tendency for even fewer schools at the master's than at the four-year level to dominate in training federal executives.

Although the concentration is much greater, the list of schools that produced federal executives with master's degrees is highly similar to those that produced federal executives with bachelor's degrees. George Washington, Georgetown, Pennsylvania State, and Kansas fall from the ranking, replaced by American University, Maryland, Kansas State, and Northwestern. Otherwise, the list of thirty schools producing bachelor's degrees is the same as the list for master's degrees. Within the list, however, important movements among the schools take place. Harvard moves from fourth to first position, replacing George Washington, which drops to second. Columbia moves from twenty-eighth to third position, and Chicago from twenty-first to fourth. This might be taken as reflecting a tendency for large private schools to move upward in the rankings, but if it is a trend it by no means affects all private institutions. Yale, Princeton, Pennsylvania, and Stanford either remain at the same level or lose ground. City College of New York drops from second to thirtieth place. Large state universities continue to dominate the lower half of the first ten institutions, with Ohio State, Wisconsin, Michigan, and Minnesota present. Although there is increased concentration at the master's level over the bachelor's level, this increase results basically from higher proportions of men taking degrees from the same schools. There is no clear-cut pattern of private institutions replacing public ones.

The tendency for a school to dominate in representation in the federal government is much greater at the doctoral than at either the master's or bachelor's level. Thirty institutions (see Table 20) granted over three-fourths of the doctoral degrees; of these thirty, twenty granted over two-thirds and ten granted almost half. This list of thirty is also quite different from that for the schools which produced four-year degrees. For example, nine colleges at the bachelor's level are not present at the doctoral level: City College of New York, George Washington, Benjamin Franklin, Missouri, Purdue, Pennsylvania State, Colorado, Kansas, and Syracuse have been replaced by Johns Hopkins, Maryland, American University, California Institute of Technology, North Carolina, Pittsburgh, Northwestern, Darmstadt, and Clark. At the four-year level, seven of the first ten institutions are state univer-

Table 20

Thirty Institutions Which Produced the Largest Number of Federal Executives with Doctoral Degrees

Number	Accumulative number	Accumulative percentage	Institution
85	85	7.5	Harvard
70	155	13.7	Chicago
64	219	19.3	Wisconsin
51	270	23.8	Columbia
49	339	29.9	Johns Hopkins
44	383	33.8	Cornell
42	427	37.7	California (Berkeley)
40	467	41.2	Minnesota
36	503	44.4	Yale
30	533	47.1	New York
29	562	49.6	Illinois
28	590	52.1	Ohio State
24	614	54.2	Maryland
23	637	56.3	Michigan
23	660	58.3	Iowa
23	683	60.3	Mass. Inst. of Tech.
22	705	62.3	Stanford
22	722	63.8	Iowa State
20	747	66.0	Princeton
18	765	67.6	George Washington
17	782	69.1	Pennsylvania
17	799	70.1	American University
16	815	72.0	Calif. Inst. of Tech.
12	827	73.1	North Carolina
10	837	73.9	Pittsburgh
10	847	74.8	Nebraska
9	856	75.6	Georgetown
9	865	76.4	Northwestern
8	873	77.1	Tech. Univ. of Darmstadt
8	881	77.8	Clark

sities, and City College of New York is a municipal school. Only two, George Washington and Harvard, are privately sponsored institutions. At the doctoral level are seven private institutions—Harvard, Chicago, Columbia, Johns Hopkins, Cornell, New York University, and Yale—with only three state universities represented—Wisconsin, California, and Minnesota. At the doctoral level the great state universities are still present but now with probably the greatest concentration in the second ten. District of Columbia schools continue to be represented, although Benjamin Franklin has been replaced by American University.

These figures taken together indicate that, as the level advances from the bachelor's to the doctor's degree, the private universities play an increasingly important role. They do not, however, dominate to the exclusion of the public institutions since those with strong graduate programs—Wisconsin, California, Minnesota, and others—continue as a group to produce a large number of federal executives.

Factors involved in the high rates of these schools are extremely complex, but trends do seem to be present. First, proportions of degrees granted at the doctoral levels by the thirty top institutions are much greater than at the master's and bachelor's levels. Second, there is some tendency for private universities with more prestige to achieve higher rankings at the doctoral than at the bachelor's level. This has to be interpreted in light of stronger graduate programs offered by these schools. Finally, the factor of geographic proximity, as exemplified by George Washington, Georgetown, and Benjamin Franklin at the four-year level, is no less important at the doctoral level. The geographic area involved, however, is somewhat enlarged with Johns Hopkins and Maryland appearing at the doctoral level. These schools are well within the commuting reach of men stationed in or near Washington, D. C. Throughout, one constant is that about two-thirds of the schools represented at the bachelor's level are represented at the doctoral level. Schools that produced men with four-year degrees are, on the whole, the schools producing men at the master's and doctoral levels, but at the doctoral level the private universities rank higher within the thirty institutions than at the bachelor level.

Geographic proximity to the District of Columbia is of even greater importance in determining where federal executives take law degrees than it is for the academic bachelor's, master's, and doctoral degrees. Among thirty schools producing the most law degrees five are in the District of Columbia. Two of these, Georgetown and George Washington, produced one-fourth of all the law degrees reported by civilian executives. Five of the first twelve are within the environs of the District of Columbia; and the Universities of Maryland and Virginia—both near Washington—are among the first twenty. Seven of the first twenty schools are, therefore, on the list in part because of proximity to places of federal employment. The importance of this factor is shown dramatically by the fact that Southeastern University, a commuter institution of about 600 students and catering to federal employees, is in fourth place. It is probable that many men took law degrees after coming to Washington to work for the government, but some men who first came to Washington as students may have chosen to work for the government after taking their law degrees. Either way, geographic proximity to Washington is important. Among the other colleges and universities, the privately and publicly controlled schools are rather equally divided and are interspersed in the rankings.

Thirteen institutions appear on all four of the lists for academic and law degrees. Four are Ivy League: Harvard, Columbia, Yale, and Pennsylvania. Five are Big Ten: Wisconsin, Michigan, Minnesota, Illinois, and Iowa. California and Nebraska are the only state universities not in the Big Ten and represented on all the lists. George Washington is the only District of Columbia school represented on all the lists. Here again, the quality of each school seems to be the fundamental element in determining its production of federal executives. Many colleges have excellent programs in a few areas, at either the undergraduate or graduate level; only a

The Colleges and Universities That Produce Executives

few are excellent in many areas and at all academic levels. Excellence is, however, not enough. The college must be available—geographically, financially, and socially—to the men who are to become federal executives. At the same time, attending one rather than another college may have great influence on whether a man follows the career routes leading into the federal elites.

The institutions that produce business leaders[1], are strikingly similar to those producing federal executives. (Except that, as we might expect, the District of Columbia colleges did not produce large proportions of business leaders. This reinforces the notion that they served as part-time institutions for the federal executives after they came to work in Washington.) The division between public and private institutions is somewhat the same. The institutions that produced higher than expected proportions of federal executives are those that produced higher than expected proportions of business leaders.

Occupational Mobility and Individual Institutions

This section concerns the first twenty colleges in production of bachelor, doctoral, and law degrees. It examines the differential functioning of institutions of higher learning in the process of occupational succession and mobility. Since these colleges produced about one-third of all the four-year degrees, we can see a substantial proportion of the college graduates in the federal service in their movement through specific institutions.

Table 21 was prepared by dividing all the men holding four-year degrees from each college into three broad groups of occupational origins. Since the number of cases involved here is relatively small, and since differences in percentages between any two adjacent schools are not large, this table represents a gradient of colleges in which the absolute position of any one college is not important.

In none of the twenty colleges and universities did more

1. See p. 51 of *Big Business Leaders in America.*

Table 21

Civilian Executives from Each Occupational Origin Group Who Received Four-Year Degrees from Twenty Institutions, in Rank Order

Father's Occupation

Lower range*		Middle range†		Upper range‡	
Benj. Franklin	39%§	Missouri	67%§	Princeton	74%§
Cit. Col. of N.Y.	37	Minnesota	65	Yale	64
G. Washington	27	Purdue	65	Harvard	52
Washington	25	Cornell	61	Michigan	37
Ohio State	23	Illinois	58	Pennsylvania	33
Illinois	23	Wisconsin	57	Cornell	32
Pennsylvania	22	Ohio State	56	Mass. Inst. of Tech.	30
New York	22	New York	56	California	29
Mass. Inst. of Tech.	21	Cit. Col. of N.Y.	55	Georgetown	28
Georgetown	18	Georgetown	54	Wisconsin	25
Wisconsin	18	California	53	Washington	25
California	18	Benj. Franklin	51	G. Washington	25
Minnesota	15	Washington	50	Purdue	22
Michigan	13	Michigan	50	N. Y. Univ.	22
Missouri	13	Mass. Inst. of Tech.	49	Ohio State	21
Purdue	13	G. Washington	48	Missouri	20
Harvard	8	Pennsylvania	45	Minnesota	19
Cornell	7	Harvard	40	Illinois	19
Yale	3	Yale	33	Benj. Franklin	10
Princeton	2	Princeton	24	Cit. Col. of N.Y.	8

*Includes unskilled and skilled workers, and farm workers and tenants without paid help.
†Includes white-collar workers, minor business executives, foremen, small business owners, farm owners, and tenants with paid help.
‡Includes major business executives, professional men, and owners of medium and large business.
§Percentage of all executives holding four-year degrees from each institution, by occupational origin group.

than half of the executives come from the lower occupational range, although Benjamin Franklin and City College of New York drew over a third from this level. Most institutions drew primarily from the middle range, although six of the twenty colleges drew less than 50 per cent from this range. The greatest span of percentages is for colleges drawing from the upper range, with Princeton drawing 74 percent and City College of New York drawing 8 per cent.

Princeton, Yale, and Harvard drew over 50 per cent of their federal executives from the upper range, with only about 2 per cent of the Princeton men and 3 per cent of the Yale men coming from the lower range. About half of the Harvard men came from the upper range, and only about 8 per cent from the lower range. Cornell, an Ivy League and land grant college, drew only 7 per cent from the lower range but, unlike the three Ivy League colleges above, it drew primarily from the middle range. Pennsylvania drew a larger percentage of its men from the lower range than did the other Ivy League colleges but, unlike Cornell, did not rank high in the middle range. The five Ivy League schools rank among the first six drawing from the upper range, but there is a considerable span between the percentages, with Princeton drawing 74 per cent from this range, Pennsylvania only 33 per cent, and Cornell 32.

The colleges ranking highest in proportion of federal executives from the middle range are state universities: in rank order, Missouri, Minnesota, Purdue, Cornell (land grant, and partly state), Illinois, Wisconsin, and Ohio State tying for seventh place with New York University—a private school. Three state universities depart from this pattern, each in a different direction. Michigan follows the pattern of the Ivy League schools, ranking low in proportions drawn from the lower range and high in proportions from the upper range. Washington ranks high in proportions from the lower range and just below the center for men from the middle and upper ranges. California is in the center of the rankings for all three ranges. On the whole, however, state universities rank high in drawing from the middle range.

Two institutions stand out as providing mobility from the lower range—Benjamin Franklin University and City College of New York; one is a private school, and the other is municipally supported. George Washington, another private institution, ranks third in proportions drawn from the lower range but is not especially low in the rankings for colleges drawing from the upper range. Three other private institutions (each in many respects different from the other) all rank at about the center for proportions drawn from each of the three ranges: Massachusetts Institute of Technology, New York University, and Georgetown.

From the foregoing it is evident that, although differences among these colleges are somewhat patterned, each also has an individuality that makes it unrealistic to force it into a public-private, large-small, or city-rural category. For example, Ivy League colleges draw most often from the upper range, but both Cornell and Pennsylvania fit this pattern only partially. Or again, Princeton and Benjamin Franklin are both private institutions, yet they are at opposite extremes for proportions of men drawn from the upper and lower ranges.

At the doctoral level individual characteristics of colleges are even more pronounced in determining places in the rankings (Table 22). Private and public, city and rural, and large and small institutions are interspersed throughout the rankings for all three occupational ranges. This can be seen to result in part from the fact that the percentages at the top and bottom of the rankings are much closer together than was the case for four-year degrees. In part, however, it probably also results from the fact that, at the doctoral level, occupational status of the father is no longer so important as it was at the A.B. level. No college granted the doctorate in over half the cases to men from the upper range, and only four colleges granted it in less than half the cases to men from the middle range.

Princeton, Yale, and Harvard continue at the doctoral level

Table 22

Proportions of Men from Three Occupational Origin Groups Who Received Doctor of Philosophy Degrees from Twenty Institutions

Father's Occupation

Lower range*		Middle range†		Upper range‡	
Minnesota	29%§	Iowa State	82%‡	Yale	48%§
Maryland	26	Iowa	65	Michigan	41
Stanford	23	Columbia	60	Princeton	40
Columbia	20	G. Washington	59	Illinois	38
Ohio State	19	Maryland	57	Harvard	36
California	18	Johns Hopkins	56	Chicago	35
Mass. Inst. of Tech.	18	California	56	Ohio State	35
G. Washington	18	New York	56	Mass. Inst. of Tech.	32
Illinois	17	Wisconsin	56	Iowa	31
Cornell	16	Princeton	55	Johns Hopkins	31
New York	15	Minnesota	55	Cornell	30
Wisconsin	14	Harvard	54	Wisconsin	29
Michigan	14	Chicago	54	New York	29
Johns Hopkins	13	Cornell	54	California	26
Chicago	11	Stanford	54	Stanford	23
Harvard	10	Mass. Inst. of Tech.	50	G. Washington	23
Iowa State	9	Ohio State	46	Columbia	20
Yale	6	Yale	46	Maryland	17
Princeton	5	Michigan	45	Minnesota	16
Iowa	4	Illinois	45	Iowa State	9

*See Table 21 for notes.

not to produce federal executives from the lower range, but another Ivy league school—Columbia—ranks fourth in production of men with doctorates from this range. Michigan, a state controlled university in the Midwest, fits much more closely the Princeton—Yale—Harvard pattern than does Cornell. State universities are interspersed throughout the ranking, with Iowa State having the interesting distinction of drawing 82 per cent of its men from the middle range.

Five of the District of Columbia schools rank high in producing lawyers from the lower range: Southeastern, American, Catholic, George Washington, and Georgetown. This clearly underscores the importance of law as an avenue from the lower occupational groups into federal executive status, since many of the graduates of these schools secured law training after coming to the District of Columbia to work for the government. Otherwise, no clear-cut patterns emerge between father's occupation and individual schools at which law degrees were taken.

PART V

The Careers of Federal Executives

CHAPTER 10

Career Lines

The chain of events which leads to a man's movement into the federal elites begins as far back at least as his grandfather's generation. The occupational and social characteristics of his forebears enhance or reduce his chances for movement into high position. The size of the city in which he was born and the geographic region from which he came are important; the educational level he attains, the subject of study he elects, and the college or university he attends are all part of the long selection process which determines whether he will become a federal executive. These antecedent characteristics, however, are not an iron mold that controls the subsequent steps in the man's career. The process goes on after he finds himself in his first occupation—a process related to the executive's own volition, his ability, and his energy resources.

The main career routes from first occupation to present position were studied to determine whether they varied among the four federal elites and between federal and business executives. What are the relative rates of movement out of the lower and into the higher-status occupations?

Three-fourths of all civilian federal executives (Table 23) began their careers in one of the professions or in a white-collar occupation. Only 14 per cent began as laborers. Five per cent were in the uniformed services—probably a reflection

Author of this chapter: Orvis F. Collins

Table 23

Career Sequence of 1959 Civilian Federal Executives

Occupation of federal executive	First occupation	Five years later	Ten years later	Fifteen years later
Laborer	14%	6%	4%	2%
White-collar worker	25	17	8	3
Minor executive	5	17	28	26
Major executive	0*	2	7	21
All professions	46	46	45	42
Uniformed service	5	8	5	3
Business owner	1	1	1	1
Other occupations	4	3	2	2
Total	100	100	100	100

The professions in detail

Engineer	15	16	16	14
Lawyer	6	7	8	8
Medical	2	2	2	2
Professor	4	4	3	2
Public school teacher	6	2	1	0*
Scientist	5	7	8	8
Accountant	1	1	1	1
Management	1	2	2	2
Other professions	6	5	4	5

*Less than 0.5 per cent.

Career Lines

of the fact that many of these men were beginning their careers at the time of World War II. Within the professions, 15 per cent of civilian executives began in engineering, 10 per cent began as teachers—4 per cent at the college level, 6 per cent at the public-school level. Only 6 per cent began as lawyers—highly concentrated in the political executive. These men did not in any meaningfully large proportions begin as laborers and then make a crossover to higher occupational status.

Over the fifteen year period shown in Table 23, percentages for men in the professions remained quite stable, but during the same period the men who started outside the professions moved quite rapidly into the status of minor and major executive; and between the ten and fifteen year periods, major executives jumped from 7 to 21 per cent.

At the end of fifteen years two occupational areas, the professions and the executive statuses, comprised 89 per cent of all federal executives. Many began their careers in the laboring and white-collar ranks; many passed through one of the professions in making the transition. Those men who moved out of the laborer and white-collar occupations did so in a decisive manner. Few men who after ten years had not made the move later become federal executives; time, from this point on in their careers, weighed too heavily against them.

The sequences of career civil service executives paralleled, on the whole, those for all civilian executives. Forty-three per cent of career civil service executives began in the professions, 27 per cent in the white-collar occupations, and 16 per cent as laborers; slightly larger proportions began, then, in the laborer and white-collar categories, and slightly smaller proportions in the professions than is true for all civilian executives. Within the professions slightly larger proportions were engineers than for all civilian executives, and smaller proportions were lawyers. On the whole, however, career civil service executives began in much the same occupational areas as did the total civilian executives, and movement during the fifteen year span also closely reflects the same pattern. Percentages in the professions are relatively stable, whereas movement out of the laborer and white-collar occupations into the minor and major executive statuses takes place.

Unlike career civil service executives, political executives followed routes different in one significant way from all civilian executives. Seven per cent more political executives than civilian were in the professions at the beginning of their careers; five years later the margin increased to 14 per cent, ten years later to 17 per cent, and fifteen years later it was also 17 per cent. This widening margin over time largely results from an increase in the proportion of political executives entering law: 22 per cent of political executives began their careers in law, compared with only 6 per cent of all civilian executives; and at the end of fifteen years 33 per cent of political executives were in law, compared with only 8 per cent of all civilian executives.

Political executives in overwhelming proportions either entered a profession when they were quite young or in the first years of their careers studied until they had attained the formal education necessary to enter a profession. At the end of fifteen years, 92 per cent of all the political executives had moved into the professions or into the status of minor or major executive. Our present analysis cannot show how many of the men from the laborer and white-collar occupations went first into the professions and then into executive status.

Foreign-service executives differ from both civil service and political in the proportion who anchored their careers in the professions. Only 38 per cent of foreign-service leaders, compared with 43 per cent for career civil service and 53 per cent for political executives, began in the professions. Moreover, foreign-service executives who started in the professions left them more rapidly than did career civil service and political executives. In contrast, the 38 per cent of foreign-service executives who were in the professions when they were first self-supporting fell to 20 per cent at the end of fifteen years.

Larger proportions of the foreign-service than of career or

Career Lines

political executives, furthermore, did not move into but began their careers in executive status: 15 per cent of foreign-service executives, compared with 4 per cent of career and 5 per cent of political executives, reported first occupation as minor executive. At five years, 35 per cent of the foreign-service executives had become minor executives and 4 per cent major executives. At ten years, 47 per cent had become minor executives and 12 per cent major executives—a total of 59 per cent. At fifteen years the percentage for minor executive fell to 43 but the percentage for major executive increased to 28—a total of 71 per cent. At fifteen years almost three-fourths of the foreign-service men had begun to climb the executive ladder.

After fifteen years, members of the three elites so far observed were concentrated in two areas, the professions and executive positions. The marked difference, however, in the concentration becomes apparent if we extract relevant figures from the tables:

	Minor or major executive	Professions
Civil service	47%	40%
Political	33	59
Foreign service	71	20

Career civil service executives emerged after fifteen years in about equal proportions through the professions and through the executive statuses. The road into the political executive elite leads through fairly extended practice in the professions. Foreign-service men, in sharp contrast, enter the executive ranks fairly fast, moving out of both the white-collar ranks and the professions. At the end of fifteen years, the proportions of men in the career civil service and political elites who are following the professional route as against the white-collar to minor executive to major executive route are quite large, while future foreign-service executives have moved out.

Men who become top-level military leaders follow a career pattern sharply different from men in any of the three civilian elites. The road to high position in the military service began, for two-thirds of these men, by immediate entrance into the military. This percentage increased to 81 after five years, 89 after ten years, and 94 after fifteen years. When we recall that over 90 per cent are college men, it becomes clear that those who aspired to high position in the military service first secured a solid educational background and then entered the service. It is within the service itself, then, that these men laid the foundation for their future careers.

Among those who did not enter the military as their first occupation, the largest proportion is the 12 per cent who entered one of the professions. Practice of the profession as a civilian, however, was not protracted. At fifteen years, only 4 per cent remained in the profession. Among those men who did attain professional standing, practice of the profession seems to have been conducted in the majority of cases within the military service. Eventual promotion into the military elites seems dependent upon early entrance into the formal age-rank promotion system. Lateral entry into high military rank is relatively rare; promotion is from within, and men must get in at an early age to qualify.

For each of the federal elites, relatively few men made the long jump out of the laborer occupations, and this occurred relatively early in the career. Remaining too long a "worker" makes it extremely difficult for a man to achieve upward mobility. There is evidence that a large number of men born into the laborer ranks become federal executives, but most of these men began their own careers on a new plateau, at a higher level than their fathers.

Career Patterns of Business and Federal Executives

Before examining the effects of occupational origin on career patterns, let us compare the careers of federal and business executives.[1] Three basic differences can be summarized: (1) much higher proportions of civilian federal executives than of business leaders are professionally trained; (2) much higher proportions of business leaders rise through laborer and white-collar occupations: and (3) much higher proportions of busi-

1. See *Occupational Mobility*.

ness leaders reach minor and major executive status during the first fifteen years of their careers than do federal executives. Let us discuss each of these differences.

Almost one half (46 per cent) of all civilian federal executives entered a profession as their first occupation, and after fifteen years 42 per cent were still there. Only 24 per cent of the business leaders, on the other hand, entered a profession as their first occupation; they did not stay long, for fifteen years later the percentage had dropped to 10.

Men in these two worlds of business and government do not share the perspectives generally shown by men with a common experience in education and training. Government at the higher levels is a world dominated by professionally trained men, showing in common the perspectives and attitudes of a long period of specialization. In this it is in strong contrast with the world of business, dominated by men who move up into their high positions through the white-collar route of clerical work and sales. Forty-four per cent of business leaders began their careers in these occupations, compared with only 25 per cent of the federal executives—a difference of 19 per cent. Movement out of laborer and white-collar occupations is equally rapid for the two major elites, but the fact remains that a second basic difference in experience exists here. Business leaders are, in the formative years of their careers, in much higher proportions exposed to hierarchical disciplines and training than are federal executives.

Finally, and perhaps most important, business leaders move much more rapidly into administrative posts than do federal executives. In lieu of experience of a professional nature, they receive experience in organizational activities which is translated into leadership roles in their organizations. At the end of their first fifteen career years, 25 per cent of the business leaders had become minor, and 57 per cent major executives, a total of 82 per cent. At the same point in their careers only 21 per cent of federal executives had become major executives and only 26 per cent had become minor executives, a total of 47 per cent.

The implications of these differences may be of fundamental importance. One stereotype shared by most Americans is that of the government administrator as a hierarchical personality —a personality in sharp contrast to the "entrepreneurial" personality of the business leader. The stereotype means that the government executive, disciplined and trained in large-scale organizations from the beginning of his career, is dependent upon the authoritarian system for definition of his goals and purposes. He is re-active rather than active, behaving only as the system requires, seeking protection through adherence to rules and precepts. He lacks the aggression, the drive, the imagination, the decisiveness of his counterpart in business.

Yet our analysis of career sequences of business and federal executives indicates that much larger proportions of business than of federal executives followed the organizational route through white-collar to minor executive to major executive. The typical career of the civilian federal executive has been graduate or professional school, practice of a profession, and then into the government at a rather high level, escaping the routinizing influence of white-collar bureaucracy.

Comparison of business leaders with each of the civilian elites shows that between business leaders and political executives the contrasts discussed above are even more extreme, and that they are only somewhat less so between business leaders and career civil service executives. On the other hand, foreign-service executives are much more like business leaders than they are like either career civil service or political executives.

It is not germane to this chapter to discuss implications for social tensions arising from these differences in the career experiences of federal and business executives. One question, however, should be raised here: How much of the conflict arising between men in government and men in business is rooted in these quite different career experiences and the resulting cleavage in perspectives, rather than in—on a rational level—differences in interests and in policies?

Career Pattern and Father's Occupation

The influence of the father's occupation upon the career patterns of federal executives might contribute to the varia-

Career Lines

Table 24
Fathers' Occupations and Career Patterns of Civilian Federal Executives

Occupation of Federal Executive

Occupation of father	Laborer	White-collar worker	Professional man	Minor executive	Major executive	Other*	Total
First Occupation
Laborer	23%	28%	37%	6%	0%	6%	100%
White-collar worker or minor executive	14	28	42	7	0†	9	100
Owner of small business	13	24	43	7	1	12	100
Farmer	12	19	48	5	0	16	100
Professional man	9	19	55	7	1	9	100
Major executive or owner of large business	8	22	43	14	1	12	100
Five Years Later
Laborer	9	18	39	21	1	12	100
White-collar worker or minor executive	6	14	43	22	2	13	100
Owner of small business	5	10	51	21	1	12	100
Farmer	6	11	49	19	1	14	100
Professional man	3	7	57	20	2	11	100
Major executive or owner of large business	3	9	42	29	3	14	100
Ten Years Later
Laborer	5	4	42	36	6	7	100
White-collar worker or minor executive	4	4	41	37	6	8	100
Owner of small business	3	4	49	31	6	8	100
Farmer	4	2	49	29	6	10	100
Professional man	2	2	52	29	7	8	100
Major executive or owner of large business	3	2	48	35	12	10	100
Fifteen Years Later
Laborer	3	1	39	32	21	4	100
White-collar worker or minor executive	2	2	37	32	22	5	100
Owner of small business	2	1	45	26	21	5	100
Farmer	3	1	43	27	20	6	100
Professional man	1	1	48	26	18	6	100
Major executive or owner of large business	1	0†	36	28	27	8	100

*Includes military service, training program, and business owners. †Less than 0.5 per cent.

tions. In Table 24 the father's occupations of laborer, farmer, and professional are treated separately, and white-collar workers, minor executives, and supervisors are combined, as are major executives and owners of large business. The occupations of federal executives are divided into five categories of importance in understanding the career movements of these men. Each of the blocks down the table advances the careers of federal executives five years.

This table shows the peculiar importance of the professions as the main route into the civilian federal elites. It was said earlier that 46 per cent of all civilian executives began their careers in one of the professions; Table 24 shows that men from all occupational origins in large numbers moved through the professions on their way into the civilian executive. At each one of the four five-year periods, over one-third of men from each occupational origin group was in one of the professions. If we take into account the men who at any one point in time may not have yet entered, or may already have left, the professions, the overwhelming importance of professional training for entrance into the civilian elites becomes even more evident.

The column for the professions in Table 24 forms an axis which remains fairly stable during the fifteen year period, with the civilian executives shifting out of the columns to the left and into the columns to the right. This tendency has been emphasized by underlining percentages greater than ten.

On the whole, men from all occupational origins followed similar career sequences in their movements into the civilian federal elites. They began in the professions, or as white-collar workers, or laborers. They very seldom began their careers as minor or major executives. The movement out of the laborer and white-collar ranks was, for men from all occupational origins, decisive: ten years after becoming self-employed, men from all occupational groups, in proportions of 95 per cent or over, had moved into the professions or into executive status. For men from all occupational origins, the career pattern is similar—an abrupt occupational mobility at the outset.

For some groups the father's occupation did have influence

on the first occupation of the executive. The largest proportion of men who began as laborers were sons of laborers, and the largest proportion of men beginning in the professions were sons of professional men. Sons of major executives or owners of large business began more often than others in executive status.

These differences in percentages, while fairly large and quite important, should not obscure the crucial fact that men from occupations of less prestige tended to move directly out of their fathers' occupations. Twenty-three per cent of the sons of laborers began their own careers as laborers, and this proportion is much larger than for other occupational groups. But 77 per cent, three out of four sons of laborers, moved out of the category with their first jobs, over a third of the sons of laborers moved directly into the professions and 28 per cent into white-collar status. Occupational mobility began almost at the outset of the career. Sons of men in the under-represented categories had, on the whole, overcome this handicap within ten years.

Larger proportions of men whose fathers were in the laborer, white-collar, farmer, and small business occupations began their careers at lower levels than sons of owners of large business, executives, and professional men. However, these disadvantages were of an immediate and transitory nature, for after fifteen years 27 per cent of sons of major executives or owners of large business had become major executives, compared with 21 per cent of the sons of laborers. Percentages for the other occupational groups fall between these two extremes. The difference is not great, and—when we consider that professional status for many may have been an advantage over executive status at this stage in their careers—it represents only a doubtful edge held by sons of major executives or owners of large business.

Among those men who achieved executive status, the father's occupation had spent its force after fifteen years. Much earlier, as a social factor, it operated to prevent greater proportions of men with less privileged backgrounds from entering educational and career routes leading into the federal elites. Those who overcame disadvantages of occupational origin made the break early in their careers. Those who remained in the competition, after fifteen years had reached a point approximately abreast of men whose fathers had been able to give them greater initial advantages.

Military executives, we found on the whole, entered the armed services immediately upon becoming self-supporting. Further, over 90 per cent of the present military executives had entered the service within the first fifteen years of their careers; those who did not immediately enter the military achieved a firm basis for their careers by entering one of the professions.

Military executives with different occupational background vary in their premilitary experience, but the variation is relatively unimportant. Thirteen per cent of sons of laborers began their careers as laborers, and 4 per cent of sons of professional men began their careers as laborers, a difference of nine. For those who began their careers as white-collar workers the difference between extreme percentages is only five. The same holds true for those who first entered the professions, where the difference between high and low percentages is again only five, and for the minor executives where the difference is only three. Fifty-five per cent of the sons of laborers entered the uniformed services as their first occupation, compared with 69 per cent of sons of professional men. Percentages for the other occupations fall between these two extremes. From the foregoing we may conclude that there is some tendency for men from higher occupations to move into the military services more rapidly than men from the lower occupations, but examination of figures for "five years later" shows how rapidly movement into the military service takes place, regardless of the occupation of the father. After ten years the span is only between 83 per cent for sons of farmers and 91 per cent for sons of owners of small business, a difference of 8 per cent, and at fifteen years the occupation of the father as a factor is canceled out.

Thus we see the same tendency for military as for civilian executives for the occupation of the father to become less important as the career develops. The importance here, again, of the father's occupation is to completely eliminate from the running a disproportionate number of men from certain occupational groups. Among those not eliminated, movement into the armed services comes very early.

Father's Occupation and Scalar Position

Sons of laborers and farmers are under-represented in the federal elites, since the larger proportions of men from these groups never secure the education to enter the career routes leading to high positions in government. In the last section, however, we saw that those sons of farmers and laborers who had not been eliminated closed the gap somewhat over the fifteen year span between themselves and the sons of men in occupations of more prestige and power. At the end of fifteen years these men from the lower-status occupations had moved into the professions and executive status in only slightly smaller proportions than sons of professional men, major executives, and owners of large business. Does this mean that eventually men from the laborer and farmer occupations completely close the gap, securing for themselves in equal proportions with men from more advantaged backgrounds the positions of greater honor and responsibility? Or do they continue to lag behind throughout their careers and, if so, to what degree?

Since the positions within the federal elites at the very top are those of greatest influence and control in shaping and executing the national policy, preemption of these positions by men of higher occupational origins would have grave implications for the functioning of government. The questions above have two aspects. First, there is the matter of composition of the population manning these extremely high positions. If men from the less influential occupational groups are in a substantial sense restricted to the lower levels within the elites, the upper levels of the federal elites take on the color of a bureaucratic aristocracy controlled by men whose traditions and concerns reflect only the higher occupational groups in America. Second, there is the matter of representation, which corresponds closely to the question of equal opportunity in a democracy. Are only the goals and aspirations of the higher occupations considered, with no voices speaking for the vast bulk of the population at the lower occupational levels? These are issues fundamental to our democratic society.

To examine them, men in the federal elites were separated by salary grade levels.[2] Occupational origin percentages for men at each salary grade level were then calculated by the same procedure as that used for calculating proportions of men from the occupational origin groups in Chapter 2. This gave information on differences in occupational origins at the several salary levels within the elites—the matter of composition. Percentages of men from the different occupational origins were then divided into percentages in the U.S. adult male population in 1930, by the same procedure again as in Chapter 2. This gave data with which to examine the matter of representation.

The civilian federal elite taken as a whole (Table 25) is internally highly stratified by occupational origin. Sons of laborers compose almost one-fourth of the executives at the GS-14 level, but only one-tenth of the executives at the level above GS-18. A similar pattern, although not so extreme, of greater proportions at the lower levels exists for sons of farmers and owners of small business.

Exactly the reverse is true for sons of professional men, business executives, and owners of medium and large business, who compose 58 per cent of all the executives above the General Service level 18 or equivalent, and only 30 per cent at the level of GS-14. It is clear that these men have greater proportions in the higher reaches of the civilian executive services, and that men from occupational backgrounds of less power and prestige are in greater proportions restricted to the lower levels.

It is also clear, however, that restrictions against men from the lower occupational origins moving into these high levels are far from absolute. Forty per cent of the men above GS-18 had been mobile out of the laborer and white-collar occupational

2. The "salary grade levels" used in this research are a set of "simulated" levels arrived at by equating men from the different pay systems.

Table 25

*Occupations of Fathers of 1959 Civilian Federal Executives at Several GS Levels or Equivalent**

Father's Occupation

Executive's GS level	Laborer	Farmer	Owner of small business	White-collar worker	Professional man	Business executive or owner of medium or large business	Total
Above GS-18	11.1%	10.5%	9.5%	11.3%	33.3%	24.3%	100%
GS-16 to 18	14.8	14.0	13.2	12.9	23.1	22.0	100
GS-15	21.4	13.4	15.2	14.8	18.4	16.7	100
GS-14	23.8	17.2	14.8	14.6	15.7	14.0	100

Ratios† of Father's Occupations to Occupations of U.S. Adult Males in 1930

Above GS-18	0.23	0.50	1.43	0.79	8.25	8.00
GS-16 to 18	0.31	0.64	1.86	0.93	5.75	7.33
GS-15	0.44	0.59	2.14	1.07	4.50	5.67
GS-14	0.50	0.77	2.14	1.07	4.00	4.67

*Salary grade levels for the services are equated by placing individuals in an equivalent rank within the General Schedule (GS) system.
†Percentage of civilian federal executives at salary grade level/percentage of U.S. adult males in occupational group = ratio.

levels or had moved upward from the farmer and owner of small business levels.

The ratios of men at each salary level to U.S. adult males, in the lower half of Table 25, show that men whose fathers were in the professions or owners of medium or large business are much more highly over-represented at the top than at the bottom of the scalar structure within the elites. For every professional man in the adult population in 1930, 8.25 men had reached the level above GS-18, while only 4.00 men had remained at the level of GS-14 or equivalent. In general, sons of business executives or owners of medium and large business are also more highly represented at the top. On the other hand, sons of laborers are under-represented at all levels, but most heavily under-represented at the higher levels. Sons of farmers, owners of small business, and white-collar workers are also more under-represented at the top than at the bottom of the salary grade structure. The conclusions reached for all civilian executives taken as a whole apply, with some modification, to each of the three civilian elites taken individually.

At the outset of this section we reviewed the finding that at the end of fifteen years men from different occupational levels tended to be at about the same point in their careers, with sons of laborers and farmers lagging only slightly behind. But men from the lower-status occupational groups, although they do tend to close the gap, never quite achieve the higher levels in government in the same proportions as men from the occupational groups with more prestige.

Achievement Time in Careers of Executives

As stated earlier, the fathers' lower occupational status seems primarily to eliminate greater proportions of lower-status men early in their careers rather than to retard them during the middle years.

There is at least one way this statement can be checked—by comparing directly ages and career speeds of men from different occupational origins during three time points in their careers. Age of beginning the career, length of time to reach present position, and present age will be compared by father's

Career Lines 165

occupation within each of the services. We ask if factors other than father's occupation may not have a greater influence on age differences, and we examine age in relation to the individual service, in relation to interfirm mobility, and in relation to type of organization. We can then determine whether other factors intervene between father's occupation and achievement times of federal executives.

Table 26 shows the average age at which men in business, in each of the services, and from nine occupational groups began their careers (first entered public service or business). Across the bottom of the table are figures derived by subtracting the lowest average age in each column from the highest average age to arrive at a difference between extreme averages. The differences between extreme averages are 3.2 years for civilian, 4.6 for military, and 3.2 for business executives. Among the three civilian elites the differences are 2.5 for career, 5.2 for political, and 1.7 for foreign-service executives.

The figure to the right of the average age by occupational origin for men in business and each of the services is the difference between the average age for the occupational origin group and the average age for all men in that elite. By examining the plus-minus signs we see that sons of owners of large business, major executives, and professional men all entered each of the civilian services at, or older than, the average age for all men in each of these elites. Sons of laborers, on the other hand, entered each of the civilian services at a younger than average age for all men in the elites. For these four occupational origins the directions of the derivations are consistent, but the average age of men from the other occupational groups fluctuates on either side of the averages for the elites.

These patterns hold for neither the military nor business leaders. The average age of entry of sons of laborers into the military is greater than the average for the whole elite, and the average age of sons of professional men is less than the average for all military executives. In the case of the business leaders, sons of laborers enter at a relatively young age, but so do sons of major executives, in contrast to both civilian and military leaders.

Table 26

Average Age of Entering Public Service or Business and Father's Occupation for the Several Elites

	Age Executive Entered Public Service				Age Executive Entered Business
Occupation of father	Civilian federal executives	Career civil service executives	Political executives	Foreign-service executives	Military executives	Business leaders
Laborer	26.7 −1.2	26.3 −0.9	28.0 −2.2	28.1 −0.1	23.2 +0.7	18.7 −2.7
Clerk or salesman	27.1 −0.8	26.6 −0.6	28.1 −2.1	28.7 +0.6	22.9 +0.4	19.7 −1.7
Minor business executive	27.5 −0.4	27.3 +0.1	28.1 −2.1	27.2 −1.0	22.1 −0.4	20.1 −1.3
Owner of small business	27.5 −0.4	27.2 0.0	28.6 −1.6	28.4 +0.2	22.7 +0.2	21.1 −0.3
Owner of large business	29.9 +2.0	28.8 +1.6	33.2 +3.0	28.6 +0.4	24.4 +1.9	21.1 −0.3
Major business executive	29.4 +1.5	28.7 +1.5	32.2 +2.0	28.4 +0.2	23.0 +0.5	21.6 +0.2
Professional man	29.0 +1.1	28.2 +1.0	31.2 +1.2	28.9 +0.7	22.3 −0.2	21.9 +0.5
Farmer	27.5 −0.4	26.8 −0.4	31.0 +1.0	27.6 −0.6	23.3 +0.8	21.6 +0.2
Uniformed service	0.0 0.0	0.0 0.0	0.0 0.0	0.0 0.0	19.8 −2.7	0.0 0.0
Average age for elite	27.9	27.2	30.2	28.2	22.5	21.4
Difference between executive averages	3.2	2.5	5.2	1.7	4.6	3.2

Average age of entry for men from the different occupational origins groups, then, varies from one elite to another; the difference between the services is greater than that between the occupations within each elite. Military and business executives entered their careers at the relatively early average age of 22.5 and 21.4 years respectively. This is much younger than the average entry into the civilian services: career civil service executives entered at an average age of 27.2, foreign service executives at 28.2, and political executives 30.2 years. If we recall that civilian federal executives are drawn from a population with more advanced education than military or business executives and have received professional training in much larger proportions, we understand two of the basic reasons why these men entered their present careers at a later age. We also understand why the differences by occupational origins groups are, relatively, of not great importance. The civilian services draw from all occupational origins men who have secured higher educations, advanced degrees, and professional training. That sons of laborers are slightly slower than men from other occupational groups merely reflects the fact that sons of laborers in highest proportions began their careers in the laborer occupations. Their movement out of this occupation was, however, rapid.

Large proportions of civilian federal executives are delayed in entering the public service while they finish their education and begin to practice a profession. There is also, probably, a greater shift of men out of business into government than out of government into business. In the case of men who receive political appointments, for example, lateral entry at higher levels is quite common. This, too, is reflected in the relatively higher age of entry into the civilian elites.

In general, age of entry is conditioned by the professional requirements for the several elites. Even so, is it not still possible that men with occupational backgrounds of greater prestige may advance more rapidly within each of the individual elites? After entering public service, the years required to reach present position suggest that this is the case for career and political executives and for business leaders, and that within these elites the sons of major executives, professional men, and owners of large business enjoy a fairly heavy advantage over sons of laborers and farmers. Within the military and foreign-service elites rates of movement vary, but not in a clear-cut and consistent fashion.

The difference of greatest magnitude is in the business elite, where sons of laborers took, on the average, 5.4 years longer than sons of major executives to reach present position. When we consider that the average time taken for all business leaders was 23.9 years, and that 5.4 is almost one-fourth of this, we see that sons of major business executives do have a clear advantage over sons of laborers. This advantage exists also among the political executives, where sons of major executives reached present position on the average 5.0 years faster than sons of laborers.

To summarize, in the civilian and business elites sons of major executives, owners of large business, and professional men all achieved their present positions at faster than average speeds. Sons of clerks or salesmen, minor business executives, and owners of small business maintained about average speeds of advancement. In the civilian career and political elites, and among business leaders, sons of laborers and farmers took somewhat longer than average to achieve their present positions.

As in the case of age of entry, differences in achievement time are far greater between the elites than between occupational origins within each elite. Achievement time for all the elites is closely, but inversely, related: business leaders enter business, and military executives enter the services, somewhat earlier than civilian executives enter public service. Business and military leaders, however, take considerably longer than civilian executives to reach their present positions. Men in some elites spent more time after entering their careers to achieve present position, while others waited longer before entry, but either mode leads to approximately the same net time to achieve present position.

Variations in age of entry and in years taken to achieve present position might conceivably have a cumulative effect, causing men from some occupational backgrounds to be either considerably older or younger than men from other occupational backgrounds. Such a result would show quite clearly that the advantage or disadvantage initially arising from the occupation of the father tends to accumulate throughout a man's career. A study of the average age of executives shows that age of entry and years to achieve present position tend to cancel each other out, rather than act cumulatively for men from different occupational groups.

Rather remarkable similarity is seen both by occupations within each elite and between the elites. The average age for sons of farmers is consistently higher and the average for sons of minor executives consistently lower than the average for all in each elite. The difference from one occupational group to another within each elite is never great—a matter of one or two years. At this point in their careers all have, on the average, drawn quite close to one another.

Coming from different occupational origins, and entering different career routes at different times in their lives, these men—at about the average age of fifty—had achieved entrance into the executive worlds of business and government. The selection process has consistently favored sons of higher-status groups—the men who are at present highly over-represented in the administrative elites. Sons of men, however, from the less powerful and prestigeful groups had at the age of fifty balanced early entry against lower career achievement times to reach about the same point in their careers as their more favored colleagues. Here again we see that the factor of occupational origins is selective rather than retarding.

The relative merits of staying with one organization[3] during

3. Reference to the three questionnaires will reveal that the term "organization" has different meanings as used in the study of business and of government executives. For business leaders, it means "firm" (see Item 7 of the 1952 business leader questionnaire) and for government executives (see Item 9 of the federal civilian executive questionnaire) it means "government departments, independent public agencies, business firms, or other private or-

a career compared with making repeated "moves" has been argued both verbally and in print. It has been reasoned that career advancement is faster for men who stay within one organization, outgrowing, rather than leaving, their successive career problems. It has also been argued that the more successful men are those who have the independence of mind to switch organizations whenever promotions are blocked. Regardless of the merits of this as an argument, it is clear that an important variable in the careers of men is that of interorganization mobility. It is to questions of variations in career speeds arising from organizations that we turn our attention in this section.

Executives in the several elites vary considerably in the number of organizations in which they served (Table 27).

Table 27

Total Number of Organizations During Executive's Career

Number of organizations	Civilian federal executives	Career civil service executives	Political executives	Foreign- service executives	Military executives	Business leaders
1	13%	13%	11%	12%	54%	25%
2	14	15	13	13	21	23
3	17	17	18	14	10	22
4	15	15	18	14	6	13
5	12	12	14	11	3	7
6	10	9	9	11	2	5
7 or more	19	19	17	25	4	5
Total	100	100	100	100	100	100

ganizations," a much more comprehensive definition than the one used in the business leader study. One probable consequence of these different definitions is an understatement of numbers of organizations associated with business leaders as compared with federal executives. See Appendix A.

Military executives, as we might expect in view of their career lines, show the least tendency toward interorganization mobility. Those who served in three or fewer organizations make up 85 per cent of the total of these executives—in keeping with our earlier findings that military executives are a more homogeneous group, in terms of education and experience, than members of the other elites. They are in overwhelming proportions educated in military science at the academies, enter the service young, and tend to stay within the first or second organization they enter. Movement into the higher reaches of the military hierarchies requires early concentration of energies in education and in career. At the same time Table 27 reveals that, among those who made lateral entry at a later stage in their careers, there is no wide organizational experience. The military elites are relatively parochial in experience, with little infusion at the higher levels of new men with new ideas.

Business executives are, but to a lesser degree, like military executives in the proportions who confined their careers to a small number of organizations. Seventy per cent, compared with 85 per cent of military executives, served in three or fewer organizations. It may be seen that entering a business firm is, in this respect, something like entering one of the military services. Time invested in an organization is an asset, and changes are not lightly made.

In sharp contrast to both military and business executives, federal executives in all three civilian services who made interorganizational moves four or five times are in about the same proportions as those who made such moves once or twice, with little or no difference on this score among the three civilian elites. Men in the civilian elites moved more freely from one organization to another, but this finding must be interpreted as meaning, in part, that movement from one civilian agency to another is not of such consequence as movement from one military service, or business firm, to another.

After achieving executive status, 65 per cent of all military executives served in only one organization, and 20 per cent in two. Thus 85 per cent of all the military executives served in two or fewer organizations. Business leaders, also, tend to stay within one organization after becoming executives or to make only one move—74 per cent served as executives in two or fewer organizations.

It is to be expected that the proportions of civilian executives should also increase when we consider only the organizations they associated with as executives, but even as executives these men have—in higher proportions than military or business executives—experienced considerable interorganizational mobility. The proportion of career civil service executives who moved twice or less is 60 per cent, which compares favorably with the 74 per cent of business executives with two or fewer moves.

The majority of civilian federal executives achieved executive status before entering their present organizations, which means that lateral entry into high-level positions in the federal civilian elites is the rule rather than the exception. This lateral entry is especially common among foreign-service officers in Department of State, where only 22 per cent of executives have served in only one organization at the executive level.

In the foregoing paragraphs, we have seen that interorganizational mobility has quite different meanings for federal civilian and military executives and for business leaders. We have seen that the rigorous demands of a military career require of most that they enter one service and stay there throughout their careers. Although business leaders in higher proportions than military executives made changes in organizations, they were at the same time more restricted than civilian executives in the proportions making a large number of changes. What has been the effect of these changes on the careers of executives?

The effect of interorganization mobility on achievement time is not the same for all the elites. Business leaders who stayed in one organization reached their present position more rapidly than those who changed organizations, with time taken to achieve the present position increasing progressively with the number of firms. Within both the civilian and military federal services, the effect of "organization hopping" is somewhat more complicated. Examination of the figures for each of the elites shows that a little interorganizational mobility is good for a man's career, but that seven or more moves have a retarding effect. Four to six moves are associated with the fastest career speeds for career civil service executives, foreign-service officers, and military executives. Political executives who make two or three moves have the fastest career speed. Men who were to become federal executives, who found their career routes blocked, made a change in organization and thereby actually profited from the temporary frustration. In the business world, on the other hand, staying with one organization resulted in optimum career speed.

The number of years before entering the present organization is especially informative in understanding differences in patterns of interorganization mobility. Four per cent of military executives reported they had served in seven or more organizations, with an average of only 4.1 years in these organizations. Those who had served in two through six organizations spent an average of only 2.3 years in these organizations. Military leaders, even those who reported serving in a large number of organizations, averaged little time outside the service after becoming self-supporting, and probably only in temporary jobs. Business leaders, in contrast to military executives, appear to have served quite long periods in organizations other than the one with which they are at present associated. Average years for business executives are, in fact, about twice as long as those for federal civilian executives. For example, civilian federal executives who served in seven or more organizations spent an average of only 10.4 years of their careers in the organizations, compared with business executives who spent an average of 20.0 years making seven changes.

It is evident that movement from one organization to another is not so serious a step for federal civilian as it is for business leaders. This may in part result from the fact that one agency within the government is much more like any other agency than one business firm is like another. If, on the other hand, it is borne in mind that many of the moves by federal executives took place in private organizations before coming to the government, it is possible that federal people are more willing than business people to cut organizational ties.

In fact, interorganizational mobility before entering the federal government appears to have an accelerating effect on the careers of federal civilian executives. Indeed, it appears that the wider the experience in private firms, the more rapidly these men achieved their present positions after entering the public service. Career civil service executives have faster achievement time with increasing interfirm mobility up through six firms; for political executives one private firm yields maximum results; and for foreign-service executives each increase in the number of firms is associated with increased career speed.

Lateral entry into the federal services appears to reduce considerably the number of years men have had to serve in order to achieve their present positions. Where lateral entry was preceded by experience in a relatively large number of private firms, movement is accelerated. Many of the federal civilian executives moved into the federal government after achieving a fair measure of professional or occupational status in private organizations. Even when these men had considerable interorganizational mobility in private organizations, they moved into the federal services quite rapidly. For those, in each of the elites, who had served with seven or more private organizations the average time elapsed before entering public service was only slightly more than seven years.

Although civilian federal executives did in many instances serve either in the professions or in private firms, on the average, they moved into the federal service early in their careers, the average executive spending only 5.8 years in private activities before entering the government. That this average is low for each of the three civilian elites indicates that the notion of the high levels of government being dominated by men who received their training outside government must, in part, be re-evaluated. Even for those with experience in seven or more private organizations the average time elapsed before entering public service was only slightly more than seven years.

We have examined the effect of interorganizational mobility on speed of career, finding that movement between organizations has a definite association with achievement time. Closely allied with this mobility is the nature of the organization in which a man served. Career speeds do vary by type of organization, with variation relatively slight in most instances. An exception includes miscellaneous small agencies with relatively few employees, most of whom serve as board members and chairmen. These positions are often granted to men in recognition of either political activity or distinguished work in private fields. It is for this reason that the average age of entrance into these agencies is almost forty years, that the average years to achieve the present position are only 11.7, and that executives in these agencies are older than those in the other agencies.

The men who entered the Executive Office of the President (including the Bureau of the Budget and similar satellite agencies) and the executive Departments (except Defense and components) did so at slightly earlier ages than the average for all civilian executives. Men who entered the Department of Defense did so at an average age of 27.9, which is also the average age for all civilian executives. Men who entered the regulatory and major nondepartmental agencies were slightly older than the average. The variations, however, are small.

There is a definite pattern in the years required to achieve executive position. Career speeds (excluding the miscellaneous agencies) are fastest in Defense, followed by the major nondepartmental agencies, the agencies and personnel around the Executive Office of the President, the regulatory commissions and agencies, the executive departments originated in the 20th century, and the executive departments which began in the 19th century. Close examination of this rank order reveals that career speeds are faster in the more rapidly expanding departments and agencies. Although the differences in terms of years are small, the pattern is clear-cut and consistent.[4]

Within the federal service, movement into each of the four

4. Other factors such as nativity, whether father's occupation was in the public service, and so on, were examined for effect on career speeds. None was found to have meaningful association.

executive elites follows a career route quite different from that of the other three. Career civil service executives tend to move either through the professions or through white-collar occupations. Political executives are highly similar in their career routes in this respect but within the professions tend to move through law, rather than through engineering, which is favored by the largest proportion of career executives. Foreign-service executives, however, differ from both career and political executives. Their main route is through the white-collar and minor executive status, with those entering the professions remaining for a relatively short time. Military executives moved directly into the uniformed services either at the outset of their careers or shortly thereafter.

Although foreign-service executives are more closely similar to business executives than are any of the other federal elites, they do have higher proportions of men who moved through the professions than have the business leaders. The most significant difference between business leaders and federal executives is that business leaders tend to move up through the white-collar and minor executive status, whereas the civilian federal executives tend to move up through the professions.

The occupation of the father plays an important role in the career patterns of federal executives, but at the end of fifteen years this influence is largely dissipated. The influence of the father's occupation is revealed not only in the initial occupations of federal executives, but in the fact that men from lower occupational status tend to move into the professions at a somewhat slower rate than do men from more privileged status.

Executives from all occupational levels tend to be of about the same present age; but those from lower occupational levels entered both business and public service slightly earlier than men from higher economic status; the latter moved more rapidly to their present positions, however, after they entered business or public service than those from lower economic levels.

CHAPTER 11

The Careers of Women in the Federal Executive

There were 10,851 civilian federal executives who returned schedules about their careers; only 145 were women—about one in seventy-five of the civilian federal executives. Although numerically of small consequence at present, these executives are of special interest in the study of mobility in American society. They play a new role in a society rapidly re-evaluating and discarding its old conceptions about the appropriate activity of women in the social economy. In a very real sense they represent a new professional type—the woman in administration. There is much guesswork about where these women came from geographically, what they are like in terms of occupational and family background, and whether they succeeded in rising to their high positions because of special training and education.

For many years, especially in times of emergency, women have been moving into the worlds of business and government. The proportion of women to men on the faculties of colleges and universities has steadily increased. They have entered and made a place for themselves in other professions of which their grandmothers, by the values of 1900, could not have dreamed. Since 1900 they have made certain occupations peculiarly their own. Despite the low numbers mentioned this has been espe-

Author of this chapter: Orvis F. Collins.

cially true in the federal government. Among all agencies (1959) in the General Schedule salary system, 49.1 per cent of all white-collar employees were women. Table 28 shows that the concentration of women at GS levels 2 through 5 was over 50 per cent. At GS-7 they began to fall off proportionately, at GS-12 there were only four women among every one hundred employees, and at the levels of GS-15 and above this dropped to an average of only one for every hundred. In 1959, women at the clerical levels were the largest group of federal white-collar employees, but fairly closely restricted to the clerical and lower professional positions. They worked in a world in which the positions of prestige and power went to the men. Vertical mobility into the higher levels of government was blocked by the fact that men in overwhelming numbers monopolized these positions.

Within the executive elite women tend to be concentrated toward the bottom.[1] Thirty-seven per cent of all civilian executives in 1959 were GS-14, whereas 66 per cent of all women executives in our sample were at this level. Since our definition of a federal executive is a person at or above GS-14 level or equivalent, who is in an administrative or policy-formulating position, some women at the GS-14 level were without doubt not included in the study because they did not perform in administrative and policy roles.

From the foregoing, two facts about women in the federal government emerge. First, opportunities for employment are excellent for white-collar women; second, the women in the federal government work in a world dominated by men. The higher reaches of federal employment are man's territory into which women advance only rarely. Have the women who do advance into these high levels special talents or abilities, special social and economic advantages?

1. The reader is asked to bear in mind throughout that the total number of cases discussed in this chapter is only 145. Percentages and ratios are therefore derived, in some instances, from few cases. Consequently, fluctuations will be greater than in other chapters where thousands are treated.

Table 28

Women in the Higher and Lower Ranks of Federal Government in 1959*

	Number	Women's percentage of total GS employees
Total women	476,448	49.1%
GS-1	946	27.7
GS-2	23,652	52.4
GS-3	119,276	68.7
GS-4	114,921	70.7
GS-5	68,199	62.2
GS-6	25,248	54.0
GS-7	30,021	33.1
GS-8	5,496	22.1
GS-9	13,825	13.8
GS-10	1,494	10.6
GS-11	5,974	7.5
GS-12	2,634	4.5
GS-13	1,158	3.1
GS-14	351	2.2
GS-15	90	1.2
GS-16	9	1.0
GS-17	7	1.8
GS-18	2	1.3
GS-18+	Not reported	
Grade not specified	63,145	

*Source: Employment Statistics Section, USCSC, Washington, D.C. Figures are for October 31, 1959. Included are all women in white-collar positions, employed full time under the General Schedule salary system, both in the United States and abroad. Figures for total employment taken from Table A-6, p. 26, *1960 Annual Report,* USCSC.

The Jobs They Do

As women have moved into government, they have been restricted to the more poorly paid and lower prestige positions. This is often the case with new kinds of people entering work areas. Movement upward in the occupational structures is usually not uniform along a broad front; newcomers tend, rather, to select areas of specialization for which they claim —because of special insight or ability—a certain expertise. As this expertise comes to be recognized by others in the occupational structure, the newcomers make the area of specialization pecularily their own. As their place at the new occupational status level becomes established it serves as a base from which the newcomers spread into the many different functional roles performed at that level.

When the newcomers are no longer concentrated in their original area of specialization but spread evenly throughout the level, the process of assimilation is complete. The evidence of this research shows that the process of fanning out is taking place but is far from complete for women in government.

In 1954 a Department of Labor report pointed out that "the best opportunities for women were in social administration services on such programs as social security, child welfare, public assistance, and vocational rehabilitation. Almost half the administrators in these programs were women." This concentration of women continues in specialized areas at the higher levels. The five departments having the highest percentage of women executives are, in the order named, the Department of Health, Education, and Welfare, with 26 per cent; the Department of State, 15 per cent; the Departments of Labor and of Agriculture, each with 10 per cent; and the Department of Commerce, 6 per cent. Over one out of every three (36.12 per cent) women executives are in two agencies, the Department of Health, Education, and Welfare, and the Department of Labor, which have only one out of twenty (5.3 per cent) of the total civilian executives. These two agencies are most intimately concerned with the problems in which women, in their traditional roles in the home, have always taken keen interest.

Two-thirds of the women executives are scattered elsewhere in the government agencies. In proportion to their total numbers, women are more highly represented than men in the Departments of State, Justice, and Agriculture, the Executive Office of the President, and the Civil Service Commission. The activities of these agencies are certainly not focused on problems of child bearing and the home. For the other agencies the proportions of women are less than those for men. In the Department of Defense, which carries on the traditionally male military functions, only 4.86 per cent of the total women executives are found, compared with the 23.2 per cent of the total civilian executives. Men still keep a near monopoly on the jobs that use physical power for attack and defense.

Another characteristic of newcomers within an occupational setting is the tendency first to seek positions of a staff nature in which they can exercise their expertise without generating direct authority conflicts. Acting as consultants and advisers, such people can share in policy formulation and yet avoid conflicts arising from policy implementation. Whatever their roles when they first entered the administrative elites, women in the federal government are no longer confined to the staff; about half function primarily in line positions.

Since designations of line and staff do not precisely denote authority positions, we divided the women executives into those who are heads of units, assistants to heads, and all others. About 60 per cent of these women listed their position as director, administrator, chief, head, chairman, or other executive position at the top of their units. About 16 per cent listed themselves as assistant to the head of the unit. The remainder, about 24 per cent, give their position as attorney, adviser, staff officer, coordinator, or others of this order. Women in the federal service are, then, not relegated to positions of advisory nature. Within their organizational units they assume positions of leadership and decision.

The Occupational Background from Which They Come

Did these women who accomplished the relatively rare feat of moving up into the federal elites begin life with unusual advantages? In occupational background over two-thirds of the women executives had fathers who were professional men, business executives, or owners; among these, about half are daughters of professional men. Fourteen per cent are daughters of farmers and 13 per cent are daughters of laborers (the larger proportion, daughters of skilled laborers). Only in rare instances did they make, in one generation, the move from unskilled or farm laborer into the federal elites. Their occupational origins are primarily in the professions and in the business owner and executive classes, with a significant number moving from the "respectable" farm and working groups. It is most interesting that only 7 per cent are from the white-collar group.

Women executives do not greatly differ in occupational origins from the total or individual civilian services. They are under-represented for the same occupations as the civilian executives as a whole—laborers, clerks or salesmen, and farmers. They are over-represented for the other occupational categories—as are the several elites and all civilian executives. Except for the daughters of professional men, the over-representation is not greatly different from any of the elites; those whose fathers were professional men are over-represented 8.5 to 1.0, compared to 4.0 to 1.0 for career, 6.0 to 1.0 for political, and 6.25 to 1.0 for foreign-service executives.

In relation to individual professions, except for engineers and ministers there is no clear-cut pattern. Daughters of engineers appear to be more highly represented, and those of ministers much less so compared with totals for the civilian elites.

The 18.5 per cent who are daughters of men in the "other professions" does yield a meaningfully higher ratio. In attempting to understand this difference, we examined the percentage distribution of women among the "other professions" and found that 10 per cent (or fourteen cases) had fathers in the narrow and specific category of accountant. This percentage is much higher than for the other professions, but the fact that there are only fourteen individuals involved indicates that the difference—whether statistically significant or not—has little significance for understanding the occupational origins.

In summary, women executives are drawn from occupational origins highly similar to those for all civilian executives, with the exception that proportionately more women come from the ranks of the professions and fewer from business.

Are the women executives proportionately from families who achieved during the grandparents' generation the status of professional man, business owner, or business executive and transmitted this higher status through the father to the present woman executive? In other words, do these women come from "old" high-status families? Our data do not show that this is the case. It is true that only 10 per cent of the women's paternal grandparents were workers, compared to 18 per cent for the total civilian executives. On the other hand, 50 per cent of the women's paternal grandparents were farmers, compared with 44 per cent for total civilian executives. For the other occupations at the paternal grandparents' level the percentages yield no clear-cut differences, especially when we keep in mind the small number of women executives with which we are concerned.

These women apparently did not achieve their high status only because of a high occupational starting place. Their over-representation in terms of the national population follows the pattern for other federal executives—they are predominantly from middle- and upper-middle-class occupational levels.

The Nativity of Women Executives

Women in the federal elites come largely from the same regional, urban-rural, and nationality backgrounds as the men. They are over-represented for New England, Middle Atlantic, West North Central, and Mountain regions and under-represented for the East North Central, the East South Central, and the West South Central. The ratios are not, considering the small number involved, significantly different from those for the total of all civilian executives. From this we may conclude that women do not, in any meaningful degree, differ from men in their geographic origins.

Examination of the size of cities from which these women come shows that here again they do not differ from the totals for civilian executives. Finally, there is no great difference between men and women executives for the percentages of foreign and American born. It is true that smaller percentages of women than men executives are foreign born (0.7 per cent compared to 3.8 per cent) and that a larger percentage had both fathers and paternal grandfathers born in this country; but given the small differences in percentage it can hardly be maintained that the women who are executives are significantly different from male executives in their geographic origins.

The Education of Women Executives

Women executives attained much the same educational levels as the men: 9.8 women executives are college graduates for every adult male so educated in the national population, compared to a ratio of 8.7 to 1 for the career civil servants, 9.8 to 1 for foreign service, and 10 to 1 for political executives. However, two-fifths of the 145 women received the master's degree compared to one-fourth of the male civilian executives; and 15.9, the doctorate, half again as many as the men. Although the differences do exist, they are greatly overshadowed by the fact that women—like all executives—are drawn almost exclusively from the ranks of the college trained.

At the higher levels in government almost two-thirds of the women began their careers by becoming established in a profession, over one out of five beginning as a public school teacher (see Table 29). Fifteen years later, the public school teachers were absorbed elsewhere in the population, with only 1 per cent remaining in this profession. Closely allied with public school teachers are the 4 per cent who began their careers as college professors. This 4 per cent rose to 7 per cent

Table 29

Career Sequence of 1959 Federal Women Executives

Occupation of executive	First occupation	Five years later	Ten years later	Fifteen years later
Unskilled laborer	0%	0%	0%	0%
Skilled laborer	2	2	1	2
Clerk or salesman	25	14	4	0
Foreman	1	3	6	5
Minor business executive	9	11	27	26
Major business executive	1	3	3	10
Business owner	0	1	1	1
Professions				
Behavioral scientist	5	11	12	13
Engineer	0	1	0	0
Medical	4	4	6	8
Natural scientist	2	4	4	4
Lawyer	5	6	8	9
Professor	4	7	7	4
Public school teacher	22	7	2	1
Other professions	19	20	17	15
All professions	61	60	56	54
Uniformed service	1	2	0	2
Training program	0	3	1	0
Other occupation	0	1	1	0
Total	100	100	100	100

five years later, remained there ten years later, and fifteen years later dropped again to 4 per cent. For this 26 per cent who began their careers in education, the movement out of education was quite rapid, with only 5 per cent remaining fifteen years after becoming self-supporting.

While movement out of the education profession was rapid, over the fifteen year period, movement into medicine, law, and the behavioral sciences steadily increased; the aggregate increase is from 14 per cent when first self-supporting to 30 per cent fifteen years later—an advance of 16 per cent. It is clear that these women during the first fifteen years of their careers prepared themselves through professional status.

But the route up through professional status was not by way of engineering and the natural sciences. Only 4 per cent were at any time during the fifteen year span in the natural sciences. The category of "other professions" is 19 per cent when first self-supporting and drops to 15 per cent only after fifteen years. This relatively large percentage includes journalists, public-relations people, nurses, and a miscellany of other professions each represented by only one or two members.

Among the women who did not enter the federal elites through the professions, the concentration is in two categories: 25 per cent of all women executives entered through the white-collar occupation of clerk or salesman. These are the women who came into the public and private bureaucracies in the secretarial and office ranks, moving out of these occupations rapidly: ten years after becoming self-supporting only 4 per cent were still in the lower white-collar occupations, and fifteen years later the movement was complete—none of the women remained in these occupations.

The shift out of the lower into the higher ranks of the white-collar occupations is most apparent in the occupation of minor executive: only 9 per cent began their careers as minor executives, but this figure steadily increased until, after fifteen years, one in four (26 per cent) was in this category. Those who reported themselves major executives did not increase in this gradual way, but in ten or fifteen years jumped from 3 to 10 per cent. After fifteen years, only 10 per cent were major executives.

Thus we have seen that the professions are the principal route for women into the higher ranks of government service, with only about a fourth of them coming from the white-collar ranks. When we recall that, at the lower white-collar levels, up to three-fourths of the total employees are women, it is clear that movement up out of white-collar ranks is, with few exceptions, not possible for women in government.

Women executives at the GS-14 and 15 levels (or equivalent) are slightly older than men executives at the same level. The discrepancy in average age increases sharply as the GS level increases; women executives at the higher levels are considerably older than their male counterparts. When we recall that only 21 per cent of women executives, compared with 63 per cent of men, are above GS-14, we see that not only do fewer women proportionately move above GS-14, but those who do expend more years in making the movement.

Finally, for most of these women, the classic decision between career and family also had to be made. Two-thirds (65.3 per cent) of the women executives were unmarried, compared with less than 5 per cent of the men.

These 145 women who have become federal executives have bucked a system which began working against them when they were born, around 1910. They elected not to play the highly patterned woman's role in our society. They went to college, they elected to enter the professions; many of them made, what was for some of them, the hard choice of a career rather than marriage; some had the energy and intelligence to combine marriage and career. They had the determination to stay within their chosen way of life until they achieved positions of equal responsibility with men in government.

PART VI

The Private and Public Worlds of the Federal Executives

CHAPTER 12

Personalities of Federal Executives

Method for Evaluating Personality Data

Until now our entire narrative has been about the *social* characteristics of the federal executive. The methods have been statistical and quantitative; significances were found in the variations of proportions and in percentages among the thirteen thousand men and women. The earlier study of the many thousands of big business executives clearly demonstrated that *personality* and the internal psychic life of the individual executive were of high importance in understanding the careers of these men. There, depth interviewing and the Thematic Apperception Test were combined in the study of the personalities of a small sample.[1] With the aid of expert analysis, some of the varieties of personality and the relations of personality to the business career were ascertained.

A similar nonquantitative procedure was followed in the study of the civilian federal executive. Professor William E. Henry, of the University of Chicago, was consulted in the field study and later analysis. He helped direct and guide the work of our staff experts.[2]

Author of this chapter: Noman H. Martin.
1. See Warner and Abegglen, *Big Business Leaders in America*.
2. The authors are responsible for what is said here about personality. They want to acknowledge, however, here and elsewhere in this volume, their deep indebtedness to Dr. Henry. They are particularly grateful for his acute insight into personality and for his great talent and professional skill in

A total of 257 intensive interviews, which included Thematic Apperception Test protocols, was collected on civilian federal executives. (Since this type of investigation is very expensive, we could take only a small sample.) We interviewed 1 person for every 42 in the civilian executive sample. Since the people to be interviewed were drawn at random, all the departments and agencies were not represented equally in the sample. For example, the ratio is 1 to 63 in the State Department and 1 to 22 in the Department of Health, Education, and Welfare.

The interview was scheduled for two hours but generally ran to three or four. Interviews were conducted in offices of the executives, in clubs and hotels, and in a few instances in the homes. They were of a life history form. The executive was asked to go back to his early childhood and talk about his first recollections and then was encouraged to discuss his early adult life and his career experiences in the federal service. His sentiments and views about public service, and his view of the world in general were elicited. Each interviewer had a guide of interview questions but was instructed to follow the guide only in a most general way.

Each executive was asked to respond to a selected set of pictures in the Thematic Apperception Test. For purposes of analysis of the TAT data, civilian executives were grouped in terms of high and low occupational origins, in terms of career civil service executives and political executives, by present age, and other variables.

The method for analysis of the TAT protocols was that of vertical examination. For example, the responses to the first picture in the TAT were all analyzed at the same time with no attempt to relate responses to the first picture to responses to the others. Percentage distributions of types of responses for different classes of executives were then examined. From these percentage distributions qualitative statements were arrived at. The researchers have elected not to report percentages of

---

the use of the Thematic Apperception Test. For the general method and approach to analysis of this test see W. E. Henry, *The Analysis of Fantasy* (New York, Wiley, 1956).

responses because doing so might influence the reader to believe that the percentages reflect a statistical refinement which actually does not exist in the treatment of the data. We will first report on general personality characteristics, then look at individual cases.

Personality and Its Variations

In general, the federal executive conceives of the external world as highly relevant, capable of exerting strong pressure, demanding, and complex. He applies this categorization not only to the world but also to the organization of which he is a part. In most cases he accepts this environmental pressure as a "given"; at times he attempts to change or modify it when he finds it too constricting; but usually the feedback from his actions becomes threatening, and he gives up such notions and turns to acceptance.

The external world is filled with authority figures, structural imperatives, associates, and the masses of people with whom he must deal. He sees such an environment not only as a pressure-creating medium, but also as a means of getting things accomplished. It is helpful; it gives direction and cue; it influences; it is beneficial; it provides for security; it is supportive.

On the whole, he views authority in a positive way. Authority figures are looked up to as persons of eminence and high status. They support, direct, and set goals. He cooperates with authority, and a good relationship is maintained. This is a dominant theme among most federal executives. Yet, while authority is viewed as a continuing and proximate force of good, he does at times feel conflict, resenting advice and direction even while going along with it.

In some instances he does not feel that advice and support are morally right—they may require individual behavior, behavior contrary to behavioral norms; but he follows it because the system and its representative, the authority figure, say he must. This makes it right or at least takes away the onus of guilt, except that there may be an anxiety which cannot be stilled.

This is not to say that he is an automaton. He is actively intelligent; in responding to the demands of authority he seeks to behave rationally and sometimes with independence. It is rather that he conceives of the authority system as omnipotent and omnipresent. There can be no question but that the issue of autonomy or emotional independence is crucial. Even though he accepts structure and needs it, he seeks independence, seeks to "go it on his own."

Here one must distinguish between the drive for independence or dependence and the development of anxiety about being dependent.[3] Both exist in the federal executive. American culture is clear in its mandate that men should be independent. Consequently the process of socialization is so structured that the growing child gradually assumes more and more independence. These executives, however, have retained strong needs for dependency, seeking sympathtic care and succor from others and especially from authority figures; but always, at the same time, striving for autonomy.

The achievement drives of the federal executive are like those of the average American, although quite frequently they stem from environmental pressures, from authority figures either past or present. Moreover, obstacles confront him, as he sees it, and deter him in the course of his achievement drives, which make areas of achievement and success often appear difficult. He is not certain about himself, his needs, and his personal goals.

While the federal executive is quite capable of initiating action he has a tendency to react to a situation rather than to structure it himself. This is particularly true when he is confronted with a task calling for individual action. In situations in which he is working closely with others, he tends to be more

3. The concept of "dependency" needs further elaboration. It must not be negatively valued. For we use the term in this sense (as defined by Webster): "A state of being influenced or determined by, or being conditioned upon or necessitated by, something else," or, "A resting with confidence, reliance; trust." A person who is dependent is one who requires something external to himself in order to act, to realize fully his capacities. He is one who requires association and meaningful relationship in order to come fully to light.

at ease, to initiate more freely, to activate rather than be acted upon. This disposition to avoid "going it alone" is especially noted in areas calling for achievement that must be solely self-directed; here considerable anxiety arises.

He experiences difficulty in resolving situations in which he is emotionally involved, situations in which he perceives conflict with authority figures, conflict over his drive for autonomy and his need for affiliation. When, however, he can deal with situations intellectually, when he can deflect emotion, when he can relate objectively, he can reach resolution, he can be decisive, and he can cope with situations.

In these words we seek to describe certain general psychological dimensions of the federal executive, to differentiate certain key elements rather than to truly characterize. We have heightened certain aspects of his personality structure; shadows perhaps have been overemphasized; we have undoubtedly forced order for delineation.

Variations in Style

Although the men making up the federal service display a rather remarkable similarity in psychological makeup, variations may be observed. Differences in social background, age, and position within the executive hierarchy produce variations in their psychology. The conditions of their service, whether political or civil, point up differences.

Yet these are variations in style—differences in degree rather than in kind—for there is more similarity than difference, more homogeneity than heterogeneity.

In general, the *career civil service executive* possesses psychological characteristics that may be described thus: he possesses lofty aspirations, the majority of which stem from external influences, from heroic figures or models, and from demands made upon him by the system and by his role as a career man.

Achievement orientation is strong. For the most part he achieves in a good way by direct action and mobilization of inner resources, by using assistance from his environment, by internalization of the press to achieve so that such influence from the external environment becomes an integral part of his ego-ideal. In other instances, lofty ideals are scaled to realistic proportions.

Yet the career civil service executive frequently experiences feelings of inadequacy and lack of insight into the means to be used to realize his lofty aspirations. In the majority of cases he overcomes these feelings of inadequacy in the ways we have indicated above; in the remainder he responds with feelings of hostility which in most instances take a hidden form such as resentment, or failing in tasks of "going it alone," or movement into fantasy and the realm of "magical" solutions.

Intimately part of a large and complex system of affiliation and connection, he is entangled in the dilemma of striving for independence and severing ties of affiliation and dependency, yet retaining such ties and support. In the push and pull of these emotional needs, he is able to find resolution at times by making the emotional break and asserting his independence, when he may feel emotionally positive in his freedom or retain feelings of guilt and loss.

The *political appointee* is very similar—he is of the same mold, although the shadings are not quite so vivid. He too possesses lofty aspirations but not to the same degree of intensity or commitment, for he is not certain they are worth the hard work and self-sacrifice. Sometimes he is concerned with his ability to attain these high objectives. If they should prove to be too high or unrealistic, he gives them up. Uncertainty, fear of failure, and doubt of capacity mark the political appointee to a much greater extent than the career civil service executive.

The issue of dependence-independence is also crucial to the political executive. He tries to break ties of emotional support and nurturance. Although he is often able to do so successfully, in a large proportion of cases this brings with it sorrow and more doubt. Often he completely rejects any major dependency ties, but sometimes a strong residue of hostility is retained. He wishes to be independent, but he finds it difficult. Relationships with authority are good; advice is sought, received, and acted upon with good resolution.

Although there is variation in degree and intensity, on the whole the career civil service executive and the political executive are similar psychologically. The career civil service executive most consistently and most intensely displays a lofty aspiration drive. He is committed to high achievement goals in a very genuine sense. While these ideals are primarily derived from external influences and from exemplary figures, in considerable measure he internalizes these pressures so that they become an integral part of his being.

The political executive is somewhat less committed and does not aspire to the same lofty heights. Further, the source of motivation for him is more internal, flowing directly from fundamental personality characteristics.

A second-order contrast between these two groups exists within the notion of self. The political appointee appears to be less certain of his capacities; he doubts that it is worth the effort. And while neither group could be characterized as possessing a strong sense of self-identity and self-confidence, the career civil service executive appears to possess these feelings to a greater extent. Assuming this to be so, it may well be that the individual turns to the environment for cues and direction, for emotional support and affiliation. Both groups of men have strong tendencies to identify with the system, with authority, and with structure. A sanctification of power seems to occur; the system can do no wrong or—always the crucial doubt—can it? This is a response to real or imagined weakness, but it is also an indication of the mobility drive of these men to identify with those higher in authority.

The system of authority is viewed largely in a very positive sense by both groups. Supportive, directive, and "sympathetic," it provides a definite structure within which they can adjust and carry out responsibility. Thus both characteristically defer, receive advice and direction, and move on.

Both groups are commonly more concerned with the external than with the internal. In Fromm's words, they are "afraid to fail and anxious to please." Generally lacking is any cold disdain of close emotional tie; the objective manipulator of the scene, the active protestant, or the revolutionist is not a member of these two groups. Both sincerely respect and follow the conventional values as these relate to them as persons. If they sometimes react with hostility, it is largely covert, rarely expressed outwardly.

Emotional relationships with environment and especially with the handling of close relationships with others clearly constitute one of the most difficult issues for both classes of federal executive. Here is the problem of handling dependency. Thoroughly imbued with conventional values, the federal executive, we infer, is clearly aware of the image of the American male as masculine, assertive, and independent. He wishes to fit this image, but he is never the purely independent type; he has strong needs for affiliation. And herein is the problem—the problem seen almost equally with all groups of federal executives under study. Both political and civil service executives have difficulty resolving the issue. Perhaps the political executive most frequently makes the break and asserts his independence. For the majority, however, there is no resolution. The desire is there, yet it is difficult.

Among the *mobile* and the *nonmobile* there tends to be homogeneity rather than heterogeneity; differences are a matter of degree. The socially mobile executive tends to seek autonomy, in rather definite contrast to his nonmobile counterpart who is more inclined to be concerned with achievement. Coming from a social background higher than his more mobile associate, the nonmobile executive tends to accept the social structure, the status system, and his place within it and focuses his attention upon performance and achievement within the system.

The mobile executive, on the other hand, is more inclined to

Personalities of Federal Executives

resist structure and authority. Seeking to go his own way and be autonomous, he strives for self-determination rather than achievement. Probably here, more than in any other psychological dimension observed, is a significant differentiation between the mobile and the socially stable federal executive.

Yet in this drive for autonomy, and this is particularly the case in situations wherein authority is present, the mobile executive is more inclined to passively submit to environmental demands. Although he frequently utilizes this environment as a supporting mechanism, he tends not to interact actively and mold his surroundings to fit his needs, at least not to the same degree as his nonmobile counterpart.

The nonmobile executive tends to relate more actively to his environment, to utilize it so that it serves his needs for achievement. This may be observed most clearly in his relationships with the structure of authority and with authority figures. For him the environment is also supportive, upholding, sustaining, and guiding him.

In coping with problems psychologically, however, there is little difference between mobile and nonmobile executives as to whether good or bad outcomes are expected by them. That is to say, mobility is not a particularly significant determinant of capacity to reach resolution of psychological issues.

When we turn to the problem of achieving emotional independence, however, differences again can be noted. In this area, the mobile executive resolves the issue more favorably than does the nonmobile. It appears that the executive who has not risen from a lower social background is tied with closer emotional ties to others and to the structure than is the socially mobile executive. Consequently he tends to be more dependent, seeks to retain ties. This is not to say, however, that either the mobile or the nonmobile federal executive should be characterized as possessing strongly independent personalities. Both veer toward dependency.

One of the more striking differences to be observed in comparing *older* and *younger executives* centers on the rather strong tendency for the older executive to seek autonomy. This drive is heightened in situations in which direction by authority is inherent, in situations tightly controlled by higher levels. Self-determination then becomes a concern of first-order importance. Yet in pursuing autonomy his ways of coping with the situation and with authority tend to be passive. He does not move directly in terms of actively engaging and dealing with authority, but he strives for autonomy covertly or at the level of fantasy. As a result, the older executive does not often satisfactorily resolve such problems; they remain with him.

The younger federal executive, in contrast, is more directed toward achievement. He accepts the restrictions of large organization, the many directives, and the need for coordination and cooperation. And given this acceptance he orients himself toward achievement rather than autonomy; he does not fight the system.

Being more concerned about autonomy, the older executive tends to be implicated to a high degree in the issue of emotional independence. While both older and younger men experience difficulty in resolving the problem of dependency, the older does so more often and to a greater extent. He may wish to assert himself and sever ties of affiliation but he has considerable difficulty, as though his full development were contingent upon his relationship with others and that to break such ties would threaten his integrity. Not being able to cope with such a break, he tends to remain dependent or not resolve one way or the other.

The younger federal executives, on the other hand, although they retain strong emotional feelings, more frequently do make the break and function in a self-contained way. It appears that many of these younger men are deeply dissatisfied with their self-image. Possessing lofty ideals and high levels of aspiration, they are drawn to the service and to the system of authority and structure in search of a more successful self-identity. Identifying with the system which they firmly believe to be right and good, the younger executives seek the advice and support of the system. They utilize it as they see fit and move on their own. This is not a passive reaction but an active interaction with the system and individuals and culture.

This same system of authority and structure tends to be differently regarded by the older man. He depends upon it, yet he rejects it. He does not seek its advice and direction in the same positive way as does the younger; or if he does, he does not feel capable of acting upon it or receiving support. There is more resistance, more negative reaction, more hostility, and less identification. He needs, yet rejects.

It would seem as though the older federal executive reflects the same general mode of reaction and behavior as does the older person in all walks of life in our society. His ideals tend to be less elevated in character. He is prone to be less ambitious or more realistic and less romantic than his younger associates. Regarding his capacity to achieve, he entertains more doubt. As he grows older, he has less time to attain the dreams he once held. With increasing age, many are inclined to resist the system more and more—to attribute to the system lack of success if that be the case.

The younger, in contradistinction, still has time to realize his aspirations. He seeks to achieve; he still has confidence in his abilities and can effectively relate to the system and utilize it.

Undoubtedly the differentiation is overdrawn. Many older executives clearly possess effective psychological mechanisms of adjustment; many relate effectively to the governmental system and their role within it; many strive for achievement or autonomy with great success. We point out, however, what is a quite clear variable of differentiation among federal executives —the element of age. Here, as is frequently observed in society at large, aging brings increasing vulnerability.

The Federal Executive by Grade Classification

Executives in our sample were all drawn from the upper levels of the federal hierarchy—General Schedule grade levels 14 through 18 and above. The research question asked was, "What psychological differences, if any, may be observed to exist in individuals occupying positions among these top levels? Is there greater similarity or difference?"

On the basis of their general role in the "top management" of the government, it could be predicted that a core or basic personality pattern could be isolated. On the other hand, some fairly well-defined differences in environment among these levels probably exist[4] and consequent variation in psychological characteristics.

Our findings indicate a much stronger tendency toward similarity than difference. It appears that the role of a "government man" exerts a considerably stronger influence than the executive role per se. That is to say, the differential demands made at the highest executive levels, compared with lower levels, are not of such magnitude as to attract or mold a significantly different personality type. In general, the same type of individual is found at the top grade as at the relatively lower levels of top management in the government service.

Differences here are of the order of magnitude of "slightly less" or "slightly more." Thus as one ascends the hierarchy of federal executives, achievement tends to become an issue of more and more relevance. Conversely, autonomy is the psychological issue found with increasing frequency as observation proceeds from higher to lower levels, but it is present at all levels. This is especially noted if authority is present when lower levels appear to push very hard for autonomy.

All levels tend to be more passive (as, for example, compared with business executives) than active in their relationships with the environment. Little real differentiation is to be found between grades. Acted upon rather than acting, they are all in considerable measure sharply affected by outside forces. The majority are not self-assertive and do not typically demand recognition of their own thinking and needs; they adjust to environmental demands.

4. Undoubtedly, executives at higher levels carry more responsibility, must deal with more abstract data, and have wider social contacts and interdepartmental involvement. See Norman H. Martin, "Differential Decisions in the Management of an Industrial Plant," *Journal of Business, 29* (1956), 249–60.

However, in direct dealings with associates, superiors, and subordinates within the structure of government active and effective coping mechanisms increase with executive level. There is a greater tendency for individuals in top positions to view the environment as supportive—to utilize it, to receive counsel and guidance, and to cooperate with it. This is of course consistent with, and directly related to, our earlier point that lower levels are more concerned with the issue of autonomy and higher levels with the issue of achievement.

It is perhaps in the issue of emotional dependency that the clearest difference in executive levels may be noted. On the whole, lower levels strive for emotional independence and succeed in making the break with greater frequency than do their higher level associates. It would appear that higher levels are more emotionally tied to the structure, to their informal groups, and to the system than are those who occupy relatively lower positions.

One last point remains to be made with respect to differences among executive levels. The ability to arrive at satisfactory resolution of psychological issues tends to increase with higher executive level; lower levels have more of a problem. Indeed, executive position or level within the hierarchy appears to be one of the best indices for predicting capacity to produce good resolution. Perhaps this is because the men in lower positions are striving more for autonomy, a goal that would be exceedingly difficult to realize in as persuasive a structure as the federal government; perhaps it is because those at higher levels tend more actively to relate to the structure and see it as a support rather than a hindrance.

At lower levels, our observation of the psychological data indicate a much greater tendency to engage in resentment and ineffective resistance. Here there would be more feelings of inadequacy, and fear of rejection, reprimand, and hostility. One seeks for self-determination, but the way is not clear.

It may now be fruitful to summarize what has been said. With decreasing executive level, lower social class origins and older age, there is an increasing tendency to seek autonomy.

Thus, at one extreme, the younger, nonmobile, top executive presents the achievement issue 70 per cent of the time; at the other, the older, mobile, GS levels 14 through 16 or equivalent, present the autonomy problem 77 per cent of the time. An individual in the former group is most likely to perceive himself as an achievement-oriented person undisturbed by conflicting pressures from the outer world or by unresolved internal doubts. He tends to know what he wants and the primary question for him is what, if anything, he will do to win his objective and what, if anything, will result from his efforts. The basic question here is, "Is it worth it?"

Since the more mobile, the older, and those occupying lower levels are more concerned with autonomy, they feel pressure from the outer world and specifically from the structure of which they are members. In this world of pressure, they question the extent of their own motivation toward success and mastery; they question their capacities. Thus it is the socially stable, younger, high-level executive who relates most easily and well to the authority structure and to the total system. It is this group who are most prone to view the governmental complex as supportive and who blend their own personalities to it in the most active manner. And it is this group who are most capable of achieving a psychologically adequate resolution of the problems of achievement, autonomy, and emotional independence.

The nonmobile, younger man who occupies higher position seems to be best able to cope with the independence-dependence issue. Either he is able to achieve emotional independence or he is happily dependent. In either event, he adjusts. The older, lower-level executive is more apt still to be emotionally involved and unable to resolve this problem.

We thus observe the federal executive, the basic form of his personality, and how the general diversifies into several types or styles. One such style emerges in the form of an individual intensely committed to high achievement who is uncertain of goals and lacks the coping mechanisms to resolve the many issues deriving from role and environment. Still another resists the structure of authority and its many directives. Either covertly hostile or undermining, he nonetheless cannot break dependency ties and is caught. Here too is the conformist. Deferring to the system, his own needs are subservient to external pressure. Here is the "organization man."

The personality structure we have here portrayed, nevertheless, in both its general form and variations, fits the role defined by a vast, large-scale organization—even though some of the individuals currently filling governmental roles appear to be out of phase.

There is in the federal executive much of the universal. We see in the personalities sketched in these pages much of what is seen in man in general—the same feelings of inadequacy, the same uncertainty, the same desire for guidance and social ties, the same deference to authority. We see the same tendency to rebel against authority, to be self-determining, and to realize independence. We see the same ambivalence, the same clash of needs.

He is not different, yet he is. A particular constellation of psychological characteristics draws him to the federal service; a particular role permitting the gratification of both dependency feelings and a drive for autonomy exists within that structure. In this sense, personality and role are functional—one fits the other. For here is a body of men in the Sunday dress of common men. Possessing ideals which raise them above that level, possessing a strong and lofty sense of values, they identify with national purpose. They raise themselves literally by their bootstraps. They feel, in a sense, men of destiny.

Three Personality Profiles

To the government mind, the sphere of the relevant and the important extends well beyond mastery over material things and self to the province of public service and to the intellectual sphere of the humanities and social sciences, the arts, and the physical sciences. There is a time depth here which extends beyond the challenge of immediate circumstances and the day-to-day problem of existence. Founded not on specific events but on a heritage of service, the time world of the federal executives ideally tends to be abstract rather than particular, global rather than provincial, eternal rather than worldly.

They are different. They constitute, as it were, a select group living a style of life that has a special accent. In them—on the lofty plane of idealism—power, compassion, and justice are united. They have a strong humanistic tendency, a belief in the advance of man. Federal executives all have this as a common point of departure: they are to be evaluated not so much by material success as by their mission, and that mission is service to mankind.

Within this general character there is, of course, variation. No occupational group is entirely homogeneous. Varying personality types work side by side in the government as they do in any organization. The particular combination of individual psychologies in any group is determined by the vagaries of total emotional climate, the demands of the situation, and by chance.

Among the many subtypes, some fairly well-differentiated forms can be distinguished. From among these it is possible to construct a series of representative profiles, personality sketches that help give a better picture of the federal executive as a person.

Three such profiles are presented here. The reader should hold in mind that they do not represent a full or complete picture of the many forms to be found in the government service. Among other varieties present is, for example, the mobile businessman temporarily in government or the young mobile man whose entire life is committed to government service. These three vignettes simply portray three representatives of personality types frequently encountered in our studies.

The first of these is Henry Page Osborne.

HENRY PAGE OSBORNE: A REASONABLE MAN

> All these were honored in their generation.
> And were a glory in their day.
> There are some of them who have left a name,
> So that men declare their praise:
>
> *Ecclesiastes 44.*

Henry Page Osborne, born in Concord, Massachusetts, the son of a highly educated man of letters and a mother whose lack of fame in the world of writing could only be traced to the fact that she was a woman, entered the government service after a year of graduate work in political science. Under the shadow of such an illustrious literary heritage, which extended back through generations, and himself not capable of being a scholar, he turned to an occupation comparable in scope and acceptance—the government service.

Had he been born of less endowed parents in Ohio, Texas, or innumerable small or large towns elsewhere, he might have turned to the world of business where, unhandicapped by lineage, he could well have been an outstanding success. As it was, his destiny was set. He inherited a social position, a mission of service, a position of sensibility in ministering the world's purpose. Had he been consulted, he might have chosen a less difficult, less ambiguous career to follow.

As it happened, he never reached the point of making any conscious, deliberate choice of career at all; given his predilections he naturally gravitated into the federal service. Washington, now as for others in the past, provided an atmosphere stimulating and exciting—the center of world events and of portentous decisions, yet socially and occupationally secure. Here in this atmosphere of education, knowledge, and charm, he could fulfill his role and his potential. In such a fellowship the standards he inherited could be met.

Osborne's ideal of life is a servitude to the realization of great ends: to be a great American with a place in history, a place justified by having influenced domestic and world events in a direction correlated with the advance and betterment of mankind. His own personal success and welfare is subordinate to the larger end. Above the mundane, daily scuffle of interpersonal competition for status and gain, he need not be self-assertive or grasping, for his goals are beyond. He need not think of himself.

His ideals are of heroic proportion. He embraces them fully and with intensity. He enters into no compromise with them;

there is no flagging of effort, no dim perception of their ramification, no question of their validity; they are right because they are right. They are "givens"—premises from which all questions may be resolved. To him, anything less is trivial and of little moment.

Socially and intellectually the ideals of monetary and material success are negative. Gaining mastery over material things, realizing profit, selling products, and all the many petty (to him) transactions of business are abhorrent. To him such a life is without meaning, without worth, and without growth. He sees his counterpart in the world of business as possessing a mind prematurely aged by the shut-in world of an enterprise of limited scope and impact. Tied to the commonplace, the businessman stands no chance for a place in history; such a man is alien to Osborne's values and his way of life.

Thus with the best of will, Osborne seeks out the "better things of life"—the arts, the humanities, and above all, the society and companionship of those who are conversant in these areas. Hoping in some way to align worldly affairs with the morality of the intellect and the gentleman, he labors diligently to demonstrate the validity of this belief. Seeking to understand, to learn, to think through, to inform, to enlighten both himself and others, he firmly lives out his belief in the supremacy of the mind and the intellect.

He cannot accept the utter "grossness" of the political process as a necessary condition for the conduct of human affairs. While he sees the rough-and-tumble of practical politics and is realistic about it, he displays a certain amount of embarrassment whenever he is caught up in the tangle of getting things done. He has no illusions about politics and is adept, yet he does not accept it as what "ought to be."

These are the terms under which Osborne views his life and his career. Knowing him and his lofty principles, one could have some doubt that Osborne would be effective in the give-and-take characteristics of the governmental process or in any large organizational activity. Others, less principled and less hampered by moral and intellectual determination, would maneuver around him.

Yet the very intensity of his purpose, together with the power of his reasoned way, carries him through and enables him to function effectively. He plays the political game to a minimum and does not seek political connections. Nothing is more important to him than his obligation to advance the welfare of man and play a part in shaping world events. Such a mission has its own rewards: to have done something of lasting value, to have made a contribution to society and—what is most significant—to have gained self-respect.

> I have only rarely encountered a man with the integrity of Henry Osborne. His is a mind of the highest order—absolutely incorruptible. He thinks for himself. And what is more, he is a doer. He combines thinking and action.
> [From a conversation with a close associate]

Osborne's ties to tradition and the life of reason enable him to achieve a strong sense of objectivity, a detachment from situations and events, and a structured approach to decision. Possessing an intelligence of a high order, well educated and knowledgeable, he can cope with complexity, reach resolution, and carry through.

He is not creative. Except through the accidents of reason, his ties to the past, habits of mind, and complete adherence to ideals are such that he is unable to break out along new avenues of thought. His ideas are innate, imposed upon situations rather than derived therefrom. His is an inherited taste, an endowed style. He proceeds, therefore, from a clear and definite structure—a framework of values, a definite and systematic approach to problems, a statuesque attitude.

So he finds the governmental structure a suitable milieu. Its structure, policy, and rules correspond to his own psychological structure, and so he experiences no conflict with his external world, no collision of his own drives and orientation with dictates of the organization. He does not rebel against the organization or against its authority system. It is internalized—easily and without emotional residues. Moreover, this occurs without feelings of dependency. Osborne does not feel tied to the governmental structure because he needs a strong father figure or because he needs emotional and social support. He is capable of operating on his own, of assuming complete responsibility for his actions, of assuming the initiative without direction and cue; he is capable of handling consequences. The reactions of others, while relevant, do not become primary determinants of his own action but are part of the many factors taken into consideration in arriving at decision. In this sense, he comes close to approximating Riesman's "inner-directed" man.

Difficulty would come from his possible lack of sensitivity to changing situations. His tendency to impose structure upon situations, his strong bias toward the intellectual and reasoned approach to problems, and his strong roots in tradition at times lead him to ignore subtleties. Thus he is not truly autonomous; that is to say, he is not capable of acting independently yet with definite sensitivity to situations. He is too formalized for that, too much cut along classical lines. As a result, certain of the nuances inherent in so many events are blurred for him.

Time for him exists in a unilineal form. The past, present, and future form a line stretching beyond. Because time is continually moving and cannot be reversed, because the present must always be seized with freshness, he experiences a strong drive to activity. Useless effort is profane. Always the direction must be in terms of advance—to move something along a little farther, to give others more of some noble ideal, to grow himself a little each day, each month, each year. In this sense, he is "activity-centered." Now at forty-seven years of age, he asks himself what better he could have done. Full of faith, energetic, confident, eager to advance the cause of mankind, capable, unselfish, virtuous, and intelligent, he possesses sufficient self-insight to ask himself this difficult question. Because he has a critical mind, he is still searching for the answers to the meaning of life and he will continue until his career is terminated, for there is no end point.

In terms of psychological adjustment, this man can only be judged as highly satisfactory. He has achieved a good ego-identity and self-acceptance. Intellectually he would fall within the upper 5 per cent of the population. His coping mechanisms are more than adequate. He can easily resolve problems, both psychological and otherwise. Control both inner and outer is good without rigidity. [Report by project research analyst]

His Family

Family, for Osborne, is highly significant—not merely in the sense of close interpersonal relationship but as a highly relevant factor in the binding of time, the continuation of a distinguished upper-class heritage. His family is for him the repository of a culture built over generations and extending into the distant future. For him, this line of descent must be preserved.

This is not to say that familial ties are cold and distant; they are very much the opposite—warm, close, and intimate. At the age of twenty-three, Osborne married a girl whom he had known since childhood. The only daughter of a close and cherished friend of the senior Osborne, she was so much like Osborne in nature, interest, and background that they seemed to think and feel as one.

This unity of spirit was not restricted to Osborne and his wife. Their children, two girls and a boy now in their teens, shared this exclusive and enduring solidarity. Their education, while thorough and traditional, was in certain measure external to their developing natures. The bulk of it came about in an indirect way through close interaction with their parents, the result of countless acts of "point and counterpoint."

The Osbornes present themselves as a self-contained cultural and social unit, an image of cool and somewhat aloof self-confidence. Definite barriers separate the family from the outside world, but they are permeable to certain individuals who are of like nature, like background, like culture.

Moreover, family does not exist separate and distinct from

work. It is clearly part of the stream of events making up Osborne's official duties.

Osborne does not take work home from the office, but he discusses abstract problems and issues inherent in his work with his family. Their views are assimilated and their opinions respected. Problems are exchanged. He does not view his children as part of a decadent younger generation or his wife as his inferior. They are equals, intellectually and socially. They are part of a common tradition of which Osborne is only the bearer —the means whereby this tradition is carried on, the vehicle through which the future will be molded. Therefore, they are essential.

Osborne represents a sizable number of executives in the service of the federal government, drawn to a considerable extent from the nonmobile, literary, upper-middle and upper classes of the East. He would function well in almost any type of organization were he so motivated. Some would characterize him as a classic executive type; others, perhaps less well endowed, might call him stuffy; still others would never understand him. His goal is to achieve a place in history and to do something worthwhile. In this he seems highly likely to succeed.

KENNETH ROBERT ELLICOTT: THE MAN AFTER STATUS

> Backward or forward, it's just as far
> Out or in, the way's as narrow
> It's there! and there! and all about me
> I think I've got out, and I'm
> back in the midst of it.
>
> *Peer Gynt*

There was little regret in Kenneth Ellicott's heart when he left his home in Chicago to attend a nearby state university. Chicago was the Midwest; it represented all that was provincial, coarse, mundane, and superficial. Since he could remember he had resented his place, his home in the northern part of the city, his schoolmates. In a sense, he resented himself.

He was part of the vast American lower-middle class, and like many others he desired desperately to rid himself of the mantle of deadly respectability. Intellectually he did not disagree with the content of that morality, but he felt hemmed in by its very goodness. He aspired to difference—specifically, to freedom. Thus, when he left Chicago, his spirit lifted to the quest before him, which was never to end. It was this way in college, in his first job, and when at the age of twenty-seven he entered the government service. It is this way now at the age of forty-three—always a never-ending search.

Like other government people Ellicott is motivated by the ideal of public service. Towering above this is the ideation of status. Ellicott aspires to be a widely respected member of society, a person looked up to by almost everyone else, a person of reputation and high rank. Indeed, this emphasis is almost monolithic, it is so dominant. This strong directing force does not exist merely in the background of his consciousness, for he is explicit about it and often speaks of it, as when one evening riding home from work with his friend, Hugh Manders, he said, "I've got to make it. I'm going to do it and I'm going to do it on my own." And only through keeping everything aboveboard; only with complete honesty and integrity.

To Ellicott anything else is secondary. To him, his job, his friends, and his family are means to one end. Not that he has no feeling for them, but they all fit into the focus of his world. He made certain that they would when he chose the government service, when he made friends, and when he married. To his intimates he is unselfish, generous, and loyal.

To this ambitious man, free movement is a must. He cannot easily tolerate direction or restriction. The basic tenets of the American system of democracy and the American heritage of free enterprise together furnish an ideological basis for his psychological makeup. He fits it perfectly. The rub comes only when he is restricted in his freedom of movement by the inevitable policies and rules of the administrative process, which he tends to resent, to rebel against, and to fuss about. Because he realizes they are necssary, he conforms; but the friction is there.

To the observer, Ellicott appears to be self-confident, poised, urbane, and somewhat aloof. In conversations he nearly always takes the initiative, for here he is an artist, the master of the deft phrase, knowledgeable and witty. He possesses the grace necessary to handle even the most difficult social situation with charm and tact. It would appear to an observer that he believes himself to be rather a superior person and, in externals, he is.

This is surface; inside he churns with self-doubt. Continually questioning his capacities, his abilities, and his apparent success, he follows a path he has most admired. Now he is not so certain that he made the right choice. He has attained a certain degree of eminence, yet nothing has happened, and nothing has been gained. He is not happy or satisfied. Restless, searching, wondering, he seeks to express something, but he does not know what. Ellicott is a complicated personality replete with paradox: he strives for freedom of expression, for autonomy, but he also seeks support. Emotionally he is quite dependent, welcoming close social ties with his associates and a high degree of structure. Thus he is caught in an emotional dilemma.

The government service with its high degree of form has slowly weakened the strong, almost violent drive he has for autonomy. Through the years it has provided him with gratification and security. While at times he still experiences a strong feeling of rebellion against the directives of higher authority, this emotion is subjugated. In its extreme form it is expressed in mild hostility—never toward the government or his fellows, but more or less free floating, directed at the abstract, outside world. His ambition is thereby channelized, his emotions and frustrations curbed under the wider impetus of social status and recognition. Year by year his drive for autonomy has diminished. Ellicott, in his search for freedom and recognition, has settled for recognition.

Life for him has but one defect—that of attainment. For someone so highly ambitious, the civil service is limited. Today he has nearly reached the top of the promotion structure. He has no place to go but he cannot bring himself to leave the social stability of the government for the possibly more lucrative field of business. Even if he were to do so, he is not at all certain that he possesses the necessary skills to succeed in the arena of close and personal competition. Also his interest is not there; he does not think the world of industry is challenging. In any event, it seems likely he will never leave the service. He enjoys more than enough power. "After all," he jokes, "what more could a guy like me expect?"

> Subject is extremely oriented in the direction of recognition. He was and is highly motivated, not so much in the direction of accomplishment, as toward status—status for its own sake. He is hindered in this drive by quite strong dependency feelings—the need for close, emotional ties and support from others, especially from superiors. He needs structure, yet he tends to rebel against it. [Report by project research analyst]

Family has many meanings, many values. To Ellicott his family by marriage is most important; it is both a means to an end and an end in itself. His family of birth he tends to forget.

As a diligent and hardworking undergraduate student he had little time for social life. Yet it was there he met the girl who was to become his wife. They were married shortly after his graduation. Mary Frances Ellicott followed her husband's career with more than usual interest. She too has high ambition; she too came from small beginnings in the Midwest. Moreover, she recognizes clearly the wife's role in furthering position and status. A devoted and capable mother, she runs her household and children with efficiency. Now at forty, her task is nearly over and she can devote her time almost fully to her own interests and those of her husband.

Thus the family became a single unified force in the case of the Ellicotts. Both understand and both accept this. Social life long since has become a game to them, a complex of moves to be played deliberately with plan and with finesse. And they play it well. Yet beneath these externals, a deep and sincere affection gives firmness and depth to their relationship. Each feels respect for the other; each feels the other's doubts as well as his own. Perhaps because of this sensitivity and mutuality, their bond is more strengthened.

Typical of the aggressive, hard-driving type so frequently associated with business, Ellicott could well have fit into industry. Yet he is basically too dependent for that kind of life. Except in very large organizations, he would find business life unrewarding. In government, along with many others like himself, he can find recognition and status and yet be secure. The only rub is that he tends to rebel against too much structure.

WILLIAM JOHN MCCULLOUGH: LOSS OF DEDICATION

> And there are some who have no memorial
> And have perished as though they had not lived
> And have become as though they had not been,
> With their children after them.
> Yet these were merciful men
> And their uprightness has not been forgotten.
>
> *Ecclesiastes 44:9*

It is probably natural for a person as he approaches sixty to believe that much of the world's work has been fruitless, that one's task is beyond the scope of reason's capacities and to feel a measure of despair. And to say along with Santayana:

> As it is, we live experimentally, moodily, in the dark; each generation breaks its eggshell with the same haste and assurance as the last, pecks at the same indigestible pebbles, dreams the same dreams, or others just as absurd, and if it hears anything of what former men have learned by experience it corrects their maxims by its first impressions, and rushes down any untrodden path which it finds alluring, to die in its own way, or become wise too late and to no purpose.

This is precisely William John McCullough's attitude toward himself, his work and the world. Today, at fifty-nine, he is weary and closely approaching cynicism. He seems to be looking beyond. Thirty-four years ago when he went to Washington he would not have uttered such thoughts nor would he have felt them. He had then a strong sense of mission, a belief in the moral goodness of man; his was a dedication to progress and a conviction of its inevitability. How then this change?

The answer is not clear, certainly not to McCullough. He has little insight into this aspect of himself, for this change took place gradually with no major shifts in his orientation and no episodes of sharp impact. The metamorphosis of his personality—a transformation from a major to a minor key through an almost imperceptible series of inevitable modifications—was inherent in McCullough the person, an intrinsic part of his developmental process, his very nature.

Except for an abiding devotion to serving mankind, he did not possess a definite and sure conception of the role of the governmental process or his place within it. His first post was an easy one, as were those immediately following. In these he was in a position to see the direct impact and relationship of his actions. He served under a strong personality; policy was clear-cut, complexities were few. Later, however, as he moved into positions of greater responsibility and more difficult administration his capacity was lacking. Or he was unable to mobilize sufficiently, either intellectually or emotionally, to cope with crisis.

Parts were parts for him and not integral sectors of a larger whole. Events existed and were interpreted only as isolated fragments. Insights into relationships among units, actions, and people were at best blurred, half-formed images. It was not that he lacked fundamental intelligence. For a number of reasons he could not integrate experience.

As a child he was what might be called precocious, and his education came easily. He achieved a mastery of both the arts and the sciences and was graduated from college magna cum laude. Nothing was too difficult for him, and he succeeded in everything he tried. After college he went on to graduate school, taking his master's degree in history, with an honors thesis.

He might well have gone farther in education but deferred work on a doctorate in order to move into the action field. At the suggestion of a professor of political science, he went to Washington and into the governmental service.

> McCullough was one of the most gifted students I have had. His mind was capable of roaming far and wide. He had what I would call the capacity of creative synthesis. Take his thesis on "Locke's Contribution to Theology"; I consider it a significant contribution to knowledge. [From a report by his faculty advisor]

But then, somehow, this great capacity was dissipated. McCullough could, in a sense, go no farther. He had reached the summit of his creative power in his early years and could not extend the boundaries of his talents. His potential had been realized and atrophy set in.

Perhaps it is this way with many individuals. Once their full productive powers have been utilized there is nothing left. The spirit withers, the world becomes sharply circumscribed, without romance, without possibility, and without dimension. Only a shell remains.

Little by little certainty was replaced by perplexity. Where once there were clarity and sureness, there was faltering, and then came a strong negative turn. Any observer of McCullough can immediately discern his defensiveness. So apparent is this orientation, so persuasive is its manifestation, that it appears to clothe his entire personality. Any suggestion made, any proposal, any idea meets with a thousand reasons why it can't be done. "It won't work," is his standard response.

Nor is this posture confined purely to a state of mind. His physical being reflects it. Sitting behind his desk, his balding head thrust forward from between his hunched shoulders, he rarely confronts a visitor directly with his gaze. Some object on his desk always appears to occupy his attention: a paper clip, a pencil, a match book. Rarely initiating conversation, he sits thus until the speaker has finished. Then he leans back.

Speaking not directly to the other person but to the ceiling or the window or some other physical object, he delivers a series of skepticisms, usually in highly abstract form, difficult to counter and frequently to understand. If pressed, he refers either to past ways of doing things, ways which support his position, or he appeals to authority, policy, and rule. If pressed even further, and especially if the other person is superior to him in authority, he usually gives in abruptly saying, "I'll try it, but it won't work out."

In time one comes to recognize this trait in men—a characteristic differing only in strength and display. Springing from different sources, it is undoubtedly quite common. In McCullough's case, this negativism stems not only from loss of a real sense of the purpose of his being, but also from a distrust of other men and himself.

He cannot relate to the world in any significant sense. No longer believing in himself and unable to establish contact with others or with events which he cannot comprehend, he moves laterally with the world rather than engaging it. His is a peculiar hesitation of action brought about by a continuing fear of separation. Yet this very fear and concern furthers such an alienation, for he cannot be himself. His only relationship with the world is through his outer self—the mask—and to sustain this he does not possess the techniques necessary to social intercourse.

As time passes, the separation becomes more and more complete. He desperately wants to relate, but he does not know how. By vigorously shutting his eyes to change he can, in a measure, live with himself. Otherwise he would be helpless and forced to admit his inability. Step by step he has been driven into this position and now there is no place else to go—nothing to do but be stubborn. Puzzled, unsure, in awe of authority and of the vast, impersonal network of relationships of which he is a part, he follows the book, drifting along on policy and the course of events.

His thoughts—and he had them at one time—remain unshared; plans and projects are formulated but never put forth.

It is as though there is no center within himself, no organizing focus, no beginning, middle, or end. At least this is the case as far as the world of action is concerned, the world in which he spends most of his working hours. His salvation is that his position has placed him in the center of power and action, into the highly structured universe of government. It is this structure that gives him direction and meaning.

It is only in the warm comfort of his family that McCullough is able, in any sense of the word, to be himself. In this atmosphere he is a warm, kind, gentle person. Here he can freely and truly relate, voice his thoughts, promulgate his plans, both give and receive. In his children, cherished and dear, his faith found its locus. They could have been the realization of all he had hoped for, the assurance, the reality. But they have gone off, busy with concerns of their own, and only his wife remains. With them there is aloneness. His circle of real relatedness is narrowed. Ultimately it will diminish to nothingness.

To fully appreciate this man, however, it is necessary to look at his spiritual life. He goes to church, as others do. Beneath this overt demonstration is a deep and firm sense of the religious. McCullough is no mere yes-seeking man; he is God-seeking. Perhaps long ago his real focus of attention shifted from the everyday universe of worldly affairs to the timeless world of the eternal.

> All these people lived all their lives in faith, and died without receiving what had been promised; they only saw it far ahead and welcomed the sight of it, recognizing that they themselves were only foreigners and strangers here on earth. [Santayana]

CHAPTER 13

Professional Pride and the Value of Service

Throughout the United States, the government civil servant evokes at best a hazy image, as if he somehow were outside the main stream of people: different from the businessman, the laboring man, the scientist, the academician, the man of arts, and even the clerk. He is stereotyped as a "bureaucrat." Such words as pedantic, narrow, stuffy, unresourceful, officious, and formal are among the more unpleasant descriptions applied, yet he is also regarded with awe, as part of that vast, impersonal, powerful domain of Washington, inscrutable, incomprehensible, and unfathomable. Holder of power, issuer of dictate and rule, judger of men, he appears to many as omnipotent, able in every respect, omnipresent and omniscient, unlimited.

The truth is we know relatively little about the government executive as a person. His ideals, his aspirations, his motives, his ways of coping with the world—in a word, his psychology —are little known. For he has not existed as an object of study nor has he been popularized in works of fiction. He has been a man from without. Yet the eyes of the world are fixed expectantly upon him and upon his decisions, for in his hands the destiny of many is increasingly being placed.

Some twenty centuries ago, Plato wrote of the philosopher-king. In this ideal, beliefs about the primacy of reason, knowl-

Author of this chapter: Norman H. Martin.

edge, honor, and justice were dominant. Dividing society into three broad classes, he visualized at the apex the aristocrats—the "elite" set apart by tradition and background to rule. Following the authoritarian man, the man of wealth and property, the tyrant, the democrat, there would rise, so Plato wrote, the reasoned man, the temperate man, the insightful man —in a word, the philosopher-king.

> Until philosophers are kings, or the kings and princes of this world have the spirit and power of philosophy, and political greatness and wisdom meet in one, and those commoner natures who pursue either to the exclusion of the other are compelled to stand aside, elites will never have rest from their evils—no, nor the human race. [From *The Dialogues of Plato*]

Today this is still a fitting yardstick against which to measure public servants—in this case, the federal executives.

As system, the beliefs and values of federal executives constitute "ideologies," or the manner or content of thinking characteristic of a group, their patterns of ideas, assertions, aims, and ideals. Not necessarily conforming with reality or how individuals act, they constitute a major influence on behavior; they have a vector quality.

Moreover, the range of these values and ideals is wide. Evolving through time, ideology reflects the personalities of individuals making up a society as they react and adjust to their unique circumstances and roles. Ideologies rationalize existence and give meaning to life.

Such a general body of ideas and values in any group, therefore, represents a totality frequently massive and complex. Composed of many diverse threads, of varying internal consistency and homogeneity, of greater or lesser rigidity, of differing degrees of persuasiveness, it can best be described in terms of selected categories of existence—categories which the observer uses to order the data. In brief form, these categories are as follows:

1. Ideas relative to the world and one's group within that world.
2. Ideas relative to the self and one's position within it: the concept of self, ego-ideal, needs, goals, and values.
3. The resolution: how one relates and adjusts to the world and to the self.

We took a body of data—interviews with federal executives—and by isolating ideas pertaining to these categories, we constructed a description of their general and specific ideologies. They represent just that: the patterns of ideas and values relative to self and the world found in a group of federal executives, 1959.

Career: Its Ideals and Ideas

The occupation of a public servant is, for the most part, highly valued by the individuals in the system. Conceived as work of major significance and magnitude, it is regarded as challenging and worthwhile. Feelings of pride and prestige are frequently engendered.

For them the occupation of public service soars high above the world of "other people." The nature of this occupational world is clearly conceived by most. Serving to direct and solidify the group, belief in the importance of their work provides a firm foundation. The following thoughts expressed again and again in the interviews illustrate the texture and flavor of this clear valuation:

> I have a feeling of participation in something important and worthwhile.
>
> These are significant days, I have a feeling of participating in them—of working on world problems.
>
> I am playing a part in the events of today.
>
> Can one possibly be involved in anything more interesting?

In contrast, the world of business is conceived as mundane:

> I don't feel I would be doing something of importance if I were to work for industry. They are not interested in the public welfare.
>
> I like hard work; the habits of business amaze me.
>
> Those organizations are so profit directed and that is all they care about. They are not interested in the public welfare, nor are they interested in law other than as it applies, or can be applied, to their desire for profit.

For them business is concerned with materialistic things. Motivation is narrowly in terms of profit and loss, of selfish interest. And while monetary rewards are much greater, it is not worth it:

> You feel that [in government] you are in the middle of things, and that makes up for several thousand a year.
>
> I don't [with reference to business] feel any satisfaction in dealing with things.
>
> Who could possibly be interested in selling soap?

They look to their counterparts in business and see them as tired, under high stress, and frequently in ill health. The businessman is in a world of "dog eat dog." Centrifugal forces prevail. In government, on the other hand, people pull together, solidarity prevails, and centripetal forces predominate.

Society is seen as external and frequently vulgar.

> I didn't like the idea that life was so social and so common.
>
> It was too small a town, too narrow in their interests, too inbred to satisfy me. [This in respect to a previous offer from business.]
>
> One has difficulty in talking to them.

However, while the prevailing ideology of doing something of lasting value and significance is strong and pervasive, some do not see it this way. For them, the government service is routine or is, at best, merely a stopping place along the route to better things. Some follow the doctrine of wealth:

> This may be a dead end. I am looking ahead to possibilities.
>
> I am trying to build up as much experience as possible, then I will move into private business.
>
> I am limited by experience. This is why I don't move into industry. I need more experience—to be stronger.

For still others, government service is conceived as a strong protective covering and a source of security. Bewildered in a rapidly changing world, they seek simplicity and structure—as they would in big business as well as in big government. But these latter views are in the minority.

A clear and firm ideology, relative to the world and to their own service, is dominant for federal executives. It is one central belief system, and no counter ideology is found in the interviews. However, as with any ideology, some do not believe it, understand it, or appreciate it. They are simply there. Rarely is a completely monolithic structure of belief and conviction present in any group; there are always the nonbelievers and the neutrals.

Some of these men embarked upon public careers with clear intent, developed in early youth and culminating in definite education and training. In other cases, talent directed the choice of career. For still others, tradition and background were decisive. For many, however, a career choice was made on the spur of the moment—the situation was occasioned by an offer, an opportunity, or by sheer chance. The routes are many.

Two basic routes are talked about most frequently by the civil servant. Background and tradition, and influence of teachers and educators are felt to be the crucial determinants, but accident or chance is also seen to operate.

For men whose views of public service are based on tradition, depth is highly relevant. Between the action of the present and anticipation of the future stands the weight of the past, buttressing, directing, and rationalizing. Serving as a major source of legitimation, the past provides a bulwark of pride against the press and uncertainty of day-to-day events. While the words deal with abstractions, they nevertheless represent a solid edge of reality for these federal executives; the past looms strongly in their ideology.

The past, becoming the present, is transformed into a "mission" or "calling." It very nearly takes the form of a divine summons to duty, a duty following logically from an individual's past.

> When one is brought up as a leader, one must accept the responsibilities.
>
> ... the background that I came from—the intellectually stimulating background that my father and relatives provided me with. Their education. The confidence that comes from background of a professional middle class—the confidence that you've got so you don't have to push too hard.

Although in a few instances this background is one of public service, a tradition of a different sort more frequently provides a basis. Such men describe family backgrounds and traditions in the arts—music, painting, literature—and in philosophy and science. The public servants did not enter into the "arts" or the humanities and science as a career. Instead, they moved into a career considered comparable in terms of acceptability and prestige—the federal service.

For many, however, movement into the federal service was by chance, without clear intent. They simply gravitated into the government. Words such as these express this orientation:

> I had no idea I would ever end up in the government. When I was a senior in college, it just happened that an examination was being given and I took it. And here I am.

A professor of mine referred me to ——— in Washington. He talked with me, offered me a position. I took it. Never even thought of government as a career.

Closely tied to one ideal of service is the belief that reward in the federal service is based on merit. In many organizations, progress through the system is a function of sponsorship, of friendship ties, dependence, intrigue. In many instances, intense rivalry colors the scene, and power struggles set the mood. Although ability and merit are important, frequently they do not pay off directly, and the "bad guys" win.

On the whole, men in the federal service believe there is no way to progress except on the basis of merit. Sponsorship is thought unreliable, nor is it regarded as a common practice. Even when they are not covered by the merit system, they believe in merit as the basis for advancement:

> One's success is due to one's self—to his ability.

> I knew I had to actively get out and seek and get what I wanted. I knew I had to work hard and to achieve it myself through my own initiative.

> It is foolhardy to attach your wagon to any superior. You cannot possibly know what is going to be the outcome of his own career.

> The worthy move ahead; the system rewards.

> Devotion to duty and assigned responsibility are rewarded by recognition and advancement.

Here is the classic "work ethic." Success and advancement are due to hard work, devotion to job, integrity, and resoluteness, with responsibility centered in the individual:

> Success is a combination of hard work and fortunate causes.

> What is needed is enthusiasm and dedication.

I think I am qualified for greater authority and responsibility.

I must learn; I must operate beyond my limits.

If one does not succeed, the fault is his.

The role of chance is recognized or, more particularly, "being in the right place at the right time and in the right circumstances." Now "chance," being the unforeseen play of forces, can operate unchecked upon the individual or it can be "manipulated," influenced, and exploited. The federal executive, no less than other men and no more, seeks to control the role of chance. By conscious and deliberate planning, he tries to direct his destiny. On the whole, however, he rests his case on devotion to his service and hard work.

In the competition for status and recognition, in the more or less normal striving for higher position, the belief is widely held that integrity and success are correlative. Moral soundness is the path upward. The system rewards those who contribute most heavily to it.

The belief system is institutionalized in the merit system, but it is extended to cover those not covered by the merit system. In most cases, both the civil servant and the political appointee see such an arrangement as a necessity. The party in power must have a leadership in the various administrative units which is loyal, sees issues as the party sees them, and carries out its objectives. As one federal executive expressed it:

> It is the obligation of the civil servant to serve with complete loyalty the objectives of the political party in power. I owe complete loyalty.

While political appointees frequently occupy the higher positions, and this may put a ceiling on higher advancement for career executives, this is more or less regarded as being part of the "nature of things." Some of the interviews with career executives revealed an attitude of wry superiority toward the transient newcomers. Interviews with career people, however, showed striking agreement that political appointees are not simply political hacks but, on the contrary, are motivated in their work by a desire to serve the ideals of the administration in power.

The Social Image—An Elite

We have described the conception the federal executive holds of his work—its worthwhile nature, significance, and value. We have described the pattern of beliefs he holds with reference to how and why he entered the service and his point of view on moving up through the career system. Let us now regard his social image:

> We are professionals; we perform our work with integrity.
>
> One's associates are worthwhile; here are men of high caliber, well-educated.
>
> I prefer to associate with the people I work with—with professionals.
>
> I had a better intellectual background and academic training than others.
>
> I have always linked myself with people who like the arts and sciences. For the most part these are government people.

If the term "elite" may be defined as a choice or select part of society, a group considered socially superior, then the federal executives may be characterized as an "elite." At least, this is the way they tend to view themselves. Clearly this conception is part of their ideology. It is expressed in the fairly frequent references they make to their surprise when they were admitted to the service, in their feeling about the important role they are playing in world affairs, and in their notion of a "calling."

In spite of this conception of themselves as an "elite" they feel that perhaps others in society do not share this belief and instead hold to the popular stereotype of the civil servant as a bureaucrat:

> People outside the government really have no understanding of how government works and how dedicated government workers are. We work harder and longer than business people but they look down on us.

These "people outside" are materialistic, less educated, and less intelligent; "they sell their souls." Because of this, their views count for little.

In spite of this rationalization, however, there is some feeling of "not being quite sure." This uneasiness is expressed in the almost exaggerated way they dramatize their work, their colleagues, and themselves.

They View Themselves

Expectations of behavior are set in considerable measure by group norms. In our terminology, this refers to the concepts held by the group in regard to the individual—his goals, his values, his code of ethics, and his character.

The source of action is held to stem from the person. He is believed to be independent, and capable of decision and of rational behavior. Endowed with education and intelligence, he will handle most situations with prudence and discretion and resolve them to the advantage of general welfare. Although the system and the structure do provide a protective covering and a general direction, the federal executive functions on his own. His success or his failure is dependent upon him; if he finds the system lacks challenge, the fault is his, not the system's. As we have seen, however, this ideology is, while important to his role, a source of conflict and anxiety.

Every individual, it is held, possesses unique objectives and goals. Resulting from his particular set of experiences, these goals become sharply molded by the frame of reference of his occupational group. In the case of federal executives, two fundamental goals stand out. The objective of public service is

Professional Pride and the Value of Service

foremost. Even more particularly, and closely allied with the doctrine of mission, is the goal of making the world a better place, of contributing something lasting and worthwhile to society:

> To contribute something that will make the United States a better country and the people in the country better for it.
>
> Leaving the world a little better place than when you came in.
>
> Organizing something of lasting value.

Of equal weight is the goal of realizing self-potential and of using that potential to its fullest extent. It is as though failure to come up to one's innate abilities is a sin, a failure to discharge a moral obligation.

The ideology is quite specific as to characteristics of personality, character, and intellect:

> A willingness for hard work; a dedication to one's responsibilities.
>
> A propensity to pioneer and innovate; not to think along conventional lines; a curiosity.
>
> Self-insight; an understanding of self and of one's purpose and mission.
>
> Courage to make unpopular or even painful decisions.
>
> A high order of intelligence and intellectual development beyond the demands of the job.
>
> A capacity to relate easily and cooperatively with others; a capacity to manage people.
>
> To be a "team member" and to subordinate one's own desires to the interests of the larger whole; unflinching loyalty.

Undoubtedly one of the major functions of an ideology is to

set the standards of right conduct for those who belong to the group. In a sense, the total ideology performs this function. However, certain elements of its body of ideas more specifically than others define "right behavior" and single out the "do-not."

More explicitly, these are the several premises of the ideology of federal executives that define a moral code:

> A fairness to people, in dealings with them, in thoughts about them and—in connection with associates and subordinates—in developing them.
>
> Not to seek political connections.
>
> To serve with complete loyalty.
>
> Devotion to God and country.
>
> Not to manipulate or scheme in order to advance one's own aims.
>
> To go beyond.

Perhaps the most effective way to summarize the basic ideology of the public servant is to select excerpts.

In relation to his background:

> Father was an architect; he came from a long line of college professors in the classics. And grandmother's family too were Greek and Latin professors. Grandfather was the director of the ——— Academy.

In relation to his education:

> We went to different boarding schools, but we were in the same class at Harvard.
>
> Education meant more to us than it did to some of the others; it was almost an end in itself.

And his brother:

> My brother is a brilliant artist—one of the best. I would say that he was a very admirable, but rather soft-headed

Professional Pride and the Value of Service

humanitarian. As we grow older I think he gets more realistic and I grow more liberal.

And when young:

I was fascinated with literature when an adolescent and wanted to write. I had studied Latin and Greek and was preparing under tutelage more Greek . . .

Following school:

I taught school for a while . . . Latin American History and Literature . . . and after my Ph.D. . . . and after the National War College.

About government service:

My feeling about government service is that if you feel you have the talent, and that the talent is needed, and if you are fortunate enough to have a little income, there is no more challenging thing to do.

On money:

The most important thing I can do with my money is see to it that my children get the kind of education that I did.

With respect to his son:

. . . he didn't want to take ROTC, but I finally persuaded him to do it, for I feel that it is necessary for him to be an officer if he does go into the service because when one is brought up as a leader, one must accept the responsibilities.

Success for him is:

I know quite definitely what I want to do. I would like to see this new ——— recognized so that it can fulfill its real potential. And I feel that I can do it, that I am one of those who can, and if I can do it I will feel that I am a success. So that you see I link my personal ambition very closely with that of the organization.

And the factors responsible:

> The background that I've emerged from. Not only my education per se, but the intellectually stimulating background that my father and relatives provided me with because of their education. And when you compare yourself with other men, it doesn't seem so remarkable that you're given responsibilities . . . The fact is that I lived abroad as a child, that I taught abroad, so that I have an affinity for foreign peoples, the historical discipline.

He is, in his own terms, an aristocrat, equipped to lead, to be in high position, and carry responsibility. While not stated explicitly, clearly there is the notion of a "calling" to public service expressed in these words.

The construction of the ideology of a group is of necessity inferential, an abstraction formed from fragments of concrete data. It represents the dream, or dreams, of the men who make up the living form of the collectivity. Here the responsibility of construction rests with the observer and the writer. Nowhere does ideology exist as a concrete totality. As for its "truth" this is a matter of logic. Ultimately it is a matter of testing first approximations by further observation and study.

There is, more specifically, the task of moving beyond first-order abstractions into notions of even greater generality and penetration in order to enrich and enlarge the description of the ideology. In this chapter we have made several such primitive generalizations, partial as they may be. It now remains to move beyond the level of direct inference from concrete data to higher orders.

Many federal executives are romantics in the sense that romance denotes events that have not yet come to pass. Or it is, in its purest expression, a concern with the place and the moment as it awakens:

> something we feel should happen, we know not what; yet we proceed in quest of it. . . . The right kind of thing should fall out in the right kind of place; the right kind

of thing should follow. [Robert Louis Stevenson, "A Gossip on Romance"]

Circumstances create events and we eagerly partake of them not knowing fully where we will be taken or when. The feeling is one of both pleasure and suspense and it is full-bodied.

For these people, coupled with the notion of romance is the gospel of action—literally, of action for its own sake. Here is an emphasis upon getting things done, of producing an effect or performing a function. In its pure form it is the sheer doing of something. Action leads somewhere and that somewhere always has a touch of the unknown within it. It will lead somewhere—they know not where.

Yet it is action in an efficient form, not merely engaging in useless activity. Both romance and action are present in the ideology of the federal executive in clear form. Certainly a good deal of the ideology as we have described it possesses both a romantic flavor and an emphasis upon useful action.

But in addition, and importantly so, there is present a strong emphasis upon idealism—the doctrine or theory asserting the central importance of mind or reason and of the value of ideal forms. For the doctrine of romance and of action taken in itself leads ultimately to pure sensation and drifting.

Plato's conception of the ideal ruling group was that of a class of men dedicated to the pursuit of wisdom and knowledge, with a taste for every type of knowledge. Such men, endowed with unquenchable curiosity, possessing courage and self-respect, sought after justice and truth. Not being concerned with the pursuit of wealth, nor allied with property, they could achieve objectivity. For them, to govern was a matter of duty and obligation—a sacred calling. They possessed the capacity for temperance, self-control, and a respect for authority. But above all they were dedicated to the pursuit of wisdom and ultimate truth.

The ideology of federal executives comes very close to this ideal. The emphasis upon intelligence, intellectual values, and culture, the notion of restraint, the drive for self-respect and the respect of others, the concept of duty and obligation—all are strikingly reminiscent of the Platonic concept of the State. Even more significant is the emphasis in the federal executive ideology upon the search for justice and the fair resolution of problems. Fairness to others, concern for the public welfare, honesty, and "goodness" are characteristics held to be decisive.

It is this part of the total ideology of the civil servant which is crucial, for it gives the direction and ultimate meaning to their role. We have already posited the romantic conception as characteristic. Now we bring in its necessary complement—the idealistic position. Together they define the broad outline of the ideology of the federal executive: the romantic-idealist-actionist.

The question remains, of course, as to how fully and deeply the federal executives live this ideology. Probably many do not; others merely imitate; others are there simply for the ride.

When they all do believe, then:

> when the true philosopher kings are born in a state, [and] one or more of them, despising the honours of this present world which they deem mean and worthless, esteeming above all things right and the honour that springs from right, and regarding justice as the greatest and most necessary of all things, whose ministers they are, and whose principles will be exalted by them when they set in order their own city. [From *The Dialogues of Plato*]

The high ideals of federal executives sustain them in the hierarchy in which they must work out their solutions, but are also a source of much of their anxiety. The peculiar demands introduced by straining between high idealism and practical reality introduce serious tensions. If they are to act effectively, these men must have the internal resources with which to resolve these demands. For them, effective functioning requires a rather special form of personality structure. It is only when as researchers we began to understand the contradictory pressures placed upon these men that we began to understand the apparently contradictory tendencies in their personality configurations.

CHAPTER 14

The World of the Civilian Executive

Determinants of human behavior are almost infinite. In order to simplify description, however, determinants may be classed as those which are internal in origin and those which stem primarily from environmental influences. Moreover, in many instances there may be conflict between the various determinants of behavior. Multiple internal needs may arise which conflict with one another; internal needs may conflict with environmental influences. The determinants, arising internally or externally, are not often sharply focused. They may exist as vague presences rather than as clear-cut and perceptible entities.

From this point of view personality is an always emerging process of ongoing activity developing out of the necessity for reconciling internal needs and external environmental situations. There is an almost infinite range of possibilities through which resolutions may be sought. Each person is unique in the way in which he mobilizes his internal resources, seeks for and utilizes help from his environment, faces uncertainties, and perceives and resolves conflict between his own self and the external world. Each person is, in other words, unique in the way he goes about relating his own actions to the life area in which those actions are carried out.

This approach to personality has the corollary that personality is not something that exists of itself as a steady state. It is

Authors of this chapter: Orvis F. Collins and Norman H. Martin.

a dynamic interplay of the individual with the world in which he lives. Yet, although each man's world is unique to him, men doing the same kind of work to a high degree share a common world. All American civilian federal executives share the world of higher-level governmental position. An understanding of their personality structures requires an understanding of that world.

In describing the world of the federal executive in broad enough terms to fit all civilian federal executives, two points must be made: first, this describes a "universal" world and not the "unique" world of each executive; second, this is the world of the civilian executive seen by outsiders—the researchers. No one federal executive would see it quite as we have described it for purposes of this research and, indeed, on any one dimension many will have seen it in quite a different way. This facility, unique to each person, for perceiving the common world from where he sits is an important function of personality and a characteristic to which we will constantly refer in our analysis.

The World of Civilian Executives: An Abstraction

The civilian executive is a member of a multiple, massive, and highly structured formal organization. Always contextually of great significance to all his actions are distinctions of this order: bureau level—department level; chief—deputy; headquarters—field; executive—legislative. Both cognitive and unreflective action must be geared to these referents of explicitly described and formally codified relationships. It is the exactness of these relationships, rather than their complexity, that is most typical of the federal world—and for that matter all worlds of large organizations. Most systems of social relationships are intricate and complex, but the large bureaucratic systems of government and business formally express relationships with exactness.

Within such a system of exactly determined relationships the individual must always act with correct superordinate, subordinate, and associational behavior. The cognitive process of identifying other positions as they have bearing upon his own situation places a not inconsiderable intellectual demand upon the civilian executive. The demands of the situation call for intelligence of a high order. For example, the process of identifying an "opposite member" in another structure (perhaps even another government), and of determining through knowledge of regulations and protocol how he may address himself to this "opposite member," is something of an intellectual feat in itself.

Intellectual capacity is, however, not enough. There is required also a sensitivity to environmental demands: first of all, to the actions and reactions of others—subordinates, superordinates, peers—and to both individuals and groups of individuals; then to both the small groups of men who surround the individual and the larger organizational systems which his actions will affect.

The world of the federal executive, however, is shaped by something beyond the web of personal and organizational interconnections. There is always present the overweening condition of policy. At one level, shaping one's actions to policy requirements is an intellectual problem. One reads and studies the congressional acts, the executive orders, and the departmental regulations and directives. One arrives at an intellectually balanced position and issues his own "paper" to conform.

At another level, however, functioning within policy demands is a more subtle and intricate process. Policy, from this point of view, consists not only of the formal statements that appear in distributed papers but also of the people who are directly and indirectly involved in the formulation of policy. Policy is—for the civilian executive—the congressman, the Cabinet official, and the general public. It is also a political process which originates and grows beyond his own tightly structured organizational world. It comes from the "Hill," from the White House, and ultimately from the public. It comes in the form of clearly defined written statements but also in the form of involved clues and subdued nuances. In determining the nature of policy, of its scope and direction, the civilian executive must have sensitivity beyond the mechanical ability to read, digest, and codify written materials.

Further, his role in relation to policy is not simply one of ingesting and passively reacting. The civilian executive in his day-by-day activity remakes policy to fit his immediate situation and his continuing intentions. At his own particular point in the organizational network he functions to rationalize and restate the broad directives which flow down through the system to him. At times this policy function is formal and explicit, as when he is called to the Hill to testify or to deliberate with legislators on new legislation. At other times the shaping of policy may be inadvertent and implicit, as when a personal aversion between two executive colleagues means that the two men never "get their heads together," and a pet project of a congressman becomes law but in the executive process never gets off the ground.

The men in these positions, although operating within their tightly structured organizational world and within the direct mandate and indirect strictures of policy, have great power. As formal agents and members of the enormous federal government, their decisions and actions convey authority which affects the lives of people throughout the nation, often throughout the world. They are at the control panel of a vast apparatus of far-flung and interconnected organizational systems.

Such power carries with it a heavy load of responsibility. Consequences of action are far-ranging, affecting wide segments of the society in the present and shaping and determining aspects of the immediate and distant future for millions of people. Reactions of others to their decisions can in proportion be swift, bitter, and ruthless. Censure may strike directly at the executive or may descend suddenly upon the head of a subordinate or superior who may not even have suspected that a decision had been made. The power of the civilian executive is subject to immediate and absolute recall.

The word "servant" in the phrase "civil servant" is not an empty expression, and it applies equally well to career civil service, political, and foreign-service executives. The civilian executive is both immediately and ultimately responsible to the very people over whom he exercises great authority. His situation is paradoxical and anomalous.

Traditionally suspicious of "bureaucracy" and hereditary guardian of individual rights and freedoms, the public militantly makes known its standards of right conduct for its servants—career, political, and foreign-service. Swift to censure and slow to praise, the public exerts its pressures upon the federal executive in no uncertain terms. The public image of the bureaucrat may be just or unjust; it may be highly rational or hysterical; criticism may be clearly directed at one man and one action; or it may be a shotgun attack on a whole agency, a whole program, or a whole administration. It does not matter. The civilian executive suddenly finds himself in the position of a meek subordinate answering to an overbearing master.

The public, in making its demands known, makes use of (and is used by) a whole arsenal of weapons. There is the irate congressman making the headlines by defending the interests of the people back home. There is the syndicated columnist, the new press phenomenon with his outlets in hundreds of cities and towns. There is the Executive Mansion, dissociating itself in order to leave responsibility with the executive only. There is the rival executive in another department moving at the tactically correct moment to expand his own domain at the expense of a colleague held up to public censure.

For a person functioning within such a system, there is an Indian behind every tree. The executive cannot, however, in a fit of aggressive action simply go out and scalp the Indian. The system, with its carefully balanced set of structures, obligations, and rewards, demands above all both correctness and a show of deference. The entrepreneurial type, with his propensity for sudden and unexpected lashing out, cannot fit into the world of large organizations, either government or business. Action may be (and often must be) firm and decisive, but it must always be cloaked in a mantle of deference and executed with an air of quietude. To move aggressively, or even noisily, may invite undesirable or even disastrous attention from superordinates, opposite numbers, or the public at large.

The men who go about resolving these peculiarly contradictory external demands do so within a framework which is at once world-wide and insular. Sitting in his administrative office, an executive may be highly familiar with the price of rice in China, and with the nutritional problems of the factory worker in Shanghai. In the course of his day's activities he may even make a move which affects the standard of living of the Chinese. At the same time, he may be isolated from the main stream of the society in which he lives and the lives of the people whom he serves.

At Washington, he lives a life of government in a city of government workers. His view of the "outside" world may become colored not only by the demands of his own job, but by the fact that his social intercourse is almost entirely with people whose job demands are highly similar. Even his wife and children may come to hold a parochial point of view. The fact that the republic insists upon underpaying him results in his having inadequate financial resources with which to do reciprocal entertaining with executives of industry and business whose jobs bring them to Washington. His tastes in life style, his opinions, and his interest may cut him off from other people in Washington. He falls back on people of his own kind—other civilian executives. He "lives" government in Washington, and if his post is in the field he may, with his few government associates, tend to feel he is a person apart.

Material and social rewards in the present and the immediate future are not great, and the public servant can foresee in the more distant future a highly structured career route with a definite ceiling. If he intends to play out his career within his present service and agency, he can calculate with nicety the possible points he can reach at retirement time. Unless he elects the big break and leaves the service, his future is fairly well plotted. Unless he chooses to go into business or back into the "free" profession from which he may have come, he must find his rewards at a more abstract level than wealth and social prestige;

his self-fulfillment must lie in the direction of satisfying his ideals of public service, in playing out to its ultimate the role of public servant.

The Conflicting Demands of the Executive Role

From the foregoing general abstraction derived from interview material, it can be seen that the role of civilian executive is one that places conflicting pressures and demands upon the individual. Any person who assumes a social role will succeed only if he has the psychological or internal capacity to perform adequately in that role. This leaves aside questions of technical ability and physical energy. The social role of civilian executive implies a series of psychological characteristics which, taken together, can be thought of as the role demands of that position. It is axiomatic, and the empirical evidence bears this out, that the men who function successfully in a given position possess the psychological capacity required by that position. Over time, occupants of such positions will come to have rather similar psychological equipment. Men who do not have such characteristics will either not have gravitated to such positions in the first place, or will have given them a trial and then moved on to other fields, often having failed. The failure, however, is situational. A man who fails as assistant to the president of a corporation may start his own business and emerge rapidly as a corporation executive in his own right. Traits of innovation and aggression may cause failure in the role of assistant but be of prime importance in the role of corporation president.

If there is one salient feature of the role of civilian executive it is the conflicting demands placed upon men in these positions. Intellectually, we can separate and state some of these contradictory demands if the reader will remember that in so doing we are abstracting the demands from their contextual setting.

The basic, and in a sense all-pervading, conflict for the men in these positions may be illustrated by setting in juxtaposition the terms "public servant" and "federal executive."

In their capacity as public servants these men are called upon to subordinate themselves to the legislative and judicial branches of the government in a relationship in which the legislative branch interprets and codifies the public will; and the judicial branch stands as guardian of the national heritage of liberty and equalitarian justice. In this aspect of their roles, these men must be highly reactive to pressures, must be sensitive to demands and, above all, must be deferential. Strictly within the confines of the role denoted by "public servant," these men are subservient not only to others in government but to the public. Any show of determination may be interpreted as "arrogance" and "dictatorship."

However, the executive role implies a mandate for action and license to perform that action. The mandate cannot be responded to in a purely reactive and passive manner. As the mandate comes to the executive, it is high-level policy to be implemented and executed; and as high-level policy it tends to be broad or general. The executive must accept it, shape it, and put it into operation. In so doing, he is necessarily creative and innovative. The very act of executing policy implies judgment, decision, and action. The executive at every point is called upon to make decisions and alter directions, and in the end his performance is necessarily different in that it is beyond what the original policy statement required.

In a sense, then, the federal executive must conceal his true power. His most decisive and far-reaching operations must be cloaked as simple extensions of policy. The overweening power of his license to act must always be expressed as something outside and beyond him. He must always appear only as the instrument and vessel of policy.

The civilian executive functions in an organizational reference of strict, formal controls over his behavior and power. He is in a direct-line relationship with superordinates who have legally defined controls over him. His every action is scrutinized by Congress and the press for possible violations and irregularities. His advancement and his reputation are closely tied to his ability to function in a highly dependent manner. He must constantly check his plans and ideas against the impersonal authority of the system itself and with his associates above and below him. Just as his role calls for complete subordination to policy, it also calls for complete subservience to superior individuals and organizations. He must act only in accordance with the wishes of others, and every action must be conditioned by reflection on whether others will be pleased.

There is, again, the other side of the coin. The Cabinet member, the bureau chief, or the executive head in government who cannot act with courage and independence is worthless. His superior must do his own work and the work of the timid subordinate. The man's own subordinates are confused and frightened. The system of delegation breaks down. The demand of the job is also, then, that the executive act with self-determination, with courage, and with decisiveness—in a word, with autonomy.

These men must, to function adequately in their roles, act within a framework of cooperation and interdependence; and yet they must act firmly and independently. In terms of their interpersonal relations they must respond to structure and direction, and yet they must act when necessary outside such structure.

The world of government, our interviews show, is a highly personal one, interlaced with ties and involvements. The career executive counts as major assets the transient people he knows on the Hill and in the White House, or the other permanent people in the agencies and departments and in the offices of unions, business, and education located in Washington. The relationships are reciprocal. The congressman who can pick up the phone and call a friend in one of the departments or agencies may be able to call into play unexpectedly powerful support for one or another piece of business he has on hand. Opportunities for better jobs, the facility to slip around a roadblock, and the ability to take care of protégés are only a few indications of the functioning of the network of interpersonal relationships in the city of government. Through the years one's ties with this network come to have close personal and emotional meanings. Violations of the feelings of trust, loyalty, and moral obligation which are implied by these relationships can have serious psychological implications for these people. The system has an integral condition for smooth functioning —the presence of warm personal ties—but here again there is conflict in the demands of the role. The executive who places personal ties above the impersonal mandate of the job fails in his role of public executive and public servant. In fact, the man who allows personal involvements to affect the conduct of his office is defined as corrupt, and his behavior is defined as corruption. The conflict is obvious. In performing their public responsibilities these men at one time or another are called upon to betray their personal loyalties, to set aside the needs of old, cherished friendships, and to disregard obligations of a personal sort which they may have incurred through the years.

In resolving such conflicts, mature men cannot make a facile decision to jettison friends and destroy old bonds. Such easy solutions are the privilege only of those who are not capable of deeper emotional involvements. For mature men such issues and choices are accompanied by feelings of doubt, shame, and guilt. Handling such emotional conflicts may require great internal strength and clear vision of where one's ultimate responsibility lies.

Having laid this groundwork, we can now ask this question: What does it take to be a federal executive? In other words, what kind of internal structuring of this external world is necessary for functioning adequately in a world of such conflicting demands?

It is our belief, based on interview data, that most executives would agree with what we have just said about the conflicts inherent in their jobs. If one probes, however, to the level of emotional set toward the world in which they live, the analysis finds some sharp divergences in the way the world is viewed.

To most federal executives, the external world looms strong, formidable, rigidly structured, and relatively intractable. There is little room for free play of the imagination, of independent and unilateral action, for going it alone without fear of consequence. To these people a world closely bounded by rule and regulation, by situational demands, and by structural imperatives is a real world which must be coped with at all times and in all ways.

Still, and this might be expected, there are both exceptions to this world view and variations of it. A significant group of executives simply would not understand our delineation of the tight controls existing in the federal world. It is not that these men would not agree; they would not understand. To them the organizational interconnections are not restrictions but represent a vast expansion of possibilities and opportunities. Such men move through the intricate interlockings of bureaucracy easily and skillfully, pursuing their own ends and fulfilling their own purposes.

Even when the system is formidable and threatening, to the executive it appears the source of help and nurture. He is dependent upon it, and this dependency tends to pervade his thinking. Severing this dependency implies a major wrench which may transcend the practical problems of finding a new job and moving to another city. For many of these executives the dependency has become symbolic and—the TAT protocols strongly suggest—represents unresolved dependency problems experienced in earlier years and carried over to the federal executive situation. In fact, there is evidence from the material that movement into these positions is in part determined by a need for escape from the more vulnerable situations in the "free" professions.

The view of the system as a source of nurturance, and the consequent feelings of dependence upon it, has as a natural corollary a strong tendency on the part of the executive to approach situations with deference. One tends to approach problems with care not to upset the state of affairs, nor to call too much attention to oneself, not to push issues to the crisis stage. To do so may cause a retraction of the supportive and nurturing aspects of the system and a frightening pushing forward of its domineering side. In the coping mechanisms of most of these men, there is a strong element of system-deference.

Here again, the mode of adaptation is not one that can simply be assumed at the moment in time when a man becomes a federal executive. The mode must, and the Thematic Apperception Test data bear this out, have been learned earlier in the life of these men. It is a mode that requires adapting oneself to other people, to handling situations within a framework of cooperation and interdependence, of holding in check one's own piercing desires and aspirations until the moment is judged propitious. Such is the positive side of the characteristic of deference, and the data indicate that most of the federal executives developed such adaptive patterns early in life and approached their federal positions with these patterns as an integral part of the self.

In such a situation there is always a temptation for the person to seek emotional withdrawal, to live in but not be a part of the interpersonal world, to make a show of deference and cooperation while remaining aloof from real meanings and consequences. Some executives find this solution to the problem, but most do not. If most of them did, the service as a social system would collapse upon itself. What is required of them is another solution.

These men have to a high degree the psychological capacity to function within large, complex organizations. They can be part of a larger whole and can subordinate themselves to the welfare and purposes of the organization. It requires above all the capacity, and these men have this capacity, to internalize the needs of the organization so that its needs become the needs of the self.

In general, the sort of person who finds innovation in itself rewarding and stimulating cannot well fit the role. It is for this reason that federal executives in their interviews and TAT protocols appear by comparison reacting rather than activating. In a system in which the wider ranges of innovation are restricted by law and policy, these men are characterized by a tendency toward circumspection and caution in putting their own ideas into effect.

As a whole, they are men with ideas and intentions. They

know at both the cognitive and emotional levels why they are in government service. In fact this belief in a duty to be performed, in a cause to be forwarded, is a distinctive characteristic of federal executives. It is an integral part of their makeup and, viewed in context, goes a long way toward explaining the motivating force which causes these men to remain in a service that places so many contradictory demands upon them.

They are, in vast majority, idealists. They have a vision of a cause and a way beyond themselves. These statements are not empty platitudes. They are based on careful analysis of interview data, where such sentiments are not present as direct statements but can only be indirectly determined from latent elements in what was told us.

This overweening idealism does not contradict the dependency leanings and the subservience to authority in the case of these men. It is precisely the capacity to strive within constricted situations onward toward high ideals which is the keystone of the entire edifice. They are men with a cause, but men who cannot (within the organizational context within which they function) be rebels. To rebel is to destroy the very possibility of bringing the cause to fruition.

The fundamental difficulty confronting these men is only partially explained by talking of the bureaucratic network itself. Much of the difficulty lies in the nature of the causes they support. Issues of public health, education, care for the aged, and national defense are involved here as they are at the national political-legislative level. At the political-executive level, however, the cause is fought out in the arenas of the headlines and the national party conventions. Speeches, allegations, and demands for special legislative deals are one part of the furore of determining action at this level.

When the civilian executive takes over, the cause is still there, but it has been transformed. His job is that of taking the mandate and making a living reality of it. A man who furthers a cause of this kind in a vast organizational system must be a crusader in his heart, and the civilian federal executives are such crusaders. They must never, however, be crusaders in their department. This is the paradox of service, and the paradox which accounts for the many apparent contradictions in their personality structures.

It is this belief in mission and calling and the importance of his work that buttresses the strength of the civilian executive and furnishes a firm foundation for his actions. It is not, however, as this figure of speech implies, something apart from him to which he turns. It is, and must be if he is to function, part of his integral self. In a real sense, what sets these men apart from other men is their sense of serving a cause.

# APPENDIX A

Theory and Method

APPENDIX A

Theory and Method

Theory and Literature

"Social mobility" is a comprehensive term referring to many varieties of movement within a social system. In this study the interest is in social mobility as occupational succession, which can be considered as the relationship between the occupations of father and son or as the general movement in and out of occupational position. The more inclusive term, "occupational mobility," may refer to other occupational career movements—changes from one job to another within a community, between communities, or both—and is not of primary interest to this research.

Sociological investigations undertaken by Sorokin in 1927, Davidson and Anderson in the mid-thirties, Rogoff, Centers, the National Opinion Research Center in the mid-forties, and Lipset and Bendix in 1949-50 reached similar conclusions: mobility is substantial in terms of occupational succession but limited in range and amount.

Evidence regarding mobility through time, rather than at a point in time as in the studies above, is not so complete or persuasive and has led to arguments for a reconstruction of history with the suggestion of a growing rigidity in American life.

Recent studies challenge our historical traditions with respect to occupational mobility in both business and government. Most of the American business leaders of the late nineteenth and early twentieth centuries, studied under the auspices of the Harvard Research Center in Entrepreneurial History, came from upper- and upper-middle-class backgrounds. One of the studies concludes:

Authors of this appendix: Paul P. Van Riper and Orvis F. Collins.

Was the typical industrial leader of the 1870's then a "new man," an escapee from the slums of Europe or from the paternal farm? Did he rise by his own efforts from a boyhood of poverty? Was he as innocent of education and of formal training as has often been alleged? He seems to have been none of these things. American by birth, of a New England father, English in national origin, Congregational, Presbyterian or Episcopal in religion, urban in early environment, he was rather born and bred in an atmosphere in which business and relatively high social standing were intimately associated with his family life.[1]

At first glance historical analysis seems almost as unkind to our traditions concerning opportunity in government. Several twentieth-century studies have only confirmed the fact that our entire political structure under the Federalists, the first of our ruling groups after 1789, was overwhelmingly manned by the well-educated, the well-born, and the prosperous.[2]

The Jeffersonian Republicans succeeded the Federalists in 1801. Then, and later, Jefferson was frequently portrayed as a radical who would destroy our institutions and upset the class structure. In office Jefferson was anticlimactic in his appointments, and he actually did little to disturb the upper-class monopoly of office-holding throughout the federal government. Leonard D. White's summary reflects current historical opinion: "Standards of appointment from 1789 to 1829 conformed to a single pattern."[3]

However in 1829, with the accession of Andrew Jackson to the Presidency, a true counterpart of the "rags to riches" tradition in business was firmly established in popular views of our political

1. Frances W. Gregory and Irene D. Neu, "The American Industrial Elite in the 1870's," in *Men in Business*, ed. William Miller (Cambridge, Harvard University Press, 1952), p. 204.
2. See such varied sources as Charles A. Beard, *Economic Interpretation of the United States* (New York, Macmillan, 1913); Carl R. Fish, *Civil Service and the Patronage* (New York, Longmans, Green, 1905); Leonard D. White, *The Federalists* (New York, Macmillan, 1948); and Paul P. Van Riper, *History of the United States Civil Service* (Evanston, Ill., Row, Peterson, 1958).
3. Leonard D. White, *The Jeffersonians* (New York, Macmillan, 1951), p. 368. See also Arthur J. Alexander, "Federal Patronage in New York State: 1789–1805" (unpublished Ph.D. dissertation, Philadelphia, University of Pennsylvania, 1945) for a comparative analysis of Federalist and Jeffersonian appointment policies in this major state.

Appendix A 255

history. In the personal case of Jackson the "log cabin" motif had some validity. The "people" were coming to claim the government. Did they get it? Certainly not right away. Both Fish and White have presented data which suggest a stubborn persistence in office of many persons more reminiscent of Washington, Jefferson, and the two Adamses, than of any Jacksonian frontiersman.[4]

Analyzing the occupations of the fathers of the 513 men who between 1789 and June, 1953, occupied the positions of President, Vice-president, Speaker of the House of Representatives, Cabinet member, and Supreme Court Justice, Mills concludes:

> Six out of ten of the 500-odd men who have come to the top of the government during the course of United States history have come from quite prosperous family circumstances, . . . two or three out of ten (24 per cent) have come from that middle class which is neither rich nor poor . . . the final two out of ten (18 per cent) originate in lower-class families. . . . Occupationally, in each and every generation, the statesmen have come from business and professional families in much greater proportions than the proportions of such families in the population at large.[5]

Unfortunately, Mills' data have not been broken down in terms of historical eras, and the heavily "aristocratic" Federalists and Jeffersonians are lumped in with everyone else.

Considered as a whole, Anderson's data—for 311 men holding positions as President, Vice-president, and Cabinet member between 1789 and 1934—strongly suggest middle- or upper-class origins for over 90 per cent of this segment of our political elite. However, Anderson has broken his data down into appropriate time periods, with results which coincide much more with our traditions than the grand total analysis of Mills. The key figures are Table 1A.

Certainly these figures suggest a considerable shift from strictly upper- to middle-class, and some lower-class, origins during the half century after 1825. Moreover, the investigations of both Anderson and Mills indicate that a greater proportion of our public leadership

4. Fish, Ch. 2 and Appendix B; and Leonard D. White, *The Jacksonians* (New York, Macmillan, 1954), p. 552 and Ch. 18 on "The Career Service."
5. C. Wright Mills, *The Power Elite* (New York, Oxford University Press, 1959), pp. 400–01.

Table 1A

Type and Percentage of Occupational Climbing of Rulers as Compared with Their Fathers*

	Per Cent of Climbing by Period			
	All rulers (1789–1934)	Modern (1877–1934)	Commoner (1825–1876)	Colonial (1789–1824)
Type of climbing				
Total climbing	25.7	24.4	30.6	13.9
Climbing from medium to high levels	23.1	21.4	27.5	13.9
Climbing from low to high levels	2.6	3.0	3.1	0.0

*Percy E. Davidson and H. Dewey Anderson, *Occupational Mobility in an American Community* (Stanford, Calif., Stanford University Press, 1937), Table V, p. 517. Anderson's choice of 1825 rather than 1829 to begin the "commoner" period is strange in light of the fact that the effective shift of power from East to West is usually conceded to be 1829. Likewise, 1883, which saw the effective beginning of Civil Service reform, provides a better date than 1875 for ending the "commoner" period.

came from middle-level agricultural and professional families (as opposed to extremely wealthy and upper-class commercial and landowning families) than entrepreneurial history has shown was the case in business. We know also that by 1829 the almost universal repeal of property qualifications for both voting and holding elective office, together with the growing political doctrine of rotation in appointive offices, had removed many barriers to political leadership. Despite their recognition of some tenure in public office between 1829 and 1860, both Fish and White note a distinct shift in the social and other characteristics of federal officeholders as a whole, beginning with Jackson. The historian Dixon Ryan Fox has come to similar conclusions with respect to politics in New York State during our early history.[6] Even Mills concedes a "status revolution" after 1829.

6. D. R. Fox, *The Decline of Aristocracy in the Politics of New York* (New York, Columbia University Press, 1919). See also Fish, pp. 79–104, for a general interpretation suggesting that the leveling effects of Jacksonianism had their roots in the states well prior to their acceptance at the national level.

Regarding the decades following 1860, can we accept as completely valid White's conclusion that, "the relationship between the people and their administrative system was not again to suggest preference to the well-born and the well-to-do"?[7]

It would appear that White has overstated the case with respect to both the Jacksonians and their successors. For the period after 1860, again the evidence is fragmentary, but a few considerations stand out. In his study of top political leaders Mills also states:

> The industrialization of the American economy is directly reflected in the fact that over three times as many were businessmen immediately after the Civil War as just before it. Since then that fact has remained more or less constant: nearly one-third of the higher politicians since World War I have been businessmen; over 40 per cent of the most recent men, those of the Eisenhower administration, have been.[8]

This is as might be expected; but these proportions have apparently never reached those found in the backgrounds of business leaders. As far as upward movement in general is concerned, the scanty available evidence points to as much fluidity, and in turn mobility, in politics during the first two or three decades of post-Civil War Republican rule as under the Jacksonians.[9]

Has the situation changed since the late nineteenth century? Here again the evidence with respect to government is partial and inconclusive. Almost the only data permitting time perspectives have been developed by Brown and Janowitz for generals and admirals between 1898 and 1950, and by Bendix for a small sample of the top levels of the career civil service as of 1940.[10] Together

7. White, *The Jacksonians*, p. 556.
8. Mills, p. 402.
9. For two somewhat different approaches to analysis of the class composition of the federal service between 1860 and 1900, but with broadly similar conclusions in respect to the point at issue here, see Van Riper, Ch. 7; and Ari Hoogenboom, "The Pendleton Act and the Civil Service," *American Historical Review*, 64 (1959), 301–18.
10. C. S. Brown, "The Social Attitudes of American Generals, 1898–1940" (unpublished doctoral dissertation, Madison, University of Wisconsin, 1951); Morris Janowitz, *The Professional Soldier* (Glencoe, Ill., Free Press, 1960); and Reinhard Bendix, *Higher Civil Servants in American Society* (Boulder, University of Colorado Press, 1949).

these studies suggest an increasingly broader base of social recruitment for the governmental elites since 1900. Comparing these data with those concerning business leaders developed by Taussig and Joslyn for 1928 and Warner and Abegglen for 1952 does not, however, solve the problem of whether the governmental hierarchy as a whole has, at any time point, been more or less open than business to persons of low socioeconomic status.[11] It has remained for the present study to give concrete evidence on this point.

We may conclude five things from this very brief and general summary of historical considerations relating to occupational and social mobility in the United States. (1) While it is clear, as one recent analyst has stated, that "the log cabin to White House myth is rather far from the truth,"[12] there is no doubt but that many new opportunities in government opened up for individuals of lower- and middle-class origins after 1829 as compared to the four previous decades. (2) During the nineteenth century there may well have been some differential between government and business with respect to opportunity for those lower on the socioeconomic scale; but just how much, and whether the differential in fact operated in favor of government as suggested here, is still open to question. (3) Any judgments with respect to general occupational mobility in the twentieth century, as compared to the nineteenth, depend upon further analysis of the earlier period in order that a more precisely delineated historical base may be available for comparison. (4) The historical progression of social mobility in the United States cannot be adequately or accurately portrayed through an analysis of what has been, or is, happening in only one type of hierarchy, be it business, government, or any other. (5) It should be clear from the above discussion that the study of mobility among government officials in the United States is subject to certain historical and, as discussed just below, legal considerations which are significantly different from those relevant to the study of business leadership.

Toward the end of the nineteenth century, with the passage of

11. F. W. Taussig and C. S. Joslyn, *American Business Leaders* (New York, The Macmillan Co., 1932); and W. Lloyd Warner and James C. Abegglen, *Occupational Mobility in American Business and Industry, 1928–1952* (Minneapolis, University of Minnesota Press, 1955).

12. Donald R. Matthews, *The Social Background of Political Decision-Makers* (Garden City, N.Y., Doubleday, 1954), p. 28.

Appendix A 259

the Pendleton Act of 1883, we come to a major dividing line for the federal civil service. This is the statute on which is based the great career civil service of the federal government as we know it today and as it is outlined in this study. It is crucial for any interpretation of occupational mobility within the federal structure since 1883—and especially since the turn of the century when this statute first began to govern 50 per cent or more of the civil service—that the implications of certain provisions of this and a few subsequent legislative enactments be understood. For together they form a legal framework which, while undoubtedly reflecting the views of a society predisposed to mobility, was probably not without some reciprocal effects.[13]

Most important, the Pendleton Act provided, for the first time in our history on a general and permanent basis, an emphasis upon recruitment into the federal civil establishment through examinations, mainly competitive, and largely open to all. The Act also provided that positions filled through examination were to be held on good behavior, and that no one in such positions was to be required to perform partisan political service or to be removed for political reasons. For purposes of this study the only other significant provisions were those reinforcing the concept of preference for war veterans[14] and directing, "as nearly as the conditions of good administration will warrant," for an "apportionment" of the career positions in Washington, D.C., among citizens of the various states, according to population. Promulgated by Executive Order, the first "rules" of the Civil Service Commission, the agency set up by the Pendleton Act to administer the new appointment system, not only forbade discrimination in appointments on the grounds of religion as well as politics, but also opened up nearly all examinations to women. Racial information was not requested on early application blanks but, under Woodrow Wilson, photographs were required. The Ramspeck Act of 1940 formally prohibited discrimination in federal employment because of race, creed, or color. Although citizenship was necessary to eligibility for the examinations, it was not

13. For a general discussion of the administrative implications of the Pendleton Act see Van Riper, Ch. 5 and following. The comparable watershed for the military came only a little later, with the various reforms—culminating in the creation of the General Staff—under President Theodore Roosevelt and Secretary of War Elihu Root.
14. Under varying interpretations this concept has a history as old as the United States.

formally required for most federal positions until just prior to World War II. Finally, in approving the Pendleton Act, Congress specifically eliminated a provision which would have restricted entrance into the federal civil service to the bottom—in, for example, the British manner. Since 1883, as before, one may move in and out of the federal civil service at almost any level and at almost any age. This tradition of "lateral entry" is thus long standing in the American civil service. It has been significant at all points in our history but, for purposes of the present research, was especially so during the great civil service expansion periods of both World Wars, the Depression era of the thirties and, to a lesser extent, the Korean conflict of the fifties.

The total impact of the statutory guidelines for the federal civil service as contained in the Pendleton Act and related laws and regulations cannot be evaluated precisely. But it is clear that this basic law of 1883 has never operated to limit the service to any special social class or segment thereof. The legal base of the American national civil service appears to be as little biased in favor of any social class as any in the world today. Indeed, the generally nondiscriminatory regulations, the opening of most examinations to all, and the apportionment requirement would suggest greater opportunities in government for members of minority groups and for all persons, regardless of economic or social status, from all geographical sections, than in much of private enterprise. In this study it has not been feasible to test this hypothesis with respect to racial and religious minorities;[15] but a special effort has been made to examine the role of the female executive in government and, to some extent, the effect of the apportionment provision of the Pendleton Act upon the geographical origins of the civil service.[16]

Veterans, to be sure, and especially disabled veterans—and in

---

15. By law, government officials and agencies may not inquire into the partisan politics, race, religion, or national origin of career civil servants; hence there are few statistics on these topics as they relate to the federal civil service. Reasons for the omission of racial, religious, and partisan data from the present reseach have been given.

16. Residence requirements, never very stringent in the federal civil service, have become less so in recent years. But the apportionment provision of the Pendleton Act, affecting original entry into the civil service in the District of Columbia, was applied fairly strictly between 1883 and World War II. It has thus had some effect on the careers of those in this study whose service falls within this period.

Appendix A

some cases their wives, widows, and mothers—have received preference in appointments. But none of these groups can be considered a social class; rather, they represent broad cross sections of most of American society. As for the foreign born, only in the last twenty years has the citizenship requirement seriously affected their potential rise and, even then, only long enough (usually five years) for naturalization to be accomplished. Nevertheless, some efforts were undertaken in this research to consider the meaning of military service and veteran preference within the civil establishment and to examine the rise of the foreign born.

Through its examination provision, the Pendleton Act did, however, implicitly stress education. To be sure, American civil service examinations have always been of a practical nature and oriented much more to a specific and current job than has been the case in almost any other country. Moreover, eligibility to take an American civil service examination has seldom depended upon the prior acquisition of any academic degree. Nevertheless, even a statement of general requirements for a position and, in turn, an examination for that position suggests the utility of education. And since 1883 education has apparently become more and more the touchstone to initial and, frequently, promotional appointments in the career civil service. The creation of the military academies of West Point and Annapolis before the Civil War signified the beginning of a similar emphasis in the military service at an even earlier date. Generally speaking, only for top-level political executives (bureau chief to Cabinet levels), attorneys, and several fairly specialized lower categories of personnel have examination procedures of some sort never applied in the federal service. One might therefore expect to find education playing an especially significant role among the factors involved in a study of mobility within the federal service, as compared to business, since 1883. Fragmentary data available for the period between 1884 and 1896, and for specific time points in 1940 and 1955, indicate that this indeed appears to have been the case.[17] Education, therefore, has from the beginning furnished a main focus of concern for the present investigation.

17. See, in order, Van Riper, pp. 165–66; Reinhard Bendix, pp. 33, 58, 92; and USCSC, Bureau of Programs and Standards, *Study of Backgrounds and Reported Training Needs of a Sample of Federal Executives* (Washington, The Commission, 1955).

Methods and Techniques

The research reported in this volume is one of a series begun in 1932 when Taussig and Joslyn published their *American Business Leaders*. In 1955 Warner and Abegglen published, in *Occupational Mobility in American Business and Industry,* and *Big Business Leaders in America,* the results of a study designed to compare movement into the business and industrial elites in 1928 with movement in 1952. Warner and Abegglen designed their study to repeat operations performed by Taussig and Joslyn in 1928, but expanded the scope of investigation to obtain data with which to test empirically current understandings of occupational mobility and to utilize new research techniques. Repetition in 1952 of research operations performed in 1928 proved fruitful in increasing knowledge about occupational mobility in big business and industry in America. The present researchers have designed their study to secure knowledge about movement into the federal elites of American government comparable to that obtained for business leaders in 1952. Collection and analysis of comparative knowledge of this order necessarily involved a series of difficult decisions.

The design of the research implied from the outset that methods and techniques used in the 1952 research for collection, analysis, and preparation of data be adhered to at every possible point, and that where alterations and innovations were made they be so incorporated into the instruments of the study as not to destroy comparability of data from the two populations. This guiding principle was followed throughout the study. The mandate that we follow so closely the 1952 research carried with it a series of problems which had to be met.

Data comparable to those collected for the 1952 business leaders had to be secured. These data had to be obtained from men at levels of power, prestige, and responsibility comparable in their systems to the business leaders in the business systems. Ideally, the same questionnaire incorporating the same items expressed in the same words would have been the best solution to the problem. Differences in position terminology, organizational structure, and advances in knowledge about occupational mobility all made necessary, however, certain revisions of the 1952 questionnaire for use in the present investigation. These revisions were based on information gained through a pilot study.

Appendix A

It was clear from the beginning that it would be necessary to use two questionnaires for the present study, one for civilians and the other for the military. There were too many differences in civilian and military terminology and organizational structure to permit the use of one instrument. As the civilian group of federal executives was by far the largest and most diverse in background, agency affiliation, pay system, etc., it was decided to work out a questionnaire procedure which, hopefully, could be utilized for both civilian and military personnel, through a pilot test on civilians alone.

A draft of a civilian questionnaire was prepared by our research group, based on the earlier Warner and Abegglen questionnaire, revised to fit civilians in the federal service. Interviews were conducted with people in the federal government to isolate special problems of research in the federal system. Several other drafts of the questionnaire, based on criticisms raised during these initial interviews, were then prepared. These drafts were also circulated informally and confidentially among certain groups of federal executives. The executives were asked to fill them out, discussing, as they did so, items they found difficult to interpret and to answer.

Three intermediate versions of the final questionnaires of varying length were then designed. These versions were different in length, in format, and in content of the questions. Some versions, for example, solicited information on racial and religious matters. Some versions contained detailed questions; others contained the same type of question but phrased more generally. Quite different forms of a covering letter accompanied the three versions.

The questionnaires were mailed, half to offices and half to homes, of 240 government leaders in Chicago and in Washington, D.C. Returns were analyzed for differences in rate and quality of return, time elapsed before return, and completeness of replies. Follow-up interviews were then conducted with both respondents and nonrespondents. These interviews focused on three vital questions: (1) Do responses to the questionnaire accurately describe the experience of the respondent? (2) Are the questionnaire items sufficient to secure the needed data? (3) Is the questionnaire with its covering letter a positive and unequivocal mode of communicating with federal executives?

A systematic attempt to isolate important factors contributing to nonreturn of the questionnaire was made. Analysis showed that no items in any of the three versions significantly affected the rate of return. Questionnaires mailed to homes and offices were returned at the same rate, in terms of both quantity and time. The respondent's rank, department or agency in which employed, age, and level of education were found to have no significant effect on the rate of return. Finally, it was found that federal executives returned the longer version of the questionnaire even more often than the shorter version, but they expressed concern about questions seeking information on race and ethnic background, political affiliation, and religious beliefs. Some of the men interviewed raised the question whether it was proper to ask federal employees to supply such information. Since these questions were not essential to comparison with 1952 business leader data, they were dropped.

In addition to the mailed questionnaire, the 1952 researchers conducted interviews with business leaders. These interviews included administration of selected pictures from the Thematic Apperception Test (TAT). To secure data parallel to the 1952 study it was necessary that the present researchers follow much the same interviewing method and that identical pictures from the TAT be used. In the pilot study phase a number of civilian government leaders were asked to participate in such interviewing sessions, as distinct from sessions intended to secure data about the effectiveness of the questionnaire, and were asked to participate in the TAT. In no case was an interview refused, and in only one case did an executive refuse to take the test.

The results of the pilot study were most reassuring. The rate of response to the various pretest questionnaires ranged from 60 to 70 per cent. Government leaders showed, in their response to both the pilot study questionnaires and the interview sessions, eagerness to participate in the study.

A final step in preparation for full-scale field work was now taken. The researchers discussed, as they had during all earlier phases of preparation, the revised questionnaire and interviewing method with high-level personnel people in the federal government. For example, the researchers appeared before the Interagency Advisory Group of the Civil Service Commission, which is made up of personnel officers from the departments and agencies. Press releases, announcing the study to federal employees, were circulated by means of the house organs of the departments. The press releases were written to clarify such matters as voluntary participation, the nonofficial role of the federal government in the study, the interests and backgrounds of

Appendix A

the researchers, and the Carnegie Corporation's financial support of the research. They were timed for publication about ten days before the first civilian questionnaires were mailed, early in 1959.

Since the pilot test of the civilian questionnaire demonstrated that this general procedure was completely feasible, work had begun on a parallel questionnaire for the armed services during the summer and fall of 1958. It was quite similar, although somewhat less exhaustive techniques were used. However, in its final form the military questionnaire was designed to include all persons in the various federal uniformed services. This proved quite simple to do, for terminology and conditions of service are similar, and the uniformed services questionnaire was ready for administration only a few weeks after that prepared for civil officials.

No preparations were made, however, for administration of the Thematic Apperception Test to the uniformed services. After considerable discussion and consideration of this problem, it was felt that the time was not appropriate for this kind of personal inquiry into areas which might well relate to national security. This represents the only segment of the study, as originally contemplated, that was not carried out.

The Final 1959 Questionnaires

A questionnaire communicating adequately with people in the many different departments and agencies and assuring uniformity of responses was difficult to design. The difficulty was increased by the necessity for so wording questions that responses could be compared to those secured in 1952 from the business leader population. Difficulties arose in comparing rank and position systems, in comparing organizational levels, and in reconciling variations in functions of people in these differing systems. In actual construction of the questionnaires these difficulties all resolved themselves into finding terms with meanings sufficiently general to transcend all the systems, and yet sufficiently specific to make possible realistic comparisons.

The first major difficulty was resolved by a decision not to prepare one questionnaire for both civilian and uniformed executives. The "civilian" questionnaire was worded in the special terminology of the world of civilian federal executives. The second, finally termed the "uniformed services schedule," was designed not only for men in uniform in the Armed Services, but also for uniformed personnel in, specifically, the U.S. Public Health Service, the Coast and Geodetic Survey, and the Coast Guard.

In addition to these two instruments, a supplementary question patterned on part of the employment form of the U.S. Government (for civilians) and on the typical service record form (for uniformed personnel) was mailed to one in ten of the federal executives. The researchers believed that complete career histories would be important both as sources of data for special analysis and as internal checks on meanings of responses. This question yielded a career sequence profile for each of approximately 750 executives who filled out and returned it. These profiles were of considerable assistance in interpreting career information.

Both 1959 questionnaires were more detailed and more comprehensive than those designed for the 1952 and 1928 business leader studies. In this section we will compare items in the 1959 with those in the 1952 questionnaire. Since the order of items varies, the items in the three questionnaires will be, for purposes of this discussion, divided into seven major areas: time; occupational origins; geographic origins; education and formal training; career, both within and outside the federal service; present organizational place; incidental questions used to qualify respondents for special purposes.

Appendix A

STUDY OF FEDERAL EXECUTIVES
CORNELL UNIVERSITY · THE UNIVERSITY OF CHICAGO

Strictly Confidential

1. What is your present age?.. —— 6-7
2. At what age did you first enter the public service?........................ —— 8-9
3. What position-title do you now use in official correspondence?_____ 10-11
4. What is the title of your present position as shown on official position-classification or job-description records?_____ 12
5. At what age did you first assume your present position?................ —— 13-14
6. What is the grade level of your present position

	if under General Schedule		if under another system, write in your classification rank
	Above GS-18	☐ 1	
	GS-18	☐ 2	
	GS-17	☐ 3	_____
	GS-16	☐ 4	
	GS-15	☐ 5	
	GS-14	☐ 6	

15

If below GS-14, please specify_____

7. At what age did you first enter the department or independent agency in which you are now employed? —— 16-17

8. Your present position is within which one of the following groups of offices:

   Schedules A or B .... ☐ 1
   Schedule C .... ☐ 2
   Excepted by statute .... ☐ 3
   Competitive under Civil Service Commission .... ☐ 4
   Competitive under separate civil service system .... ☐ 5
   Other (*please specify*)_____ ☐ 6

18

	In any capacity	In a minor or major executive capacity

9. With how many government departments, independent public agencies, business firms, or other private organizations have you been associated during your career, including your present organization? (For the period since 1947, consider the Army, Navy, Air Force, and Office of the Secretary of Defense as separate agencies.) .... ——   (19 .... ——   (20

   a) How many of these organizations were *federal*?................. ——   .... ——

   b) How many of these organizations were governmental but *non-federal* (state, local, international, public school, state university, etc.)?... ——   .... ——

   c) How many of these organizations were *private*?................. ——   (21 .... ——   (22

(We would find any comments you might have on the above questions very helpful. If you have any further remarks, would you turn the page and enter them on the back of this page.)

Appendix A

10. What are the organizational levels between the top of your agency and your present organizational unit?

Official name of organization

Department or independent agency _____

Intermediate unit(s) .... _____

_____

_____

_____

_____

Your present unit . . .. _____

11. Your present *position* is best characterized as .... Line ☐ 1
    Staff ☐ 2

12. Your present *unit* is best characterized as .... Line ☐ 4
    Staff ☐ 5

13 (a). After becoming self-supporting, what occupation did you engage in

Occupations	(24-25) when you first became self-supporting	(26-27) 5 years later	(28-29) 10 years later	(30-31) 15 years later
Worker—unskilled or semiskilled (blue collar)	☐ 01	☐ 01	☐ 01	☐ 01
Worker—skilled or mechanic (blue collar)	☐ 02	☐ 02	☐ 02	☐ 02
Custodian, messenger, or guard	☐ 11	☐ 11	☐ 11	☐ 11
Policeman, fireman, or mailman	☐ 12	☐ 12	☐ 12	☐ 12
Inspector or investigator	☐ 21	☐ 21	☐ 21	☐ 21
Farmer ⎰ farm worker or small tenant	☐ 31	☐ 31	☐ 31	☐ 31
⎱ farm tenant with paid help	☐ 32	☐ 32	☐ 32	☐ 32
⎰ farm owner without paid help	☐ 33	☐ 33	☐ 33	☐ 33
⎱ owner or manager with paid help	☐ 34	☐ 34	☐ 34	☐ 34
Clerical worker	☐ 41	☐ 41	☐ 41	☐ 41
Retail clerk or retail salesman	☐ 42	☐ 42	☐ 42	☐ 42
Salesman	☐ 51	☐ 51	☐ 51	☐ 51
Foreman	☐ 61	☐ 61	☐ 61	☐ 61
Other first-line supervisor	☐ 62	☐ 62	☐ 62	☐ 62
Junior or minor executive (middle management)	☐ 71	☐ 71	☐ 71	☐ 71
Major executive	☐ 72	☐ 72	☐ 72	☐ 72
Owner small business (sales under $50,000)	☐ 81	☐ 81	☐ 81	☐ 81
Owner medium business (sales between $50,000 and $100,000)	☐ 82	☐ 82	☐ 82	☐ 82
Owner large business (sales over $100,000)	☐ 83	☐ 83	☐ 83	☐ 83
Profession ⎰ Engineer	☐ 91	☐ 91	☐ 91	☐ 91
⎱ Lawyer	☐ 92	☐ 92	☐ 92	☐ 92
⎰ Doctor (M.D.)	☐ 93	☐ 93	☐ 93	☐ 93
⎱ Scientist	☐ 94	☐ 94	☐ 94	☐ 94
⎰ Minister	☐ 95	☐ 95	☐ 95	☐ 95
⎱ Professor	☐ 96	☐ 96	☐ 96	☐ 96
⎰ Public schoolteacher	☐ 97	☐ 97	☐ 97	☐ 97
⎱ Other (*please specify*) _____	☐ 98	☐ 98	☐ 98	☐ 98
Formal training program	☐ Y1	☐ Y1	☐ Y1	☐ Y1
Uniformed military service	☐ Y2	☐ Y2	☐ Y2	☐ Y2
Other (*please specify*) _____	☐ —	☐ —	☐ —	☐ —

13 (b). For each of the four time points above, please indicate whether your occupation was in the public service ....

Yes ☐ 1   Yes ☐ 3   Yes ☐ 5   Yes ☐ 7
No ☐ 2   No ☐ 4   No ☐ 6   No ☐ 8

(We would find any comments you might have on the above questions very helpful. If you have any further remarks, would you turn the page and enter them on the back of this page.)

Appendix A

14. When you first entered the federal civil service, did you enter through
    - Competitive examination and selection from a register .... ☐ 1
    - Non-competitive examination procedure .... ☐ 2
    - Temporary or indefinite appointment not requiring examination or political clearance ..... ☐ 3
    - Appointment involving senatorial confirmation .... ☐ 4
    - Political appointment without senatorial confirmation .... ☐ 5
    - Other procedures (*please specify*) _____ ☐ 6

15. Where do you consider that the bulk of your governmental experience falls?
    - Research and development .... ☐ 1
    - Insurance, retirement, social security .... ☐ 2
    - Natural resources management or development .... ☐ 3
    - Economic or business regulation .... ☐ 4
    - Procurement, supply, manufacturing, maintenance, etc., of material ...... ☐ 5
    - Military operations and training .... ☐ 6
    - Administrative staff services (personnel, legal, public relations, budgeting, O & M, etc.) .... ☐ 7
    - Other (*please specify*) _____ ☐ 8

16 (a). Principal occupations of others in your family (if deceased, please indicate previous occupation):

Occupations	(35–36) Your father (when you became self-supporting)	(37–38) Your father's father	(39–40) Your mother's father	(41–42) Your wife's (or husband's) father
Worker—unskilled or semiskilled (blue collar)	☐ 01	☐ 01	☐ 01	☐ 01
Worker—skilled or mechanic (blue collar)...	☐ 02	☐ 02	☐ 02	☐ 02
Custodian, messenger, or guard	☐ 11	☐ 11	☐ 11	☐ 11
Policeman, fireman, or mailman	☐ 12	☐ 12	☐ 12	☐ 12
Inspector or investigator	☐ 21	☐ 21	☐ 21	☐ 21
Farmer { farm worker or small tenant	☐ 31	☐ 31	☐ 31	☐ 31
{ farm tenant with paid help	☐ 32	☐ 32	☐ 32	☐ 32
{ farm owner without paid help	☐ 33	☐ 33	☐ 33	☐ 33
{ owner or manager with paid help ..	☐ 34	☐ 34	☐ 34	☐ 34
Clerical worker	☐ 41	☐ 41	☐ 41	☐ 41
Retail clerk or retail salesman	☐ 42	☐ 42	☐ 42	☐ 42
Salesman..............................	☐ 51	☐ 51	☐ 51	☐ 51
Foreman...............................	☐ 61	☐ 61	☐ 61	☐ 61
Other first-line supervisor	☐ 62	☐ 62	☐ 62	☐ 62
Junior or minor executive (middle management)	☐ 71	☐ 71	☐ 71	☐ 71
Major executive	☐ 72	☐ 72	☐ 72	☐ 72
Owner small business (sales under $50,000)..	☐ 81	☐ 81	☐ 81	☐ 81
Owner medium business (sales between $50,000 and $100,000)	☐ 82	☐ 82	☐ 82	☐ 82
Owner large business (sales over $100,000)..	☐ 83	☐ 83	☐ 83	☐ 83
Profession { Engineer.....................	☐ 91	☐ 91	☐ 91	☐ 91
{ Lawyer......................	☐ 92	☐ 92	☐ 92	☐ 92
{ Doctor (M.D.)...............	☐ 93	☐ 93	☐ 93	☐ 93
{ Scientist.....................	☐ 94	☐ 94	☐ 94	☐ 94
{ Minister.....................	☐ 95	☐ 95	☐ 95	☐ 95
{ Professor....................	☐ 96	☐ 96	☐ 96	☐ 96
{ Public schoolteacher	☐ 97	☐ 97	☐ 97	☐ 97
{ Other (*please specify*)_____	☐ 98	☐ 98	☐ 98	☐ 98
Uniformed military service...............	☐ Y2	☐ Y2	☐ Y2	☐ Y2
Other (*please specify*)_____	☐	☐	☐	☐

16 (b). For each member of your family, please indicate whether the occupation was in the public service .... Yes ☐ 1   Yes ☐ 3   Yes ☐ 5   Yes ☐ 7
                                                                                                                        No ☐ 2   No ☐ 4   No ☐ 6   No ☐ 8

(We would find any comments you might have on the above questions very helpful. If you have any further remarks, would you turn the page and enter them on the back of this page.)

17. Did you, during the first five years of your working career or thereabouts, receive substantial financial aid (not less than $10,000) from any of the following sources:

	Yes	No
Inheritance	☐ 1	☐ 2
Relatives	☐ 3	☐ 4
Friends	☐ 5	☐ 6

44

18. If your father was in the public service, are you now connected with the same department or independent agency that he was?

Yes ☐ 9   No ☐ 0   44

19. If your father was in the public service, he was primarily in which one of the following:

	Appointive Office	Elective Office
Federal executive civilian service	☐	1
Federal legislative service	☐	☐ 2
Federal judicial service	☐	3
State government	☐	☐ 4
Municipal government	☐	☐ 5
County, town, or township government	☐	☐ 6
Public schools	☐	☐ 7
State college or university	☐	8
International civil service	☐	9
Uniformed military service	☐	0
Other (please specify) ————	☐	☐ x

45

20. At what age did you first engage in any of the following types of work on a full-time basis as a regular employee (on your own and self-supporting)?

	Age on entrance into any appointive office	Age on entrance into any elective office
Federal executive civilian service	——	
Federal legislative service	——	
Federal judicial service	——	
State government	——	——
Municipal government	——	——
County, town, or township government	——	——
Public schools	——	——
State college or university	——	
International civil service	——	
Uniformed military service	——	
Business firm or other private organization	——	
Other (please specify) ————	——	——

21. Are you entitled to veteran preference?
No ☐ 1
Yes, five point ☐ 2
Yes, ten point ☐ 3   46

22. If you have had military service, how much of this service was as an officer?
All ☐ 5
More than half ☐ 6
Less than half ☐ 7
None ☐ 8   46

23. If you have had military service, how many years of active military duty have you had? ——   47

24. If you have had military service, with what service were you connected?
Army ☐ 1
Navy ☐ 2
Air Force ☐ 3
Other (please specify) ————   48

(We would find any comments you might have on the above questions very helpful. If you have any further remarks, would you turn the page and enter them on the back of this page.)

Appendix A

25. If you have had military service, what is the highest military rank you have ever held (whether on active duty or not)?

    Enlisted man or noncommissioned officer .... ☐ 5
    Warrant Officer .... ☐ 5
    2d Lieutenant or Ensign .... ☐ 6
    1st Lieutenant or Lieutenant (j.g.) .... ☐ 6
    Captain or Lieutenant .... ☐ 6
    Major or Lieutenant Commander .... ☐ 7
    Lieutenant Colonel or Commander .... ☐ 7
    Colonel or Captain .... ☐ 8
    Brigadier General, Rear Admiral (lower half) or Commodore ... ☐ 9
    Major General or Rear Admiral (upper half) .... ☐ 9
    Lieutenant General or Vice Admiral .... ☐ 9
    General or Admiral .... ☐ 9
    General of the Army or Fleet Admiral .... ☐ 9

    48

26. Extent of schooling of yourself and your father and mother. (*Please check only the highest correct category.*)

	(49) Self	(50) Father	Mother
Less than high school	☐ 1	☐ 1	☐
Some high school	☐ 2	☐ 2	☐
High school graduate	☐ 3	☐ 3	☐
Some college	☐ 4	☐ 4	☐
College graduate	☐ 5	☐ 5	☐
Postgraduate study	☐ 6	☐ 6	☐

27. If you attended college, will you please fill in the following:

Institutions attended	Major subject	Degree	Year received degree	Last year attended	
_____	_____	_____	_____	_____	51–52
_____	_____	_____	_____	_____	53–54

28. How much formal business training have you had?

    None .... ☐ 1
    Correspondence courses, public school, or business college .... ☐ 2
    Commercial training in college or university .... ☐ 3

    55

29. In addition to any business training, what other types of formal management training have you had?

    None .... ☐ 5
    Full-time, in-service training course work totaling a month or more (including military courses with management, command, or administrative content) .... ☐ 6
    Full-time university management training program .... ☐ 7
    General political science training in college or university .... ☐ 8
    Public administration training in college or university .... ☐ 9
    Other (*please specify*)_____ ☐ 0

    55

30. Have you ever been a member of an employee association or union?.. Yes ☐   If, so, for how
                                                                       No ☐   many years?... _____

    56

31. Are you now a member of an employee association or union? .... Yes ☐ 9
                                                                                          No ☐ 0

    56

    (We would find any comments you might have on the above questions very helpful. If you have any further remarks, would you turn the page and enter them on the back of this page.)

Appendix A

	Self	Wife or husband	Father	Father's father	Mother	Mother's father	
32. Place of birth: U.S.	☐ 1	☐	☐ 3	☐ 5	☐	☐	57
Non–U.S.	☐ 2	☐	☐ 4	☐ 6	☐	☐	57

33. Are you... Male ☐ 8   Married ☐ 0   57
    Female ☐ 9   Single ☐ x

34. Were you born in one of the following cities or a suburb of one of them?
    New York, Chicago, Philadelphia, Baltimore,   Yes ☐ 1   58
    St. Louis, Boston, or Pittsburgh........................ No ☐ 2

35. What was the approximate population of your birthplace at the time of your birth?
    Over 400,000 (or a suburb of a city this size)...... ☐ 4
    100,000–400,000 (or a suburb of a city this size).... ☐ 5
    25,000–100,000................................. ☐ 6   58
    2,500–25,000.................................. ☐ 7
    Rural or less than 2,500....................... ☐ 8

36. In what state, territorial area, or foreign country
    a) was your *first* federal civil position located?............. ——————   59
    b) was your legal residence at the time of this appointment?..——————   60
    c) is your *present* federal position located?................. ——————   61
    d) is your present legal residence?......................... ——————   62

37. How many years have you served in the federal *civil* service in the following areas:
    Washington, D.C., and vicinity... ——   63
    Elsewhere in continental U.S..... ——   64
    Alaska or territories............. ——   65
    Foreign countries............... ——   66

38. Are you registered in any state as a voter?... Yes ☐ 1   67
    No ☐ 2
    If so, what is the state?........ ——————

39. Did you find it possible to vote in any of the following presidential elections?
    Yes   No
    1944.......... ☐ 3   ☐ 4
    1948.......... ☐ 5   ☐ 6   67
    1952.......... ☐ 7   ☐ 8
    1956 .... ☐ 9   ☐ 0

40. If you have succeeded the person to whom this questionnaire was originally addressed, please check ☐

41. If you are no longer a federal employee, please check.................................... ☐

42. If born in the U.S., in which state were you born?——————————————————

Please return this questionnaire to:
STUDY OF FEDERAL EXECUTIVES
5835 KIMBARK AVENUE
UNIVERSITY OF CHICAGO
CHICAGO 37, ILLINOIS

(We would find any comments you might have on these matters very helpful. If you have any further remarks, would you turn the page and enter them on the back of this page.)

Appendix A

STUDY OF FEDERAL EXECUTIVES
CORNELL UNIVERSITY · THE UNIVERSITY OF CHICAGO

Strictly Confidential   Uniformed Services Schedule

1. What is your present age? _____   6–7
2. At what age did you first enter the public service? _____   8–9
3. What position-title (not rank) do you now hold? _____   10–11
   _____   12
4. At what age did you first assume your present position? _____   13–14
5. What is your present rank?

	Temporary rank	Permanent rank	
Admiral or General	☐ 1	☐ 6	15
Vice Admiral or Lieutenant General	☐ 2	☐ 7	
Rear Admiral (upper half), Major General or equivalent	☐ 3	☐ 8	
Rear Admiral (lower half), Brigadier General or equivalent	☐ 4	☐ 9	
Captain, Colonel or equivalent	☐ 5	☐ 0	
Other (please specify) _____			

6. At what age did you first attain your present temporary rank? _____   16–17
7. With how many organizations, including your present one, have you been associated during your career? (For example: public agencies, private firms, self-employment, Army, Navy, or Air Force) _____   18–19

   With how many of these have you been associated at the job level of minor or major executive level (including your present one)? _____   20

8. At what age were you first sworn into any uniformed service? _____   21–22
9. Your present *position* is best characterized as .... Line ☐ 1
                                                                        Staff ☐ 2
10. Your present *unit* is best characterized as .... Line ☐ 4   23
                                                                     Staff ☐ 5
11. What are the organizational (or chain of command) levels between the top of your agency and your present organizational unit? (Consider OSD, D/A, D/N, and D/AF as separate agencies.)

    Official name of organization

    Department or independent agency _____

    Intermediate unit(s) .... _____
                                      _____
                                      _____
                                      _____

    Your present unit .. .. _____

(We would find any comments you might have on the above questions very helpful. If you have any further remarks, would you turn the page and enter them on the back of this page.)

Appendix A

12 (a). After becoming self-supporting, what occupation did you engage in

	(24–25) when you first became self-supporting	(26–27) 5 years later	(28–29) 10 years later	(30–31) 15 years later
Occupations				
Worker—unskilled or semiskilled (blue collar)	☐ 01	☐ 01	☐ 01	☐ 01
Worker—skilled or mechanic (blue collar)	☐ 02	☐ 02	☐ 02	☐ 02
Custodian, messenger, or guard	☐ 11	☐ 11	☐ 11	☐ 11
Policeman, fireman, or mailman	☐ 12	☐ 12	☐ 12	☐ 12
Inspector or investigator	☐ 21	☐ 21	☐ 21	☐ 21
Farmer — farm worker or small tenant	☐ 31	☐ 31	☐ 31	☐ 31
Farmer — farm tenant with paid help	☐ 32	☐ 32	☐ 32	☐ 32
Farmer — farm owner without paid help	☐ 33	☐ 33	☐ 33	☐ 33
Farmer — farm owner or manager with paid help	☐ 34	☐ 34	☐ 34	☐ 34
Clerical worker	☐ 41	☐ 41	☐ 41	☐ 41
Retail clerk or retail salesman	☐ 42	☐ 42	☐ 42	☐ 42
Salesman	☐ 51	☐ 51	☐ 51	☐ 51
Foreman	☐ 61	☐ 61	☐ 61	☐ 61
Other first-line supervisor	☐ 62	☐ 62	☐ 62	☐ 62
Junior or minor executive (middle management)	☐ 71	☐ 71	☐ 71	☐ 71
Major executive	☐ 72	☐ 72	☐ 72	☐ 72
Owner small business (sales under $50,000)	☐ 81	☐ 81	☐ 81	☐ 81
Owner medium business (sales between $50,000 and $100,000)	☐ 82	☐ 82	☐ 82	☐ 82
Owner large business (sales over $100,000)	☐ 83	☐ 83	☐ 83	☐ 83
Profession — Engineer	☐ 91	☐ 91	☐ 91	☐ 91
Profession — Lawyer	☐ 92	☐ 92	☐ 92	☐ 92
Profession — Doctor (M.D.)	☐ 93	☐ 93	☐ 93	☐ 93
Profession — Scientist	☐ 94	☐ 94	☐ 94	☐ 94
Profession — Minister	☐ 95	☐ 95	☐ 95	☐ 95
Profession — Professor	☐ 96	☐ 96	☐ 96	☐ 96
Profession — Public schoolteacher	☐ 97	☐ 97	☐ 97	☐ 97
Profession — Other (*please specify*) _____	☐ 98	☐ 98	☐ 98	☐ 98
Formal training program	☐ Y1	☐ Y1	☐ Y1	☐ Y1
Uniformed Service — Enlisted man	☐ X1	☐ X1	☐ X1	☐ X1
Uniformed Service — Warrant officer	☐ X2	☐ X2	☐ X2	☐ X2
Uniformed Service — Ensign through lieutenant; 2d lieutenant through captain; or equivalent	☐ X3	☐ X3	☐ X3	☐ X3
Uniformed Service — Lieut. commander, commander; major, lieutenant colonel; or equiv.	☐ X4	☐ X4	☐ X4	☐ X4
Uniformed Service — Colonel or captain, or equivalent	☐ X5	☐ X5	☐ X5	☐ X5
Uniformed Service — General or flag officer, or equivalent	☐ X6	☐ X6	☐ X6	☐ X6
Uniformed Service — Other (*please specify*) _____	☐ X7	☐ X7	☐ X7	☐ X7
Other (*please specify*) _____	☐ __	☐ __	☐ __	☐ __

12 (b). For each of the four time points above, please indicate whether your occupation was in the public service.

Yes ☐ 1   Yes ☐ 3   Yes ☐ 5   Yes ☐ 7
No ☐ 2   No ☐ 4   No ☐ 6   No ☐ 8

13. Where do you consider that the bulk of your service falls?

- Combat, field training or work, duty at sea, or related operational activity .... ☐ 1
- General staff, joint staff, OPNAV, Office of the Secretary, Under or Asst. Secretary, or equivalent for your service .... ☐ 2
- Administrative assignment (personnel, legal, fiscal, public relations, etc.) .... ☐ 3
- Technical assignment (medical, ordnance, communications, transport, etc.) .... ☐ 4
- Research and development .... ☐ 5
- Supply, procurement, maintenance, etc. of material .... ☐ 6
- Instructor or responsible for instruction in a service school, ROTC, etc. .... ☐ 7
- Student at a service or other school .... ☐ 8
- Attaché, MAAG, liaison, or similar special duty .... ☐ 9

(We would find any comments you might have on the above questions very helpful. If you have any further remarks, would you turn the page and enter them on the back of this page.)

Appendix A

14 (a). What types of commission have you held?

	Your first commission	Your present commission
Regular	☐ 1	☐ 4
Reserve or AUS	☐ 2	☐ 5
National Guard	☐ 3	☐ 6

14 (b). Have you ever been an enlisted man (woman) or warrant officer?   Yes ☐ 7   No ☐ 8

15 (a). Principal occupations of others in your family (if deceased, please indicate previous occupation):

Occupations	(35–36) Your father (when you became self-supporting)	(37–38) Your father's father	(39–40) Your mother's father	(41–42) Your wife's (or husband's) father
Worker—unskilled or semiskilled (blue collar)	☐ 01	☐ 01	☐ 01	☐ 01
Worker—skilled or mechanic (blue collar)	☐ 02	☐ 02	☐ 02	☐ 02
Custodian, messenger, or guard	☐ 11	☐ 11	☐ 11	☐ 11
Policeman, fireman, or mailman	☐ 12	☐ 12	☐ 12	☐ 12
Inspector or investigator	☐ 21	☐ 21	☐ 21	☐ 21
Farmer { farm worker or small tenant	☐ 31	☐ 31	☐ 31	☐ 31
farm tenant with paid help	☐ 32	☐ 32	☐ 32	☐ 32
farm owner without paid help	☐ 33	☐ 33	☐ 33	☐ 33
owner or manager with paid help	☐ 34	☐ 34	☐ 34	☐ 34
Clerical worker	☐ 41	☐ 41	☐ 41	☐ 41
Retail clerk or retail salesman	☐ 42	☐ 42	☐ 42	☐ 42
Salesman	☐ 51	☐ 51	☐ 51	☐ 51
Foreman	☐ 61	☐ 61	☐ 61	☐ 61
Other first-line supervisor	☐ 62	☐ 62	☐ 62	☐ 62
Junior or minor executive (middle management)	☐ 71	☐ 71	☐ 71	☐ 71
Major executive	☐ 72	☐ 72	☐ 72	☐ 72
Owner small business (sales under $50,000)	☐ 81	☐ 81	☐ 81	☐ 81
Owner medium business (sales between $50,000 and $100,000)	☐ 82	☐ 82	☐ 82	☐ 82
Owner large business (sales over $100,000)	☐ 83	☐ 83	☐ 83	☐ 83
Profession { Engineer	☐ 91	☐ 91	☐ 91	☐ 91
Lawyer	☐ 92	☐ 92	☐ 92	☐ 92
Doctor (M.D.)	☐ 93	☐ 93	☐ 93	☐ 93
Scientist	☐ 94	☐ 94	☐ 94	☐ 94
Minister	☐ 95	☐ 95	☐ 95	☐ 95
Professor	☐ 96	☐ 96	☐ 96	☐ 96
Public schoolteacher	☐ 97	☐ 97	☐ 97	☐ 97
Other *(please specify)* _____	☐ 98	☐ 98	☐ 98	☐ 98
Uniformed military service { Enlisted man	☐ X1	☐ X1	☐ X1	☐ X1
Commissioned officer	☐ X3	☐ X3	☐ X3	☐ X3
Other *(please specify)* _____	☐ __	☐ __	☐ __	☐ __

15 (b). For each member of your family, please indicate whether the occupation was in the public service

Yes ☐ 1   Yes ☐ 3   Yes ☐ 5   Yes ☐ 7
No ☐ 2   No ☐ 4   No ☐ 6   No ☐ 8

16. Did you, during the first five years of your working career or thereabouts, receive substantial financial aid (not less than $10,000) from any of the following sources:

	Yes	No
Inheritance	☐ 1	☐ 2
Relatives	☐ 3	☐ 4
Friends	☐ 5	☐ 6

17. If your father was in the uniformed service, are you now in the same service?   Yes ☐ 9   No ☐ 0

(We would find any comments you might have on the above questions very helpful. If you have any further remarks, would you turn the page and enter them on the back of this page.)

Appendix A

18. If your father was in the public service, he was primarily in which one of the following:

	Appointive office	Elective office
Uniformed military service	☐	0
Other uniformed commissioned service	☐	1
Federal executive civilian service	☐	2
Federal legislative service	☐	☐ 3
Federal judicial service	☐	4
State government	☐	☐ 5
Municipal government	☐	☐ 6
County, town, or township government	☐	☐ 7
Public schools	☐	☐ 8
State college or university	☐	9
International civil service	☐	X

45

19. At what age did you first engage in *each* of the following types of work on a full-time basis as a regular employee (on your own and self-supporting)?

	Age on entrance into any non-elective position	Age on entrance into any elective office
Uniformed military service	___	
Other uniformed commissioned service	___	
Federal executive civilian service	___	
Federal legislative service	___	___
Federal judicial service	___	
State government	___	___
Municipal government	___	___
County, town, or township government	___	___
Public schools	___	
State college or university	___	
International civil service	___	
Business firm or other private organization	___	___
Self employment	___	

46–47

48

20. Extent of schooling of yourself and your father and mother. (*Please check only the highest correct category.*)

	(49) Self	(50) Father	Mother
Less than high school	☐ 1	☐ 1	☐
Some high school	☐ 2	☐ 2	☐
High school graduate	☐ 3	☐ 3	☐
Some college	☐ 4	☐ 4	☐
College graduate	☐ 5	☐ 5	☐
Postgraduate study	☐ 6	☐ 6	☐

21. If you attended college, will you please fill in the following:

Institutions attended	Major subject	Degree	Year received degree	Last year attended
_____	_____	_____	_____	_____
_____	_____	_____	_____	_____

51-52-53

54

22. How much formal business training have you had?

None	☐ 1
Correspondence courses, public school, or business college	☐ 2
Commercial training in college or university	☐ 3

55

(We would find any comments you might have on the above questions very helpful. If you have any further remarks, would you turn the page and enter them on the back of this page.)

Appendix A

23. In addition to any business training, what other types of formal management training have you had?
    - None.. ☐ 5 — 55
    - Full-time, in-service training course work totaling a month or more (including military courses with management, command, or administrative content)...................... ☐ 6
    - Full-time university management training program................................... ☐ 7
    - General political science training in college or university........................... ☐ 8
    - Public administration training in college or university.............................. ☐ 9
    - Other (*please specify*) _____

24. If born in U.S., in which state were you born?_____ — 56–57

25. Were you born in one of the following cities or a suburb of one of them?
    - New York, Chicago, Philadelphia, Baltimore, Yes ☐ 1 — 58
    - St. Louis, Boston, or Pittsburgh......................... No ☐ 2

26. What was the approximate population of your birthplace at the time of your birth?
    - Over 400,000 (or a suburb of a city this size)...... ☐ 4
    - 100,000–400,000 (or a suburb of a city this size).... ☐ 5
    - 25,000–100,000............................... ☐ 6 — 58
    - 2,500–25,000................................. ☐ 7
    - Rural or less than 2,500....................... ☐ 8

27. In what state, territorial area, or foreign country
    - *a*) was your *first* full-time uniformed duty assignment?..... _____ — 59
    - *b*) was your legal residence at the time of this assignment?.. _____ — 60
    - *c*) is your *present* uniformed duty assignment?............ _____ — 61
    - *d*) is your present legal residence?....................... _____ — 62

28. How many years of active duty have you had in the following areas:
    - Washington, D.C., and vicinity... ___ — 63
    - Elsewhere in continental U.S..... ___ — 64
    - Alaska or territories............ ___ — 65
    - Foreign countries............... ___ — 66
    - At sea......................... ___ — 67
    - Total years of active duty....... ___ — 68

29. Have you ever been:

	Yes	No
on flying status...	☐ 1	☐ 2
on submarine duty...	☐ 3	☐ 4

    — 69

30. Who signs your effectiveness, efficiency, or fitness report?
    - commissioned officer of your own service... ☐ 7 — 69
    - commissioned officer of another service... ☐ 8
    - civilian in your own service organization.. ☐ 9
    - civilian connected with another service or organization............................. ☐ 0

31. Have you ever been a member of any uniformed service(s) other than your present one? (consider former USAAF and present USAF as the same)..Yes ☐ 1 — 70
    No ☐ 2
    - (*a*) If "yes," which ones?.................. _____
    - (*b*) If "yes," what year did you change over?.. _____

    (We would find any comments you might have on the above questions very helpful. If you have any further remarks, would you turn the page and enter them on the back of this page.)

32. How were you first commissioned?
   - West Point or Annapolis graduate.. ☐ 4
   - Other military school graduate.. ☐ 5
   - ROTC graduate... ☐ 6
   - Officer candidate school or V-12.. ☐ 7
   - CMTC, BMTC, or Plattsburg Plan Training Camp...................................... ☐ 8
   - Direct commission from civil life... ☐ 9
   - Direct commission from warrant officer or enlisted status.......................... ☐ 0

33. If your uniformed service has branches, corps or other major categories:
   - In which were you first commissioned? _____
   - In which are you now serving, or in which did you last serve? _____

34. How many months have you held your present position?................. _____
    How many months did you hold your last previous position?............. _____

35. How many months of service schooling (all types) have you had?........ _____

36. Are you.. Male ☐ 8   Married ☐ 0
                                                         Female ☐ 9   Single ☐ x

37.   Self   Wife or   Father   Father's   Mother   Mother's
                              husband   father   father
    Place of birth:...U.S. .... ☐ 1....☐ 2....☐ 3....☐ 1 ....☐ 2....☐ 3
                     Non-U.S..... ☐ 4....☐ 5....☐ 6....☐ 4 ....☐ 5....☐ 6

38. Are you registered in any state as a voter?....................... Yes ☐ 1
                                                                       No ☐ 2

39. Did you find it possible to vote in any of the following presidential elections?
                                                            Yes   No
                                                  1944..... ☐ 3   ☐ 4
                                                  1948..... ☐ 5   ☐ 6
                                                  1952..... ☐ 7   ☐ 8
                                                  1956..... ☐ 9   ☐ 0

40. If you have succeeded the person to whom this questionnaire was originally addressed, please check.. ☐

41. If you are no longer on active duty, please check....................................... ☐

Please return this questionnaire to:
STUDY OF FEDERAL EXECUTIVES
5835 KIMBARK AVENUE
UNIVERSITY OF CHICAGO
CHICAGO 37, ILLINOIS

(We would find any comments you might have on these matters very helpful. If you have any further remarks, would you turn the page and enter them on the back of this page.)

Appendix A

Location of respondents at time points in their lives is crucial to study of occupational mobility. Without knowledge about ages at which men have moved from one status to another, the study of career velocity is not possible. The following block of items concerned with time is arranged so the reader may compare and contrast ways the data were solicited in each of the three questionnaires.

In both 1959 questionnaires the phrase "public service" was used in place of the word "business" in the item beginning, "At what age did you first enter . . ." The reason for not using the word "business" is obvious, but finding an adequate phrase to replace it was difficult. Attempts to spell out in detail in the preliminary and pilot versions the intention of the researchers were not fruitful. Further, the researchers felt the question in the 1959 questionnaires should be phrased at about the same level of generality as that of the 1952 questionnaire. The phrase "public service" was used, but with precautions in the form of internal checks. Item 20 of the civilian and 21 of the uniformed services questionnaires asked the respondent to indicate at what age he had entered a series of services, both within and outside the federal structures. Comparison of these responses with those made to the more general phrase "public service" showed that the bulk of federal employees equate "public service" with federal employment. Since, however, non-federal public service was construed by the researchers to be a logical step for movement into federal elite status, entrance into any civilian public service was interpreted as age for first entering public service.

Data on the age at which the respondent first assumed his present position were also crucial for study of career speed. In securing this information certain adjustments again had to be made. Item 3 of the 1952 questionnaire was repeated, but with the word "business" dropped. One further complication, however, had to be dealt with here. Position tenure in the Armed Services is carefully prescribed by law, with only relatively brief tenure being permitted military executives. Items 34 and 6 of the uniformed services questionnaire were added to insure adequate information on actual position tenure, and to provide the alternative of using rank in lieu of position if this became necessary.

Item 5 of the 1952 questionnaire was altered for both 1959 questionnaires. Item 7 of the civilian questionnaire reflects the need for a term roughly comparable to the idea of the firm conveyed in

Table 2A

Comparison of the Three Questionnaires

1952 Business leaders	1959 Civilian federal executives	1959 Uniformed services
Item	Item	Item
1. What is your present age?	1. What is your present age?	1. What is your present age?
2. At what age did you first enter business?	2. At what age did you first enter the public service?	2. At what age did you first enter the public service?
3. At what age did you first assume your present business position?	5. At what age did you first assume your present position?	4. At what age did you first assume your present position?
5. At what age did you enter your present organization?	7. At what age did you first enter the department or independent agency in which you are now employed?	8. At what age were you first sworn into any uniformed service?
No comparable item	No comparable item	34. How many months have you held your present position? How many months did you hold your last previous position?
No comparable item	No comparable item	6. At what age did you first attain your present temporary rank?

item 5 of the business leader study. The phrase "department or independent agency" was chosen from several alternatives tried out in earlier versions. Item 8 of the uniformed services schedule was chosen as the best way of expressing the same idea to uniformed men, with the decision that a career begun in any of the uniformed services would be most nearly equivalent to a career begun in a business firm or in a single department or agency. Here again items 20 of the civilian and 19 of the uniformed services questionnaires were of great value in interpreting responses. These were the items used for establishing time points for the study of movement through the structures.

A most crucial set of data for these studies concerns the occupational backgrounds of men in the several elites. The business leader questionnaire in items 11 and 15 (see *Occupational Mobility in American Business and Industry*) asked for information on occupations of the respondent's father, the respondent's father's father, and the respondent's wife's father. Both 1959 questionnaires were expanded to include the respondent's mother's father. This addition reflected experience of the 1952 researchers that in the bilateral American society the occupational origin of ego's mother has impact on ego's career achievements. Further alterations were made. First, the item "when you were in grammar school" on the occupation of ego's father was dropped. The 1952 researchers had found it yielded information little different from the subitem "when you became self-supporting." Second, both 1959 questionnaires added items, 16 (*b*) on the civilian and 15 (*b*) on the uniformed questionnaires, to secure information on whether relatives of the respondent had been in the public service.

Categories of occupations were expanded and revised to take into account special problems of communicating with federal executives and special problems arising from differences in business and federal structures. In both the civilian and uniformed services questionnaires the word "blue collar" was added to "worker" to make interpretation easier for federal people; categories for "custodian, messenger, or guard," "policeman, fireman, or mailman," "inspector and investigator," "clerical worker," and "first-line supervisor" were added to make possible more refined analysis of typical government occupations. The category of profession was expanded to include "professor" and "public school teacher" in both 1959 questionnaires, reflecting experience of the business leader research that the professions are of particular importance as sources of the business elite. The uniformed services questionnaire included a division of uniformed military service into officers and enlisted men.

Items 19 of the civilian and 18 of the uniformed services schedules inquired into areas of public service in which ego's father had served. These questions permit analysis of differences between public service and nonpublic service families. This analysis of public service backgrounds was, of course, not appropriate in the study of business leaders.

Addition of occupational subcategories to the 1959 questionnaires created special coding problems in recombining them into the categories originally used in the business leader study. Coding interpretations used in the business leader study were meticulously followed in making these combinations.

Both the 1928 and the 1952 researches demonstrated that ethnic and geographic origins are important variables in occupational mobility, but not always in ways indicated by American beliefs. We wished to extend the inquiry into this area. Item 16 of the business leader questionnaire had asked for information on whether the respondent, his father, and his father's father had been born in the United States. The item was repeated in the 1959 questionnaires but expanded to include the respondent's wife or husband, the respondent's mother, and the respondent's mother's father. These additions paralleled the expansion of items about occupational origins to include information on the mother's occupational antecedents. Reproducing the "size of city" portion of item 16 of the business leader study presented special problems. The 1952 researchers, working with an average time of 1900 for the respondent's birth, had lumped together the seven cities which in 1900 had a population of over 400,000. In the 1959 questionnaires, these cities had to be held separate to allow for comparisons. Since the time of birth had shifted from 1900 to 1910, allowance had also to be made for other cities which between 1900 and 1910 had achieved a population of over 400,000. Items 34 and 35 of the civilian and 25 and 26 of the uniformed services questionnaires show how this problem was solved.

Items 36 and 37 of the civilian and 27 and 28 of the uniformed services questionnaires solicited information on geographic mobility after entering the federal service. Here, again, inclusion of these items reflected the experience of the business leader research that

Appendix A

geographic mobility is closely associated with occupational mobility although, for the military and some civilian government executives, it must be recognized that much mobility reflects the requirements of the military (or civilian federal) system rather than free occupational or positional choice.

The basic datum necessary for the study of the relationship between education and occupation is the level of schooling achieved. Item 12 of the business leader questionnaire, which solicited this information in 1952, was repeated exactly in 1959, except that the 1959 questionnaires included a column for the respondent's mother. This addition again reflected the experience of earlier researchers that in a bilateral society the distaff side of the family is important.

For these highly trained elites, most of whom have been to college, the second most important datum is the college attended and degrees received. The 1952 research, using item 13 of the business leader questionnaire, had shown that college is for the business elite the royal road to executive status. The 1959 questionnaires, therefore, expanded this area of inquiry to include in items 27 and 21 of the two questionnaires the major subject taken in college, the year the degree was received, and the last year attended.

Item 14, concerning the amount of formal business training, of the 1952 questionnaire was identical with item 28 of the civilian and item 22 of the uniformed services questionnaire. The interest here was in determining whether formal *business* training has the same effect in the public service as it has in the business world. In both 1959 questionnaires this line of inquiry was extended by item 29 of the civilian and item 23 of the uniformed questionnaires. These items inquired into formal training other than business, both inside and outside colleges and universities. Item 35 of the uniformed services questionnaire, concerning months of service schooling, extended this inquiry still farther.

Closely allied with formal education and schooling, as cumulative factors in career preparation, is experience. Items 15 and 13 of the civilian and uniformed services questionnaires asked for information on this point. Because of the differences between the military and civilian hierarchies, wording for this question had to be different for the two 1959 questionnaires.

The business leader question most basic to analysis of careers was item 10, beginning, "After becoming self-supporting, what occupation did you engage in?" Both 1959 questionnaires asked the identical question. The business leader questionnaire showed occupations for five-year intervals. Both the civilian and uniformed questionnaires repeated this. Inspection of the three questionnaires, however, will show that some occupations were itemized in greater detail in 1959 than in 1952.

The reader will also observe certain alterations in the occupational categories. In most cases changes were made for the reasons set forth in the discussion of occupational origin items. Listing ranks in the uniformed services questionnaire was necessary for examination of movement up through the uniformed services hierarchies. Items 13 (*b*) and 12 (*b*) of the civilian and uniformed services questionnaires were used to examine movement in and out of public life. Items 14 and 32 of the civilian and uniformed questionnaires solicited information on the formal mode of entry into the service. These items were used extensively in cross checking the organizational status of the respondents. No comparable items were included in the 1952 business leader questionnaire. Item 11 (*a*) of the 1952 questionnaire, whether the respondent's father was connected with the same firm as the respondent, was paraphrased in item 18 of the civilian and item 17 of the uniformed services questionnaires.

To find a phrase comparable to item 7 in the 1952 questionnaire (number of firms associated with) was most difficult because of the problem of equating the firm as an entity with the organizational entities in the federal service. The long, cumbersome, and detailed item 9 of the civilian questionnaire represents one solution to the problem, and the shorter item 7 of the uniformed services questionnaire represents another. Neither form was totally satisfactory, but the researchers believe that, by going into detail here, comparability among the three items was maintained. Item 9 of the 1952 questionnaire, concerning financial aid received at the outset of the respondent's career, was repeated as items 17 in the civilian and 16 in the uniformed services questionnaires. Item 8 of the 1952 questionnaire, whether friends and relatives were involved in the respondent's present firm, was not duplicated in the 1959 questionnaires since it proved impossible to frame a suitable question that would be even remotely equivalent.

Items 21 through 25 of the civilian questionnaire were designed to examine the relationship between military experience and civilian careers in government. These are new questions for which there is no counterpart either in the business leader study or in the uniformed services questionnaire. These questions were not used in the present volume, but the researchers intend in later publications to report on the information secured. Items 30 and 31 of the civilian questionnaire were designed to study the relationship between occupational mobility and identification with occupations. They also recognize the fact that in government, as opposed to business, civilian executives may and do belong to employee unions. Military commanders may join such organizations but, as they almost never do, these two items were not repeated in the military questionnaire. Union membership will be reported in later publications. Special questions used only in the uniformed services questionnaire were items 14, 29, and 33, exploring the influence of certain special statuses and qualifications on the careers of military executives. The results are not reported in the present volume.

Placement of respondents in their organizational structures at the time they filled out the questionnaire was relatively simple in the case of the business leader study. Only three basic items of information were necessary. The type of business engaged in was determined through the business registers used to draw the sample, and this information was later transferred to the IBM cards. Item 4 secured information on the volume of sales or gross income of the respondent's organization when he first entered the organization and at the time he filled out the questionnaire. Item 2 of the 1952 questionnaire secured information on the respondent's present business position, and item 7 (c) on the number of firms associated with at present as a member of the Board of Directors. These items were sufficient to place the 1952 business leader respondent in his current organizational context.

Placing individuals within the military services was more complicated, but not nearly so difficult as placing them within civilian organizations. For the analysis contemplated for the 1959 research, it was necessary that each respondent be placed four ways. (1) The locus of his organizational unit within the federal system of organizations was determined. (2) His individual position was so identified that it could be made comparable with similar positions in other federal structures. (3) Information on the rank and pay grade systems throughout the various structures was collected in a form that would make comparisons across the structures possible. (4) In the study of federal structures the type of service in which an individual is engaged is one of the most important distinguishing attributes, and it was important that data be obtained with which to make this placement.

The problem of organizational unit was solved in both 1959 questionnaires by securing the agency name from the register used for sampling and coding this directly into the respondent's identification number. Items 10 of the civilian and 11 of the uniformed services questionnaires, concerning the respondent's organizational unit's distance from the top of the hierarchy, were used as internal check questions enabling coders simply and easily to place the respondent's organization unit. This information was also most helpful in coding position and rank material. Finally, item 12 of the civilian and item 10 of the uniformed services schedules were used to determine whether a respondent was in a staff or line unit, a useful distinction relatively easy for respondents to make.

Items 3 and 4 of the civilian questionnaire asked for information on the position of the informant. Early interviews had made clear that federal civilian executives hold positions which can be defined in one of several ways, with an executive usually varying his position title according to the person he is addressing. The method evolved was to ask two questions. Item 3 of the civilian questionnaire asked, "What position title do you now use in official correspondence?" This item was coded. Item 4, position shown on official position classification or job description records, was used primarily to clarify responses to item 3. Item 3 of the uniformed services questionnaire asked simply "What position title (not rank) do you now hold?" This single item was found sufficient for the uniformed service executives. Item 11 of the civilian and the comparable item 9 of the uniformed services questionnaire were designed to examine relationships between people in line of authority and people in staff positions. These items were treated extensively in earlier analysis but in many instances are not reported in this volume because few differences emerged. In addition, item 30 of the uniformed services questionnaire was designed to examine military-civilian relationships by looking at military men under civilian authority in contrast to those under military authority. Analysis of this relationship has not yet been carried out.

In the study of the federal service, in contrast to the business community, the distinction between position and rank was maintained. It was neither feasible nor necessary to maintain this distinction for business. In the federal service, however, rank is not only important and easily ascertainable but also of as much or more assistance in checking the placement of persons in their proper organizational niches than is position title. Data on rank are, of course, most easily available for the military, and item 5 in the military questionnaire covered this matter. Rank in the civil service is reflected through levels of pay, for the various civil pay systems employ what is widely recognized as a rank system. The best known such system, which also related to by far the greatest number of respondents involved in this study, is termed the General Schedule (GS), which had some 18 "grades" at the time of this study. Further, since all other civil pay systems in the federal government provide quite similar ranges of pay for similar levels of responsibility, the comparative rank positions of persons in pay systems other than GS could be ascertained by a fairly simple question (item 6 on the civilian questionnaire) which asked for the person's salary system rank. The researchers could then make an equation based on standard salary data or, where a person's salary but not his official rank was known—and it is very easy to check salary in government—the researchers could deduce his rank. In other words, in the civil service salary is closely related to rank, and rank in turn reflects level of work, responsibility, and official status, all on a fairly uniform basis throughout the service. Indeed, therefore, some of the present study's analysis has been made in terms of these salary (really rank) levels.

A fourth criterion for locating an individual is the type of service. No comparable distinctions are made in business structures. The type of service item of primary importance in the civilian questionnaire was item 8. It was scored in conjunction with items 6 and 14 of the civilian questionnaire, and in the analysis stage was used to place the respondents as career, political, or foreign-service executives. Since, in the uniformed services, type of service and agency are coterminous, references to the respondent's identification number were adequate for placement. Systematic cross checking of these items made it possible to place each respondent within his service.

Each of the three schedules included questions important for qualifying respondents for special purposes and as internal checks on other items. Items 6, 17, and 18 requested special information essential only for the business leader study and were not repeated in the 1959 questionnaires. Items 33 of the civilian and 36 of the uniformed services questionnaires, concerning the respondent's sex and marital status, were necessary for identifying women executives and for examining proportions of married and unmarried people. Item 40 of both 1959 questionnaires asked if the respondent had succeeded the person to whom the questionnaire had been originally addressed. Item 40 was included because in the pilot study some executives filled out and returned questionnaires addressed to their predecessors, taking the view that the questionnaire had been sent to the office and not to the person. This item was crucial for eliminating duplicate returns. Item 41 of both 1959 questionnaires identified individuals who had retired and was helpful in interpreting age inconsistencies. Items 38 and 39 of both 1959 questionnaires were special questions designed to examine voting patterns of federal executives. They were not used in the present analysis.

The Questionnaire Returns and Their Accuracy

The civilian and military questionnaires were submitted to 18,620 executives—15,701 civilian and 2,919 military. Mailings went to every agency of the Executive Branch except, for obvious reasons, the Central Intelligence Agency; also excluded were the Federal Bureau of Investigation (Justice) and the National Security Agency (Defense); the District of Columbia "city" government and related agencies; and the so-called "legislative" agencies such as the General Accounting Office, the Library of Congress, the Government Printing Office, and the Office of the Architect of the Capitol, for these are not part of the Executive Branch proper. Finally, certain miscellaneous committees, commissions, and other units, such as the High Court of Military Justice whose managerial functions are at best nebulous, were omitted.

Each questionnaire had been precoded with an identification number permitting returns to be ordered by department or agency and by the second-level unit within each department or agency.

Each return was evaluated; questionnaires not adequate for inclusion in the study because of ambiguous or incomplete responses were rejected and not included in the total of returns. Comments written into the questionnaires by respondents, and examination of replies to internal check questions made it possible to use many returns which had not been correctly or completely filled out. Care was taken, however, that only questionnaires providing unambiguous information be retained.

A total of 12,929 questionnaires were returned in usable condi-

Appendix A

tion, 10,851 by civilians and 2,078 by the military. The rate of usable returns was 69.43 per cent for all questionnaires mailed, with the military responding at a slightly higher rate than civilians by a percentage of 71.18 compared to 69.11. See Table 3A for distribution and return of the questionnaires.

Table 3A

Distribution of Total Mailings and Returns

	Number of mailings	Number of returns	Percentage of returns
Civilian executives			
All departments	11,373	7,834	68.88
All independent agencies	4,328	3,017	69.71
Total civilian	15,701	10,851	69.11
Military executives			
U.S. Army	1,188	859	72.31
U.S. Air Force	994	708	71.23
U.S. Navy	669	465	69.50
U.S. Marine Corps*	68	46	67.65
Total military	2,919	2,078	71.18
Total, civilian and military	18,620	12,929	69.43

*For those with special interests, the returns from the Marine Corps have been kept separate from those from the Navy.

These extremely high percentages of returned questionnaires resulted from several factors. Advance discussion with federal executives, meetings with key personnel people, and circulation of press releases were steps designed to insure that the executives had positive knowledge about the study. Certainly the interest of the federal executives in the study and their belief that the undertaking was worthwhile, not only as a scientific endeavor but for information which could become available to them, helped to account for the results. The prestige of Cornell University and the University of Chicago was also a factor. A major reason for the very substantial return is without doubt also the prestige and respect accorded by federal executives to the members of the project's sponsoring committee listed on the covering letter and all other correspondence. Finally, the devotion of the project's clerical research staff in carefully controlling the mailing of the questionnaires, checking for duplications in the mailing lists, and preparing a neat and businesslike "package" to be received by the respondents affected the rate of return.

Three of ten failed to return the questionnaire. Were these three substantially different from those who returned the questionnaires? Investigation of this crucial issue began long before final versions of the questionnaires were mailed. During the pilot phase of the study, an attempt was made to call by telephone each of the 232 men in the Chicago area to whom pilot versions of the questionnaires had been mailed. This included those who had and had not returned the questionnaire. In the case of those who had not, the researcher attempted to make an appointment; if this failed, he asked questions over the telephone. Collecting information to analyze reasons for nonreturn of questionnaires was complicated by many executives' pleading overwork and promising to return it immediately. In some cases they did return it. Reasons given over the telephone for nonreturn were varied and included transfer or retirement, overwork, disapproval of studies of this type, and that questions were "too personal." After four telephone contacts, forty-seven men who had not filled out the questionnaire were still eligible for interviewing, and thirty-seven were interviewed. The interviewer at that time attempted to get the executive to fill out a questionnaire. At the same time, he asked a series of open-end questions which were also asked of men who had returned usable questionnaires.

In all, eighty-two people were interviewed during the pilot phase, including thirty-five who had filled out the questionnaire. Comparisons were made between responses returned by mail and responses collected by having a nonrespondent fill out the questionnaire during the interview. It was found that grade level, agency of employment, educational level, and past presidential preferences of respondents were not statistically different for the two groups. No variables on which meaningful differences existed could be found.

Failure to acquire clear-cut information about why some federal

Appendix A 291

executives failed to fill out questionnaires is merely negative evidence that the questionnaires returned accurately represent the total sample of federal executives. More positive tests can be made by comparing percentage of mailings to returns for several variables.

Tables 4A and 5A show proportions of the total civilian questionnaires mailed to each of the departments and agencies, and the proportions of returns from each of these departments and agencies. The relatively low return for the State Department results primarily from the large proportion of these men stationed overseas and rotated between overseas and United States assignments. After analysis of the questionnaires began, several hundred replies came to us too late for inclusion and, in fact, at present writing a few are still coming in, the bulk from men serving overseas. This was the only discrepancy of any size between rate of mailing and rate of return for the departments.

The relatively small numbers of executives in each agency led

Table 4A

Distribution of Total Civilian Mailing and Returns by Department

Departments	Mailings	Returns	Mailings	Returns	Return of each Dept.'s Mailing
State	2,525	1,419	16.08%	13.07%	56.20%
Treasury	1,151	758	7.33	6.99	65.86
Defense	3,540	2,517	22.55	23.19	71.10
Justice	466	287	2.97	2.64	61.59
Post Office	266	170	1.69	1.57	63.91
Interior	660	524	4.20	4.83	79.39
Agriculture	1,119	886	7.13	8.17	79.18
Commerce	894	697	5.69	6.42	77.96
Labor	256	181	1.63	1.67	70.70
Health, Education, and Welfare	496	395	3.16	3.64	79.64
Total	11,373	7,834	72.43	72.20	

Table 5A

Distribution of Total Civilian Mailing and Returns by Independent Agencies

Independent agencies	Mailings	Returns	Mailings	Returns	Returns of each agency
Executive Office of the President (*p. 291)	238	165	1.52%	1.52%	69.33%
Atomic Energy Commission	375	264	2.39	2.43	70.40
Civil Service Commission	147	107	0.94	0.99	72.99
Federal Reserve System	58	44	0.37	0.41	75.86
General Service Administration	208	148	1.32	1.36	71.15
Housing and Home Finance Agency	335	212	2.13	1.95	63.28
U.S. Information Agency	386	230	2.46	2.12	59.59
Tennessee Valley Authority	227	181	1.45	1.67	79.74
Veterans Administration	547	423	3.48	3.90	77.33
Federal Communications Commission	103	63	0.66	0.58	61.17
National Labor Relations Board	145	77	0.92	0.71	53.10
Federal Trade Commission	87	48	0.55	0.44	55.17
Interstate Commerce Commission	76	46	0.48	0.42	60.53
Securities and Exchange Commission	82	63	0.52	0.58	76.83
Federal Power Commission	80	62	0.51	0.57	77.50
Civil Aeronautics Board	98	67	0.62	0.62	68.37
Federal Aviation Agency	357	238	2.27	2.19	66.67
Air Coordinating Committee	85	84	0.54	0.77	98.82
National Aeronautics and Space Administration	287	204	1.83	1.88	71.08
National Science Foundation	43	38	0.30	0.35	88.37
Railroad Retirement Board	38	31	0.24	0.30	81.58
Renegotiation Board	48	38	0.31	0.35	79.17
Small Business Administration	31	16	0.20	0.15	51.61
Federal Deposit Insurance Corporation	49	28	0.31	0.26	57.14
Miscellaneous†	226	140	1.44	1.29	61.95
Total	4,328	3,017	27.57	27.80	
Total, departments and independent agencies	15,701	10,851	100.00	100.00	

Appendix A

the researchers to expect more variation between the percentage of mailings and returns in the agencies than in the departments. Table 5A shows that this did not happen. Even when the number mailed was less than 100, the proportion of mailings to returns is remarkably similar from one agency to another. Tables 4A and 5A show no sizable variation by department and agency. There is no meaningful difference by military service. We therefore conclude that proportion of mailings to returns is similar for all the departments, agencies, and military services.

It is important for analysis of possible bias to know whether men at the different scalar levels responded in equal proportions. A sample distorted by over-representation at the lower levels or, equally serious, at the higher levels would indicate a serious weakness in the study. Tables 6A and 7A show that proportions of mailings to returns are consistent throughout the scalar levels. In Table 6A we see that slightly fewer executives than expected at levels higher than GS-18 failed to return the questionnaire and that slightly fewer at GS-14 failed to return them. At the levels between GS-15 and 18 slightly more than expected filled out and returned the questionnaire. We can conclude that our sample is representative in terms of the scalar structure, with men at the two extremes slightly under-represented. In Table 7A, proportions of mailings to returns by military rank, we see that the differences between percentages mailed and returned are without consistent pattern. We may conclude that the returns are biased neither in the direction of the high nor the low scalar levels within the government service.

As one further test, let us examine the proportion of mailings to returns by geographic regions.

In Table 8A we see that 49.10 per cent of the total mailing was to executives in Washington, D.C., and that 48.04 of the total re-

---

*White House Office, Bureau of the Budget, Council of Economic Advisers, National Security Council, Office of Civil and Defense Mobilization, and staff of President's Advisory Committee on Reorganization.

†This category includes all the other independent agencies with a total mailing of fewer than 30 each: the Farm Credit Administration, Export-Import Bank of Washington, Canal Zone Government, the St. Lawrence Seaway Development Corporation, and all other "independent agencies" listed in the 1958 edition of the *Official Register of the United States*, pp. 607–731, except the following: American Battle Monuments Commission, Boston Historical Sites Commission, Committee on Purchases of Blind-Made Products, District of Columbia Redevelopment Land Agency, Jamestown-Williamsburg-Yorktown National Celebration Commission, National Capital Housing Authority, National Capital Planning Commission, National Railroad Adjustment Board, and U.S. Soldiers' Home. In total the miscellaneous agencies number 22.

Table 6A

Distribution of Total Civilian Mailing and Returns by GS Level

GS level or equivalent	Mailings	Returns	Mailings	Returns	Returns of each GS level
Above GS-18	642	344	4.09%	3.17%	53.58%
GS-18	417	296	2.66	2.73	70.98
GS-17	522	421	3.32	3.88	80.65
GS-16	1,660	1,166	10.57	10.75	70.24
GS-15	6,167	4,469	39.28	41.18	72.47
GS-14	5,850	4,012	37.26	36.97	68.58
Unknown	443	143	2.82	1.32	32.28
Total	15,701	10,851	100.00	100.00	69.11

Table 7A

Distribution of Total Military Mailing and Returns by Military Rank

Rank	Mailings	Returns	Mailings	Returns	Return of each rank
Admiral or general	37	31	1.27%	1.49%	83.78%
Vice admiral or lieutenant general	109	80	3.73	3.85	73.39
Rear admiral (upper half) or major general	653	461	22.37	22.18	70.60
Rear admiral (lower half) or brigadier general	467	392	16.00	18.86	83.94
Captain or colonel	1,653	1,114	56.63	53.61	67.39
Total	2,919	2,078	100.00	100.00	71.19

Appendix A

Table 8A

Distribution of Total Civilian Mailing and Returns by Geographical Location*

Region	Mailings	Returns	Mailings	Returns
New England	232	158	1.48%	1.46%
Middle Atlantic	930	613	5.92	5.65
East North Central	1,066	824	6.79	7.59
West North Central	369	280	2.35	2.58
South Atlantic	1,104	882	7.03	8.13
East South Central	655	478	4.17	4.41
West South Central	419	317	2.67	2.92
Mountain	484	373	3.08	3.44
Pacific	760	586	4.84	5.40
Washington, D.C.	7,709	5,213	49.10	48.04
U.S. Territories; Canal Zone	118	118	0.75	1.09
Canada	33	21	0.21	0.19
Latin America; British W. Indies	355	201	2.26	1.85
Africa	151	84	0.96	0.77
Asia	736	375	4.69	3.46
British Isles	52	25	0.33	0.23
Non-Communist Europe	466	272	2.97	2.51
Communist Europe	20	13	0.13	0.12
Australia, New Zealand, etc.	15	11	0.10	0.10
Others	27	7	0.17	0.06
Total	15,701	10,851	100.00	100.00

*For security reasons, data comparable to those shown for civilian executives in this table are not available for military leaders.

turns were from Washington, D.C.—a difference of 1.6 per cent. Examination of the other pairs of proportions of mailings and returns within the continental United States shows highly similar results; the differences are slight and form no consistent pattern. Examination of returns from overseas tells a different story. Here again the differences are slight but consistent and in their cumulative effect result partially in the slightly poorer showing of the State Department discussed above.

Examination of rates of return by three dimensions shows that those who did return their questionnaires do not differ in a systematic way from those who did not. From this the inference is made that the sample obtained is an accurate and valid representation of the total sample of federal executives as defined before the questionnaires were mailed.

A further methodological question, often raised in criticism of studies of this type, is how closely answers to items on the questionnaire correspond to events in the lives of respondents. There are usually several questions of this order raised. How can individual items on a questionnaire stand for the complex variables and interrelations among variables in the life situation? How can responses checked on questionnaires about events thirty or forty years past be accurate and not merely a reflection of cumulative distortion and family mythology? How can discrepancies between one individual's interpretation of an item and another's, and the resultant difference in answers, be reconciled?

Questions of this order are not the less crucial and important because they are difficult to answer. They are questions which have concerned the present researchers since the beginning of the study. A major portion of the research effort during the pilot study was devoted to detailed interviews with men who had filled out and returned the questionnaires, and the questionnaires were adjusted to take into account the problems raised. Life history documents were taken in semistructured interviews. Comparison of data reported in such interviews with responses to items on the questionnaires showed that the executives had common understandings about the questionnaires and that their replies could be uniformly treated.

The operations involved were too detailed to report here, but where questions were found to be vague and to elicit ambiguous replies, they were altered. The interviewers found that these executives, in the vast majority of cases, not only knew their grandfathers' occupations, but could discuss in detail the situations in which their grandfathers had carried them on.

If the present researchers could repeat this study, they would phrase few questions differently. On the whole they believe that the questionnaires as instruments for eliciting information were satisfactory within the limits necessary for the research.

Appendix A

The Selection of Population to be Studied

It was necessary that the population studied meet two basic criteria: the persons selected must represent an accurate sampling of top-level positions within the federal service as a whole, and they must be at levels of responsibility and authority comparable with the men studied in the 1952 business leader research. As we will see, this second criterion could not be directly and procedurally met by the techniques through which the 1952 researchers established a population comparable with the 1928 business leaders.

Consideration of an operating definition for federal executives immediately brought to the fore one fundamental difference between the business community and the structure of the Executive Branch of the federal government. The business community consists of a series of at least nominally independent and autonomous organizations. The federal government is one pyramid of organizations reporting to the President of the United States, but with the suborganizations in fact exercising varying degrees of autonomy. The problem facing the researchers was to determine what level of suborganizations would be comparable to the business firms studied in 1952, and what positions within these suborganizations would be considered comparable to the positions in the business leader population. That the research should extend its field of inquiry upward though the Cabinet level was obvious, but establishing a lower boundary was more difficult.

Consultation with government executives, private individuals with experience in the government, and educators working in the field of public administration led to several desirable definitions. First, it was decided that a population of federal executives more extensive than those assigned to duty in Washington, D.C. should be studied; to exclude from the population ambassadors, regional directors of large agencies, and area military commanders would exclude an important segment of the executive functioning of the federal government. Second, it was important that the population should be determined by level of responsibility rather than merely by whether a position was career, political, civil, or military. That is, this decision recognizes that career personnel in the upper echelons have very real executive functions, including considerable relationship to policy development and formulation. With these two criteria in mind, the following procedure was adopted.

Since the federal government maintains no central listing of all public employees, it had been recognized from the beginning that, for the *civilian* mailing, there was only one possible source for names and addresses, the 1958 edition of the *Official Register of the United States*.[18] The *Official Register* lists names, agencies, position titles, state and congressional district of legal residence, and salary of those "persons occupying administrative and supervisory positions in the legislative, executive, and judicial branches of the government." From this listing members of the Legislative and Judicial branches were, as indicated earlier, excluded. Discussions with those responsible for compilation of the *Register,* with a number of federal personnel officers, and with other government officials led to certain conclusions concerning the adequacy of this document for research purposes. Above all, there was complete agreement that, with some supplementation, the *Register* would serve to provide an adequate sample for this study. That is, while it was somewhat uneven in agency proportions of "administrative" personnel, it did exclude almost all persons occupying scientific, technical, or professional positions involving little executive or supervisory activity.

But before agency proportions could be further checked and, if need be, corrected, it was necessary to determine whether this was in fact feasible. In light of the great numbers of personnel at the GS-14 level or equivalent—some 19,000 by June 30, 1958[19]— it was clearly impractical to check this level further, particularly for the larger agencies. Our initial assumption was that this situation left the larger agencies under-represented at this level. But further calculations, possible after the data had been collected and tabulated, indicated that actually this is not generally the case. For example, our final returns contained information on 4,012 persons

18. Now published annually by the USCSC (Washington, Government Printing Office); names and positions were as of May 1, 1958. The *Congressional Directory* is similar, but much less complete for the Executive Branch; the 1958 edition of the *Directory* was used for a few minor supplementary reference purposes.

19. Calculated from data supplied by the federal Employment Statistics Office of the USCSC. This total breaks down into approximately 14,500 specifically in GS-14 positions plus some 4,500 at equivalent levels in other pay systems (foreign service, postal field service, medical personnel of the Veterans Administration, Atomic Energy Commission, Tennessee Valley Authority and a few others).

Appendix A

at the GS-14 level or equivalent, or about 21 per cent of the total at this level. By comparison, the subreturn for a group of six major departments (State, Treasury, Justice, Post Office, Interior, and Agriculture) was slightly over 29 per cent. The same was generally true for all other major agencies, and most minor ones, except the Department of Defense. For Defense there are data in this research for only 8 per cent of GS-14 or equivalent level civilian personnel. This, however, is not too surprising in light of the fact that many executive posts in Defense are held by uniformed military personnel, who are treated separately in this study. If one combines the GS-14 and equivalent uniformed military personnel, the representation of Defense at this level more nearly approaches a percentage similar to other major agencies. Nevertheless, the final sample must be considered to some extent to under-represent the Department of Defense at this level and, perhaps, a few of the smallest agencies. There was no way, however, to remedy this theoretical defect.

To check agency proportions for GS-15 and equivalent or above, was quite another and much simpler matter. The grand total of persons at this level or above (about 12,500 as of June 30, 1958[20]) was much smaller and our initial *Register* list much more complete. Therefore, to check whether the *Official Register* did in fact contain a full listing of executives at these top levels, the personnel directors of the departments and the independent agencies were contacted either personally or by letter. The general requirements of the study were set forth and the personnel directors asked to judge whether the *Register* was over 90 per cent (the proportion felt both desirable and feasible to obtain) complete for these purposes. All personnel directors of the sixty-one departments and agencies involved in this study responded. For the great bulk of agencies the *Register* was found to be better than 90 per cent complete for purposes of this research—in many cases, particularly among smaller agencies, nearly 95 to 99 per cent complete. But three categories of problems were discovered, all of which indicated important omissions from the 1958 edition of the *Register*.

First, for reasons undetermined, the *Register* for this year failed to make any reference at all to three agencies: the Airways Modernization Board (a small unit brought into the Federal Aviation

20. Calculated from data supplied by the federal Employment Statistics Office of the USCSC. This total breaks down into approximately 8,000 in the GS system plus some 4,500 at equivalent levels in other pay systems.

Agency in the fall of 1958), the Federal Deposit Insurance Corporation, and the Federal Reserve System. The personnel directors of the latter two agencies quickly responded to a request for suitable lists of executives.

Next, as the Federal Aviation Agency, the National Aeronautics and Space Administration, and the Office of Civil and Defense Mobilization were in process of being organized or reorganized as a result of legislation passed between the cutoff date of the *Register* (May 1, 1958) and the time of preparation of our executive mailing list (fall of 1958), special efforts were made to obtain corrections to reflect any changes deriving from this situation. Again, these efforts were successful, with any executives from the formerly independent Airways Modernization Board included with those of the new Federal Aviation Agency.

Finally, the personnel offices of some fourteen departments and agencies, although already at the 90 per cent point or better in completeness of their *Register* lists, supplied data to make their rosters even more accurate for purposes of this study. Only the Bureau of the Budget, Post Office Department, Department of State, and Department of Defense (including the Departments of the Army, Navy, and Air Force) appeared to be significantly incomplete in their listings at these top levels.

The Bureau supplied additions through its personnel office, and the Post Office Department did the same for postmasters and assistant postmasters (specifically excluded from the *Register*) and assisted in checking our postal field service listings.

The State Department informed the researchers that the *Official Register* was not adequate, but that the *Official Register* in conjunction with the *Foreign Service List* for October, 1958, would provide an adequate sample of executives in the State Department and in the International Cooperation Administration.[21] The *Foreign Service List* gives names and official addresses of members of field staffs and personnel assigned to the Department in Washington.

As the Department of Defense does not maintain an integrated listing of its executives below very top levels, it was necessary that a somewhat different procedure be followed. The *Register* listing

21. *Foreign Service List* issued quarterly by the Department of State (Washington, Government Printing Office, October, 1958). The Department's *Biographic Register* (Washington, Government Printing Office, 1958) containing similar data as of May 1, 1958, was also useful.

for the Office of the Secretary of Defense was considered sufficiently complete for this study. However, the Department provided a full list of persons at the GS-16 level and above for checking purposes. The Navy was able to supply a consolidated list of its top personnel at GS-15 and above. This left the field installations of the Army and Air Force unchecked, especially at the GS-15 and equivalent level, for which the *Register* was known to be seriously deficient. To fill this gap the two agencies directed each of their field activities to supply directly to the headquarters of this study the names, position designations, and office addresses of all personnel at GS-15 level and above.

As a result of these various endeavors to improve the *Register* listings, it was possible to obtain the names and addresses of 9,408 persons deemed to be executives from the total of about 12,500 civilians known to be at GS-15 level or equivalent or above (75 per cent). Discussions with federal officials and consultation of certain other published data suggest strongly that the great bulk of the missing 25 per cent were then engaged primarily as specialists rather than executives, and in professional, scientific, and technical rather than administrative and supervisory posts. All evidence indicates that, at the GS-15 level and above, the present study contains at least the 90 per cent of "executives" originally deemed desirable. The fact that, for each level above GS-15, the proportion of total persons included in mailings for this study from a particular level increases, provides additional evidence on this point. For one would expect a continuing rise in the proportion of executives the higher in the hierarchy one reached.

Finally, there is the question of comparative agency proportions at the GS-15 level and above. Using the same type of data and analysis—based on returns compared to total personnel at various levels—as presented earlier for GS-14 personnel, one notes first that for all agencies the returns in this study contain information on 6,696 persons at GS-15 or higher, about 53 per cent of the total number of civilians at these levels. By comparison, the subreturn for the same six major departments (State, Treasury, Justice, Post Office, Interior, and Agriculture) was sightly over 57 per cent. As a result of the augmentation of the Department of Defense by the *Register,* its returns comprised nearly 59 per cent of its totals at these levels. That is, for all major agencies, and most minor ones, the returns approximated 50 per cent of all personnel known to be at the GS-15 level or higher. At these levels all agencies, including the Department of Defense, appear to be represented in similar proportions, when returns are compared to total personnel in each agency.

From this, a definition in operational terms of civilian federal executives emerges. That is, the *Register* definition, limited by a floor established at the GS-14 level, provided the principal basis for the segregation of executives from other employees. In addition, every effort was made to exclude professional, scientific, and technical personnel serving primarily in individual capacities as specialists rather than as administrative and supervisory personnel in an executive sense. Determination of executives by such procedures is, of course, subject to some problems. But these procedures were the best possible and, as discussed later, appeared quite adequate for the purposes of the research.

At first it was thought that the *Official Register* might be suitable as a source for *military* and *other uniformed service executives,* and initial listings were prepared from this publication. Consultation with Department of Defense officials revealed, however, that the *Register* was incomplete for military personnel, with the various subdepartments of Army, Navy, and Air Force represented in widely varying proportions. It was proposed that certain official military registers, containing complete lists of all military personnel, with the various grades, be used.[22] As a second step, therefore, these special military registers were collated with the listing from the *Official Register*. At general and flag officer ranks, all personnel were included and received questionnaires regardless of official position at the time, since all such military officers are considered to be generalists of executive caliber. Those few not at the moment in executive posts either had been or, because of military rotational policies, soon would be. Because of their great numbers, colonels and naval captains were included in the military listing only if they then held positions of a managerial nature and had also been included in the *Official Register*. Military personnel at this latter level were equated approximately with GS-14 civilians and it was desired to include them in no greater proportions.

22. *U.S. Army Register,* Vol. I, Jan. 1, 1958; *Register of Commissioned . . . Officers of the United States Navy and Marine Corps . . .,* Jan. 1, 1958; and *Air Force Register,* Jan. 1, 1958 (all: Washington, Government Printing Office, 1958).

For the other uniformed services of the Coast Guard, Coast and Geodetic Survey, and Public Health Service, similar procedures were used, except that all uniformed personnel at the level of colonel or naval captain or equivalent were included. These services, however, have not been analyzed in the present study.

One difficulty in mailing to military leaders arose from security regulations which designate certain lists of high-ranking officers as "classified" information. Through cooperation of the Defense Department this obstacle was overcome. The researchers selected from the registers names of military leaders, typed the names on envelopes containing questionnaires, and sent them to the Department of Defense, which in turn forwarded them to generals and flag officers throughout the world. Without this cooperation of Department of Defense officials, relatively few individuals occupying these high military ranks could have been included in the study.

It is evident that, although the procedure for selecting federal executives was similar to that used in the 1952 business leader study, it was applied within a quite different organizational context, a fact which raises certain questions.

The 1952 research followed closely the sampling definitions and procedures used by Taussig and Joslyn in 1928. In 1928, *Poor's Register of Directors* was used as the basic sampling instrument; the 1952 study used the 1952 edition.[23] A basic criterion for the 1928 population was size of firm in terms of volume of sales or gross income. The 1952 research made use of the same criterion, adjusting for increases nationally in size of business between 1928 and 1952. The 1928 population was selected in terms of the type of industry. The 1952 research also used this criterion, making certain adjustments discussed in *Occupational Mobility*. The 1928 population was defined also in terms of position title. The 1952 research used this criterion with no adjustments in terminology necessary.

Comparing federal and business executives presents several problems not encountered in comparing 1952 to 1928 business leaders. First, the federal government is one extensive hierarchy; the business community is made up of a series of discrete hierarchies. Second, annual sales are a widely used criterion for judging size of business enterprise and were used as such in the business leader

23. *Poor's Register of Directors and Executives, United States and Canada* (New York, Standard and Poor's, 1952).

research. Since the federal government makes no comparable sales it was not possible to equate structures in terms of size. Third, the type of industry presented so many complications as to make this criterion unusable for equating the two populations. There is in the business community no industry, for example, comparable to national defense.

Similarly, positions held by men in the two different populations could not be compared. The relatively simple title nomenclature of the business world is not duplicated in the federal structures where position titles are much more diverse. Interviews with government officials focused our attention on the kinds of traps involved in assuming comparability because of surface similarity in position titles. For example, an executive in the federal government administering insurance and retirement may "write" three or four times the volume of insurance as his counterpart in the business world. To consider his organizational responsibilities as that much greater is to overlook the vital fact that the business executive is deeply involved in promotion and sales of his insurance. Examination of other "equal" responsibility levels led the researchers to believe that no such direct equations between business and the federal government could be validly made.

The only solution open to the researchers was to select from the total population of the federal government executive branch those positions which were at the highest levels and included typical managerial and executive responsibilities. The population occupying these positions would then be assumed to be in general terms equivalent to the business leader population. The critical problem was that of establishing a lower boundary for such a population of federal executives. Reasons for establishing the lower boundary at the beginning of GS grade 14 or equivalent were discussed above. An additional reason for establishing a lower boundary at this level was to insure that sufficient men from lower levels were included in the federal population to be "fair" to the business population. Obviously, to have selected only those people at the Cabinet level, and immediately below, in the government structures would have caused a bias in one direction. To select individuals at very low government levels would have been a bias in the opposite direction. The solution was made in consultation with high-level government officials, public-administration educators, and various individuals who have functioned as consultants to the government from private industry.

In the study of business leaders it was possible to treat all businessmen as one category. As research on federal executives moved forward, it became evident that the research was being directed toward several very different populations. The division of federal executives into civilian and military groups was obvious and was adopted early in the research. Less obvious, but equally important, was whether or not the research should treat all civilian executives as one group. Discussion among the researchers and with government people made clear that such a procedure would distort and conceal answers to important questions. It was decided that the civilian executives be divided into three main categories: career civil service, political, and foreign service.

Career civil service executives were defined as civilian employees, other than foreign service, who hold tenure positions in a merit system of the federal government. By far the greatest proportion of career civil servants function within the general merit system established by the Pendleton Act of 1883 under the general direction of the U.S. Civil Service Commission. Separate merit systems are operated by the Atomic Energy Commission, the Tennessee Valley Authority and, for specific groups of employees, by several other agencies. Appointments under all these merit systems were considered to be distinctly career in nature.

Political executives as a category consist of four principal groups. The first comprises individuals falling within the provisions of Sections 102 through 109 of the Executive Pay Act of 1956, the act in force at the time of this study. These provisions cover nearly all top positions in the departments and agencies. Such positions are also excepted by Congress from merit system considerations, and are clearly within a category designated as both "political" and "executive." The other types of personnel included within the general category of political executive consist of individuals holding positions that fall within the three groupings officially designated as Schedules A, B, and C by the Civil Service Commission.[24] Schedule

24. The definitions of these schedules may be found in almost any annual report of the USCSC. See, for example, *76th Annual Report* (Washington, Government Printing Office, 1959), p. 108. For a complete list of Schedule A, B, and C positions as of the time of this study see the *Federal Register*, XXIII (December 20, 1958) pp. 9810–25.

A is defined by the Civil Service Commission as, "positions other than those of a confidential or policy-determining character for which it is not practicable to examine . . . " Schedule B is defined as, "positions other than those of a confidential or policy-determining character for which it is not practicable to hold competitive examination . . . Appointments to these positions shall be subject to such non-competitive examination as may be prescribed by the Commission." Persons holding Schedules A and B positions were very few at the levels dealt with in this study. They were included within the political executive category because much discretion on the part of appointing officers is clearly permissable. Schedules A and B are, in terms of the needs of this research, highly similar categories and were listed as one in the questionnaire. The decision to include men in Schedules A and B in the political executive category was arrived at with awareness that many individuals in Schedules A and B perform duties similar to those performed by individuals categorized in career civil service. Schedule C is defined as "positions of a confidential or policy-determining character," and persons holding them are considered to hold political appointments. Quite a number of persons holding Schedule C positions are included within the political executive group.

A third category used in this study of civilian executives is the foreign service. This category consists of executives who are foreign-service officers, foreign-service reserve officers, and foreign-service staff personnel. It also includes some high ranking noncareer men who are in the State Department as political executives in, especially, the foreign-service posts of minister and ambassador. The category of foreign service, therefore, while heavily career, cuts to a limited extent across both the career-merit and the political categories.

Together these three categories of civilian executives are referred to as "civilian federal executives." Most collective references to all four (civilian plus military) are to "the several services." Although "men" is used throughout most of this study, the various tables include data on 145 women executives who, in addition, are considered collectively in Chapter 11.

The reasons for the four-way division of federal executives stem not only from the usual civil-military distinctions or from the fact that such a division assists comparison with many previous studies organized around these same, almost traditional categories.[25] Equally significant is the fact that the great bulk of federal personnel are systematically ranked and graded within two fundamental types of personnel systems.

One of these systems may be characterized as emphasizing "rank-in-the-man" and the other "rank-in-the-job." In the former an individual holds a relatively permanent rank and status (such as indicated by the personal title of "Colonel") wherever he may be moved about in the service in terms of geography or, in some cases, agency. Indeed, a main purpose of this personal rank is to facilitate the planned movement of personnel. In the American federal service the principal groups of persons with such rank are found in the traditional uniformed military services of the Army, Navy, Air Force, and Marine Corps; in the uniformed and militarily paid and ranked commissioned officer corps of the Coast Guard (with Treasury in peace and Navy in war), the Coast and Geodetic Survey (Commerce), and the Public Health Service (Health, Education, and Welfare); and in the civilian Foreign Service of the Department of State. Because of the great number of representatives in top level positions and the diverse functions involved, we have limited the study of individuals with personal rank to those in the upper levels of the military services in the Department of Defense (Army, Navy, Air Force, and Marine Corps)[26] and to their counterparts in the Foreign Service.[27]

Personnel in the other uniformed services are not analyzed, nor have distinctions among Army, Navy, Air Force, and Marine Corps been analyzed, although the data for such an analysis were

25. See Paul T. David and Ross Pollock, *Executives for Government* (Washington, Brookings Institution, 1957) Ch. 3 and 5. See also James L. McCamy and Alessandro Corradini, "The People of the State Department and Foreign Service," *American Political Science Review*, 48 (1954), 1067–82; and Second Hoover Commission, *Task Force Report on Personnel and Civil Service* (Washington, Government Printing Office, 1955).

26. Data have been collected, however, on the equivalent levels of the other three commissioned officer corps, and on the above military services as separate and distinct services. Analysis of these separate services will be made at a later date.

27. The capitalized term "Foreign Service" has not been used in this study because the "foreign-service executive" category includes a limited number of persons not formally members of the official "Foreign Service." This has been done to give a more complete composite view of that total group, including the Foreign Service, who direct our foreign affairs.

collected. For purposes of the present volume we have dealt only with military executives as one category. A subsequent volume treating the military services in detail and analyzing differences between military and other uniformed service personnel is planned by the researchers.

The remainder of the federal service, which is entirely civilian, may be characterized as position- rather than rank-oriented. In the great bulk of our federal civil establishment men and women do not carry their rank with them as they move about. There are many historical reasons for this which need not be discussed here.

Whereas the military and the foreign-service groups are relatively self-contained and easily separable for close scrutiny, the position-oriented portion of the civil service is not so easily handled. It too must be divided for purposes of a study such as this, but in a horizontal rather than vertical manner characterized by no neat and precise line of demarcation. At the levels dealt with here one may say that the dividing line is roughly at the bureau chief level, with many bureau chiefs and nearly all those below categorized as "career," and with some bureau chiefs and nearly all those above categorized as "political." The reasons for distinguishing between career and political posts and the persons holding them are well known, and it is enough to say here that this classification stems especially from the differing modes of appointment and tenure and from the differing roles with respect to partisan politics traditionally ascribed by both law and custom to these two groups of officials.

It is recognized that this four-way division of federal executives, while essential for any sensible analysis of personal characteristics, mobility, and career patterns, is artificial from certain organizational, administrative, and social-system points of view. Therefore, data have often been suitably consolidated in order to present various composite pictures. It is anticipated that more analysis of this type will be made in subsequent reports.

The Use of Census Data in the Study

The present study relied heavily on the reorganization of census data undertaken for the 1952 business leader study. In both studies national population data on occupational distributions, nativity, and educational levels have been used extensively as central standards around which samples are compared. The 1952 researchers set forth (pages 237 to 240 of *Occupational Mobility*) the reorgan-

Appendix A

ization of census data and the reasons for it. The present study has followed these decisions as closely as possible, but the primary rationale does not remain the same for the two studies. The rationale for reorganization of census data in the 1959 study is that at every step procedures used in the 1952 study be followed as closely as possible. Failure to do so would have invalidated at the outset many of the comparisons between business leaders and federal executives. In one sense, this restriction of the 1959 research greatly simplified operations. It was necessary only to ascertain what the 1952 researchers had done and then repeat the operation. In another sense, this restriction made the 1959 research more complicated and difficult. Decisions made in 1952 had to be carefully isolated and examined. While isolation of such decisions in the summary form presented in the methods chapter of *Occupational Mobility* was relatively simple, isolation of detailed decisions was much more difficult. The process became one of following step by step the operations performed in 1952 and available in the records.

As one example, the 1952 researchers reclassified the hundreds of occupations listed in the occupational statistics census volumes into broad occupational groups. If comparability were to be insured, exactly the same census occupations had to be combined in exactly the same way for the 1959 research.

These operations could have been avoided in 1959 if the same census data could have been used. Seven years, however, had elapsed between the two studies. Further, the 1952 business leader sample averaged slightly over fifty years in age, whereas the 1959 civilian federal executives averaged slightly under fifty. The cumulative effect of these factors made an adjustment by one ten-year census period necessary in comparing such factors as occupational origins and nativity of executives.

Since the operations used in 1959 followed as closely as possible those of 1952, the reader is referred to pages 237–240 of *Occupational Mobility* for further discussion of some of the points that will be raised. As in the 1952 study, the most important single set of census data in the present study relates to distribution of occupations. For the comparisons of father's occupation with occupations in the national population, the 1952 research used data from the 1920 census. To make the comparison accurate, however, they used only male adults, defined as twenty years of age and over. Further, to examine the role of place of birth (U.S. and non-U.S.) and region of birth, they reorganized the 1920 census data on occupations by state and region and by nativity. The federal executive research made the same comparisons but used 1930 census data.[28] The rationale behind the 1952 decisions is quoted here for the reader's convenience:

> The importance of these qualifications of the basic definition of the comparison figures should not be overlooked. All the factors—age, sex, and nativity—have an accumulative effect on occupational proportions in the population. Thus, younger workers, female workers, and foreign-born workers had to be concentrated in the lower occupational statuses, which substantially alters the proportions in these occupations. An underestimation of occupational mobility would result if the comparisons were made simply with the entire U.S. population by occupation. [*Occupational Mobility*]

The 1952 researchers report two major difficulties encountered in categorizing 1920 census data. The first of these was an undercount by 500,000 of agricultural workers, resulting from the fact that the 1920 census was taken in January of that year. The business leader researchers elected not to correct for this undercount, stating as their reason that, "the majority of the 500,000 not counted would in all probability be excluded from our estimates of total male adults by reason of age and/or sex." After some consideration, the 1959 researchers also elected not to correct for this undercount. Their principal reason was that to do so would have meant that the 1920 figures compiled for the business leader research would then have had to be computed again, and the fact that such a recomputation would have injected more uncertainty than it would have resolved.

The 1952 business leader research also had a major problem to solve in dividing owners of large business from owners of small business. The census data on occupations do not make this distinction—a very important one in these researches. Using census data on size of business, the 1952 researchers evolved a formula by which they divided all business into two size categories, with the percentage of owners of small business in the total population set

28. Bureau of the Census, *Fifteenth Census, 1930*, Vol. IV, Occupations by States, Table 11.

Appendix A

at 5 per cent and the proportion of major executives and owners of large business at 4 per cent. The 1959 researchers used exactly the same formula for arriving at percentages of small business owners, and of major executives and owners of large business, for the 1930 census data.

The figures for U.S. adult males used in the 1952 study include Negroes, although Negroes do not appear in significant numbers among the business elite. The 1952 researchers reasoned:

> There is no question that Negroes are concentrated in large proportions in the lower occupational levels. Further, Negroes tend to be located in particular geographical areas. When the problem is viewed in terms of social structure, however, it will be seen that limiting the population data to white workers is unjustified. That is, in terms of occupational mobility, the general absence of the Negro from positions of business leadership is an element in the total recruitment process of the United States. Estimates of mobility based on the white population alone would be inaccurate. Further, in the social structure of the South particularly, the very presence of Negroes in large numbers would presumably serve to accelerate the mobility of whites in the business structure. Thus, valid study of the representation of occupational groups in business leadership must include the Negro and other disadvantaged racial groups in the occupational distribution on which the mobility estimates are based. [*Occupational Mobility*, pp. 239–40]

Arrangement of data for 1900 and 1910 to make possible comparisons of rates of birth by size of city and by region presented no difficulties to the 1959 researchers. The major problem had been in rephrasing item 16 of the business leader questionnaire to secure comparable responses from the federal executives. How this was done is discussed in the section comparing the questionnaires. Once comparability of questionnaire items was achieved, the use of 1900 and 1910 census data was simple, with no adjustment necessary.

One should also note that the business leader researchers, for reasons discussed on page 240 of *Occupational Mobility*, used 1940 census data for comparing educational levels of business leaders with the nation as a whole; the 1959 researchers elected to use 1957 data. To make comparisons between 1952 business leaders and federal executives possible, the 1950 census data, rather than 1940, have been used for computing business leader ratios. This adjustment brings the two samples into correspondence.

The cautionary remarks made by the 1952 researchers about hazards in using census data apply as well now as then. Changing occupational definitions from one census to another, undercounting and overcounting, and other necessary adjustments all introduce possibilities for error. Both the 1952 and 1959 researches have been careful not to place finer interpretations on figures resulting from the use of census data than the accuracy of census data warrants.

APPENDIX B

Supplementary Tables

APPENDIX B

Supplementary Tables

Chapter 2 *Page*

1B. Occupational Distribution of Fathers of Civilian Federal Executives and of U.S. Male Adult Population for 1930. 321
2B. Sources of 1959 Civilian Federal Executives: Ratio of Proportion of Fathers in Occupational Group to Proportion of Occupational Group in Adult Male Population in 1930. 322
3B. Occupations of Fathers of 1959 Military Executives 323
4B. Sources of 1959 Military Executives: Ratio of Proportion of Fathers in Occupational Group to Proportion of Occupational Group in Adult Male Population in 1930 324
5B. The Professions as Sources of 1952 and 1959 Executives: Ratio of Proportion of Fathers in Professions to Proportion of Professions in Adult Male Population in 1920 and 1930 Respectively 325
6B. Sources of 1952 and 1959 Executives: Ratio of Proportion of Fathers in Occupational Group to Proportion of Occupational Group in Adult Male Populations 326

Chapter 3

7B. Comparison of Place of Birth of 1959 Federal Executives 327
8B. Ratio Comparison of 1952 Business Leaders and 1959 Federal Executives by Region of Birth with

		Page
	1900 and 1910 Adult Population, Respectively, by Region of Residence	329
9B.	Distribution by Region of Present Legal Residence of 1959 Civilian Federal Executives and 1950 Adult Male Population	330
10B.	Regional Retention of Potential Civilian Federal Executives	330
11B.	Geographical Mobility Ratios: 1959 Civilian Federal Executives' Movement out of Region of Birth into Region of Present Legal Residence	331
12B.	Comparison of Geographical Mobility of U.S.-Born 1952 Business Leaders and 1959 Federal Executives	332

Chapter 4

13B.	Size of Birthplace of 1959 Civilian Federal Executives and Size of Community of Residence of 1910 U.S. Population	333
14B.	Occupations and Types of Communities of Fathers of 1959 Civilian Federal Executives	334
15B.	Ratio of Nativity of 1952 Business Leaders and 1959 Federal Executives and U.S. Population	336
16B.	Occupational Mobility and Nativity: Occupations of Fathers of 1959 Civilian Federal Executives in Four Nativity Categories	337
17B.	Distribution by Nativity and Occupation of 1959 Federal Executives' Fathers and of 1930 U.S. Adult Males	340
18B.	Comparisons among the Services of Native and Foreign-Born Executives' Fathers	341

Chapter 5

19B.	Occupational Mobility in Three Generations: Occupations of Fathers and Paternal Grandfathers of 1959 Civilian Federal Executives	342
20B.	Movement of 1959 Civilian Federal Executives' Fathers out of Occupations of Paternal Grand-	

Appendix B

Page

fathers: Distribution of Fathers in Each of Ten Occupational Groups According to Occupation of Father's Father   343
21B. Ratios of Movement out of Occupations of 1959 Civilian Federal Executives' Paternal Grandfathers into Occupations of Fathers   344
22B. Civilian Federal Executives: Sources and Channels of Mobility   345
23B. Occupational Mobility in Three Generations: Occupations of Fathers and Paternal Grandfathers of 1959 Military Executives   346
24B. Military Executives: Sources and Channels of Mobility   347
25B. Big Business Leaders: Sources and Channels of Mobility   348

Chapter 6

26B. Occupations of Father's Father and Mother's Father of 1959 Civilian Federal Executives   349

Chapter 7

27B. Occupations of Civilian Federal Executives' Fathers and Occupations of Spouses' Fathers   350
28B. Comparison of Occupational Origins of Wives in the Several Services   351
29B. Education and Marriage of Civilian Federal Executives and Business Leaders when Both Father and Father's Father Were Major Executives, Owners of Large Business, or Professional Men   352
30B. Marriage and Achievement Time: Mean Number of Years to Achieve Federal Position for Executives by Occupation of Father and Spouse's Father   352
31B. Nativity and Marriage of 1959 Civilian Federal Executives   353
32B. Nativity and Marriage of 1959 Military Executives   353

Chapter 8

		Page
33B.	Comparison of Education of 1959 Federal Executives and 1952 Business Leaders with Population of the United States	354
34B.	Ratios of Educational Levels of Men in the Elites to Educational Levels of U.S. Adult Males	355
35B.	Percentages, by Education of the Father, of Executives at Three Educational Levels	356
36B.	Executives Who Reported College Degrees	357
37B.	Sons of Fathers in Each Occupational Group Who Reported Master's Degrees	358
38B.	Sons of Fathers in Each Occupational Group Who Reported Doctor of Philosophy Degrees	359
39B.	Sons of Fathers in Each Occupational Group Who Reported Medical Degrees	360
40B.	Sons of Fathers in Each Occupational Group Who Reported Law Degrees	361
41B.	Degrees and Area of Specialization of 1959 Civilian Federal Executives	362
42B.	Degree and Area of Specialization of 1959 Career Civil Service Executives	363
43B.	Degree and Area of Specialization of 1959 Political Executives	364
44B.	Degree and Area of Specialization of 1959 Foreign-Service Executives	365
45B.	Degree and Area of Specialization of 1959 Military Executives	366

Chapter 9

46B.	Types of Institutions from Which Master's Level Degrees Were Received	367
47B.	Types of Institutions from Which Doctoral Level Degrees Were Received	368
48B.	Types of Institutions from Which Law Degrees Were Received	369
49B.	Types of Institutions from Which Medical Degrees Were Received	370
50B.	Types of Institutions from Which Second Degrees at All Levels Were Received	371

Appendix B

		Page
51B.	Thirty Institutions Which Produced the Largest Number of Four-Year Degrees Reported by Civilian Federal Executives	372
52B.	Thirty Institutions Which Produced the Largest Number of Master's Level Degrees Reported by Civilian Federal Executives	374
53B.	Thirty Institutions Which Produced the Largest Number of Federal Executives with Law Degrees at All Levels	375
54B.	Institutions Attended by American Business Leaders	376
55B.	Men from Three Occupational Origins Who Received Law Degrees from Twenty Institutions	377

Chapter 10

56B.	Career Sequence of 1959 Career Civil Service Executives	378
57B.	Career Sequence of 1959 Political Executives	379
58B.	Career Sequence of 1959 Foreign-Service Executives	380
59B.	Career Sequence of 1959 Military Executives	381
60B.	Career Sequence of 1952 Business Leaders	382
61B.	Father's Occupation and Career Pattern of Military Executives	383
62B.	Father's Occupation and Years Required to Achieve Present Position after Entering Public Service	384
63B.	Comparison of Age at Entry and Time to Achieve Present Position by Men in Each of the Elites	385
64B.	Average Age of Executives by Occupation of the Fathers	386
65B.	Number of Organizations Associated with as an Executive	387
66B.	Interorganizational Mobility and Speed of Career	388
67B.	Experience in Private Enterprise and Speed of Career	389
68B.	Occupational Mobility and Types of Public Organizations of 1959 Civilian Federal Executives	390

Chapter 11

69B.	Proportions of Women Executives and of Total Civilian Executives in 1959, at the GS Levels	391

Page

70B. Departments and Agencies in Which 1959 Civilian Federal Executives and 1959 Civilian Federal Women Executives Served — 392

71B. 1959 Civilian Federal Women Executives by Line and Staff Position in the Federal Hierarchy — 393

72B. Occupations of Fathers of 1959 Civilian Federal Women Executives — 394

73B. Ratios of Women Executives and of Total Executives in the Several Services to Adult Male Population in 1930 — 395

74B. The Professions as Sources of Women Executives: Ratios of Women Executives and of Executives in the Several Elites to Adult Male Population in 1920 — 396

75B. The Professions as Sources of 1959 Civilian Federal Women Executives — 396

76B. Occupational Mobility in Three Generations: Occupations of Fathers and Paternal Grandfathers of 1959 Civilian Federal Executives and of 1959 Civilian Federal Women Executives — 397

77B. Ratios of 1959 Civilian Federal Executives and of Civilian Federal Women Executives by Region of Birth to 1910 Adult Population by Region of Residence — 397

78B. Ratios of Size of Birthplace of 1959 Civilian Federal Executives and of 1959 Civilian Federal Women Executives by Size of Community of Residence to 1910 U.S. Population — 398

79B. Nativity of 1959 Civilian Federal Executives and of 1959 Civilian Federal Women Executives and U.S. Population in 1950 — 398

80B. Ratios of Educational Levels of Women Executives and of the Three Civilian Elites to the Adult Male Population — 399

81B. Present Age of Women Executives and of Executives in the Three Civilian Services by GS Level — 399

82B. Marital Status of All 1959 Civilian Federal Executives and of 1959 Civilian Federal Women Executives — 400

Appendix B

TABLE 1B (Chap. 2)

Occupational Distribution of Fathers of Civilian Federal Executives and of U.S. Male Adult Population for 1930*

Occupation	Fathers of 1959 civilian federal executives	Total U.S. male adult population in 1930
Unskilled or semiskilled laborer	4%	33%
Skilled laborer	17	15
Owner of small business	14	7
Clerk or salesman	9	12
Foreman	5	2
Minor or major business executive; owner of large business	17	3
Professional man	19	4
Farm laborer	0†	6
Farm tenant or owner	14	16
Other occupations	1	2
Total	100	100

*Fifteenth Census, 1930, Vol. IV, Occupations by States, Table 11.

†Less than 0.5 per cent.

TABLE 2B (Chap. 2)

Sources of 1959 Civilian Federal Executives: Ratio of Proportion of Fathers in Occupational Group to Proportion of Occupational Group in Adult Male Population in 1930

Occupation of father	Ratio*	Rank order (1–9)
Unskilled or semiskilled laborer	0.12	8
Skilled laborer	1.13	5
Owner of small business	2.00	4
Clerk or salesman	0.75	7
Foreman	2.50	3
Business executive or owner of large business	5.67	1
Professional man	4.75	2
Farm laborer	0.00	9
Farm tenant or owner	0.88	6

*Proportional representation = 1.00.

TABLE 3B (Chap. 2)

Occupations of Fathers of 1959 Military Executives

Occupation of father		
Laborer		14%
Unskilled or semiskilled	1.9%	
Skilled worker or mechanic	12.1	
White-collar worker		9
Clerk or retail salesman	3.0	
Salesman	6.1	
Business executive		20
Foreman	4.9	
Minor executive	9.8	
Major executive	5.5	
Business owner		19
Small business	13.4	
Medium business	4.0	
Large business	1.8	
Professional man		18
Doctor	3.9	
Engineer	2.8	
Lawyer	5.1	
Minister	1.7	
Other profession	5.1	
Farmer		10
Farm tenant or farm worker	0.4	
Tenant with paid help	0.6	
Farm owner without paid help	3.0	
Owner or manager with paid help	5.7	
Uniformed service		9
Uniformed service	8.5	
Other occupations		1
Government service	0.4	
Other occupation	0.3	
Total per cent	100.0	100
Total number	2,078	

TABLE 4B (Chap. 2)

Sources of 1959 Military Executives: Ratio of Proportion of Fathers in Occupational Group to Proportion of Occupational Group in Adult Male Population in 1930

Occupation	Fathers of 1959 military executives	Ratio[*]	Rank order (1–10)
Unskilled or semiskilled laborer	2%	0.06	10
Skilled laborer	12	0.80	6
Owner of small business	13	1.86	5
Clerk or salesman	9	0.75	7
Foreman	5	2.50	4
Business executive or owner of large business	21	7.00	1
Professional man	18	4.50	3
Farm laborer	1[†]	0.17	9
Farm tenant or owner	9	0.56	8
Uniformed service	9	5.00	2
Other occupations	1		

[*] Proportional representation = 1.00.

[†] 0.4 rounded to 1 per cent.

Appendix B

TABLE 5B (Chap. 2)

The Professions as Sources of 1952 and 1959 Executives: Ratio of Proportion of Fathers in Professions to Proportion of Professions in Adult Male Population in 1920 and 1930 Respectively

Profession of father	Business leaders	Civilian federal exec.	Career civil service exec.	Foreign-service exec.	Political exec.	Military exec.
Lawyer	8.00	8.44	5.56	10.00	20.44	11.33
Minister	5.48	6.67	5.71	11.90	6.90	4.05
Engineer	4.80	4.77	4.77	4.92	5.08	4.31
Doctor	4.78	5.95	5.24	8.09	7.14	9.29
Other professions*	1.89	2.74	2.52	3.87	2.61	2.22

*Includes:

| Teachers | 2.24 | 2.24 | 1.90 | 2.24 | 2.07 |
| Professors | 14.17 | 11.67 | 27.50 | 14.17 | 7.50 |

TABLE 6B (Chap. 2)

Sources of 1952 and 1959 Executives: Ratio of Proportion of Fathers in Occupational Group to Proportion of Occupational Group in Adult Male Populations

Occupation of father	Business leaders	Civilian federal executives	Career civil service executives	Foreign-service executives	Political executives	Military executives
Unskilled or semiskilled laborer	0.16 (9)*	0.12 (9)	0.12 (9)	0.09 (9)	0.06 (9)	0.06 (9)
Skilled laborer	0.63 (7)	1.13 (5)	1.27 (5)	0.73 (7)	0.87 (6)	0.80 (6)
Owner of small business	3.60 (2)	2.00 (4)	2.14 (4)	1.71 (3)	1.86 (4)	1.86 (5)
Clerk or salesman	0.80 (6)	0.75 (7)	0.83 (7)	0.58 (8)	0.75 (8)	0.75 (7)
Foreman	1.33 (5)	2.50 (3)	2.50 (3)	1.50 (4–5)	2.00 (3)	2.50 (4)
Minor or major business executive; owner of large business	7.75 (1)	5.67 (1)	4.67 (1)	8.00 (1)	6.67 (1)	7.00 (1)
Professional man	3.50 (3)	4.75 (2)	4.00 (2)	6.25 (2)	6.00 (2)	4.50 (3)
Farm laborer	0.00 (10)	0.00 (10)	0.00 (10)	0.00 (10)	0.00 (10)	0.00 (10)
Farm tenant or owner	0.45 (8)	0.88 (6)	0.94 (6)	0.75 (6)	0.81 (7)	0.56 (8)
Uniformed service, etc.	2.00 (4)	0.50 (8)	0.50 (8)	1.50 (4–5)	1.00 (5)	5.00 (2)

*The numbers in parentheses indicate the rank order of each occupation for the several categories.

Appendix B

TABLE 7B (Chap. 3)

Comparison of Place of Brith of 1959 Federal Executives

State	Career civil service exec.	Foreign-service exec.	Political exec.	Civilian federal exec.	Military exec.
New England					
Maine	0.5% ⎫	1.2% ⎫	0.7% ⎫	0.6% ⎫	0.8% ⎫
New Hampshire	0.4 ⎟	0.4 ⎟	0.3 ⎟	0.4 ⎟	0.6 ⎟
Vermont	0.2 ⎬ 7.1	0.3 ⎬ 9.5	0.5 ⎬ 8.5	0.3 ⎬ 7.7	0.8 ⎬ 8.1
Massachusetts	4.3 ⎟	6.4 ⎟	4.4 ⎟	4.7 ⎟	4.4 ⎟
Rhode Island	0.6 ⎟	0.7 ⎟	0.7 ⎟	0.6 ⎟	0.5 ⎟
Connecticut	1.1 ⎭	0.5 ⎭	1.9 ⎭	1.1 ⎭	1.0 ⎭
Middle Atlantic					
New York	12.4 ⎫	13.2 ⎫	12.6 ⎫	12.5 ⎫	8.8 ⎫
Pennsylvania	7.3 ⎬ 22.1	6.4 ⎬ 22.7	7.4 ⎬ 22.1	7.1 ⎬ 22.0	5.0 ⎬ 16.0
New Jersey	2.4 ⎭	3.1 ⎭	2.1 ⎭	2.4 ⎭	2.2 ⎭
South Atlantic					
Delaware	0.1 ⎫	0.4 ⎫	0.2 ⎫	0.2 ⎫	0.4 ⎫
Maryland	1.9 ⎟	2.0 ⎟	2.0 ⎟	1.9 ⎟	2.2 ⎟
Virginia	2.3 ⎟	2.7 ⎟	2.0 ⎟	2.3 ⎟	2.0 ⎟
West Virginia	1.0 ⎬ 9.5	0.7 ⎬ 9.7	0.8 ⎬ 9.0	0.9 ⎬ 9.5	1.3 ⎬ 11.9
North Carolina	1.4 ⎟	1.2 ⎟	1.7 ⎟	1.4 ⎟	1.7 ⎟
South Carolina	1.0 ⎟	1.1 ⎟	0.6 ⎟	1.0 ⎟	1.3 ⎟
Georgia	1.4 ⎟	1.3 ⎟	1.4 ⎟	1.4 ⎟	2.5 ⎟
Florida	0.4 ⎭	0.3 ⎭	0.3 ⎭	0.4 ⎭	0.5 ⎭
Washington, D.C.	3.0 } 3.0	2.0 } 2.0	4.7 } 4.7	3.1 } 3.1	2.2 } 2.2
East South Central					
Kentucky	1.6 ⎫	0.9 ⎫	1.2 ⎫	1.5 ⎫	2.3 ⎫
Tennessee	2.2 ⎬ 6.7	1.1 ⎬ 3.9	1.6 ⎬ 5.1	2.0 ⎬ 6.2	2.2 ⎬ 7.8
Alabama	1.7 ⎟	1.0 ⎟	1.0 ⎟	1.5 ⎟	2.0 ⎟
Mississippi	1.2 ⎭	0.9 ⎭	1.3 ⎭	1.2 ⎭	1.3 ⎭
West South Central					
Arkansas	1.1 ⎫	1.5 ⎫	0.6 ⎫	1.0 ⎫	1.5 ⎫
Louisiana	0.8 ⎬ 6.0	0.7 ⎬ 7.1	0.6 ⎬ 6.1	0.8 ⎬ 6.0	0.9 ⎬ 11.2
Oklahoma	1.3 ⎟	2.3 ⎟	1.7 ⎟	1.4 ⎟	2.7 ⎟
Texas	2.8 ⎭	2.6 ⎭	3.2 ⎭	2.8 ⎭	6.1 ⎭

[continued]

TABLE 7B (Chap. 3)
[continued]

State	Career civil service exec.	Foreign-service exec.	Political exec.	Civilian federal exec.	Military exec.
East North Central					
Michigan	2.2% ⎫	2.7% ⎫	2.2% ⎫	2.3% ⎫	2.3% ⎫
Ohio	5.8 ⎪	4.8 ⎪	4.7 ⎪	5.5 ⎪	3.7 ⎪
Indiana	3.1 ⎬19.2	2.3 ⎬18.8	2.4 ⎬18.1	3.0 ⎬19.1	2.6 ⎬16.0
Illinois	5.7 ⎪	7.0 ⎪	6.2 ⎪	5.9 ⎪	5.5 ⎪
Wisconsin	2.4 ⎭	2.0 ⎭	2.6 ⎭	2.4 ⎭	1.9 ⎭
West North Central					
Minnesota	2.9 ⎫	1.9 ⎫	3.0 ⎫	2.8 ⎫	2.4 ⎫
North Dakota	1.0 ⎪	0.6 ⎪	0.6 ⎪	0.9 ⎪	0.6 ⎪
South Dakota	0.9 ⎪	0.8 ⎪	1.5 ⎪	1.0 ⎪	1.1 ⎪
Nebraska	2.2 ⎬16.6	1.2 ⎬13.7	2.1 ⎬16.4	2.1 ⎬16.3	1.6 ⎬13.7
Iowa	3.3 ⎪	2.7 ⎪	3.7 ⎪	3.3 ⎪	2.5 ⎪
Kansas	2.5 ⎪	2.9 ⎪	2.8 ⎪	2.6 ⎪	2.2 ⎪
Missouri	3.8 ⎭	3.6 ⎭	2.7 ⎭	3.6 ⎭	3.3 ⎭
Mountain					
Montana	0.6 ⎫	1.2 ⎫	0.7 ⎫	0.7 ⎫	0.8 ⎫
Idaho	0.8 ⎪	0.7 ⎪	0.7 ⎪	0.7 ⎪	0.6 ⎪
Wyoming	0.3 ⎪	0.1 ⎪	0.3 ⎪	0.3 ⎪	0.1 ⎪
Nevada	0.1 ⎬5.3	0.1 ⎬6.0	0.2 ⎬4.7	0.1 ⎬5.2	0.1 ⎬6.1
Utah	1.3 ⎪	1.7 ⎪	1.0 ⎪	1.3 ⎪	1.3 ⎪
Colorado	1.7 ⎪	1.2 ⎪	1.6 ⎪	1.6 ⎪	1.7 ⎪
Arizona	0.2 ⎪	0.6 ⎪	0.1 ⎪	0.2 ⎪	0.8 ⎪
New Mexico	0.3 ⎭	0.4 ⎭	0.1 ⎭	0.3 ⎭	0.7 ⎭
Pacific					
Washington	1.7 ⎫	1.2 ⎫	1.9 ⎫	1.7 ⎫	1.9 ⎫
Oregon	0.8 ⎬4.5	1.5 ⎬6.6	0.7 ⎬5.3	0.9 ⎬4.9	1.2 ⎬7.0
California	2.0 ⎭	3.9 ⎭	2.7 ⎭	2.3 ⎭	3.9 ⎭
Total	100.0	100.0	100.0	100.0	100.0
	100.0	100.0	100.0	100.0	100.0

TABLE 8B (Chap. 3)

Ratio Comparison of 1952 Business Leaders* and 1959 Federal Executives by Region of Birth with 1900 and 1910 Adult Population, Respectively, by Region of Residence

Region of birth	Business leaders	Civilian federal executives	Career civil service executives	Foreign-service executives	Political executives	Military executives
New England	1.43	1.14	1.00	1.29	1.29	1.14
Middle Atlantic	1.47	1.05	1.05	1.10	1.00	0.76
East North Central	1.18	0.95	0.95	0.95	0.90	0.85
West North Central	1.00	1.23	1.31	1.08	1.31	1.08
South Atlantic	0.57	1.00	0.92	0.85	1.08	1.08
East South Central	0.40	0.67	0.78	0.44	0.56	0.89
West South Central	0.44	0.67	0.67	0.78	0.67	1.11
Mountain	1.00	1.67	1.67	2.00	1.67	2.00
Pacific	1.33	1.00	1.00	1.40	1.00	1.40
	N=7,500	N=10,851	N=7,640	N=1,269	N=1,865	N=2,078

*Warner and Abegglen, Occupational Mobility, Table 21.

TABLE 9B (Chap. 3)

Distribution by Region of Present Legal Residence of 1959 Civilian Federal Executives and 1950 Adult Male Population

		Civilian Federal Executives	
Region	1950 male adult population		Residence ratio
New England	6%	3%	0.50
Middle Atlantic	21	9	0.43
East North Central	21	11	0.52
West North Central	10	5	0.50
South Atlantic	13	50	3.85
East South Central	7	5	0.71
West South Central	9	5	0.56
Mountain	3	5	1.67
Pacific	10	7	0.70
Total	100	100	

TABLE 10B (Chap. 3)

Regional Retention of Potential Civilian Federal Executives

	Regional Stability	Regional Gain or Loss	
Region	Executives born in region who are now in region	Increase or decrease over number of executives born in region	Average ratio mobility out of region
New England	60%	− 58%	0.52
Middle Atlantic	66	− 59	0.52
East North Central	54	− 44	0.66
West North Central	64	− 71	0.83
South Atlantic	19	+294	0.43
East South Central	46	− 16	0.58
West South Central	49	− 23	0.61
Mountain	33	− 2	0.75
Pacific	25	+ 58	0.53

TABLE 11B (Chap. 3)

Geographical Mobility Ratios: 1959 Civilian Federal Executives' Movement out of Region of Birth into Region of Present Legal Residence*

Region of Present Legal Residence

Region of birth	Distribution by region of birth	New England	Middle Atlantic	East North Central	West North Central	South Atlantic	East South Central	West South Central	Mountain	Pacific	Average mobility out of region
New England	8%		0.88	0.50	0.25	1.00	0.50	0.25	0.38	0.38	0.52
Middle Atlantic	22	0.77		0.59	0.27	1.09	0.36	0.18	0.27	0.59	0.52
East North Central	19	0.42	0.42		0.63	0.89	0.63	0.53	0.84	0.95	0.66
West North Central	16	0.38	0.38	0.75		0.94	0.69	1.00	1.19	1.31	0.83
South Atlantic	13	0.31	0.46	0.46	0.23		0.85	0.46	0.31	0.38	0.43
East South Central	6	0.33	0.33	0.50	0.67	0.83		1.00	0.83	0.17	0.58
West South Central	6	0.17	0.33	0.50	0.67	0.67	0.83		1.00	0.67	0.61
Mountain	5	0.40	0.40	0.60	0.60	0.80	0.20	1.00		2.00	0.75
Pacific	5	0.00	0.20	0.40	0.40	0.80	0.40	0.40	1.60		0.53

*Random movement into a region = 1; mean = 0.60.

TABLE 12B (Chap. 3)

Comparison of Geographical Mobility of U. S.-Born 1952
Business Leaders and 1959 Federal Executives

Percentage of Executives Who Moved

Type of mobility	Career civil service exec.	Political exec.	Foreign-service exec.	Civilian federal exec.	Business leaders
Intrastate	9	11	1	9	33
Intrastate, rural to urban	4	3	0*	3	7
Interstate, intra-region	12	10	3	11	15
Interregion	75	73	26	67	45
Abroad	0	3	70	10	0
Total	100	100	100	100	100

*Less than 0.5 per cent.

TABLE 13B (Chap. 4)

Size of Birthplace of 1959 Civilian Federal Executives and Size of Community of Residence of 1910 U.S. Population[*]

Size of community	Civilian federal executives born in community	1910 U.S. population living in community	Ratio of civilian federal executives to population
All Civilian Federal Executives			
400,000 and over	21%	11%	1.91
100,000–400,000	12	8	1.50
25,000–100,000	12	8	1.50
2,500–25,000	21	15	1.40
Under 2,500	34	58	0.59
Total	100	100	
	N = 10,692		
Washington Civilian Federal Executives			
400,000 and over	24	11	2.18
100,000–400,000	12	8	1.50
25,000–100,000	12	8	1.50
2,500–25,000	20	15	1.33
Under 2,500	32	58	0.55
Total	100	100	
	N = 5,515		
Field Civilian Federal Executives			
400,000 and over	19	11	1.73
100,000–400,000	11	8	1.38
25,000–100,000	11	8	1.38
2,500–25,000	22	15	1.47
Under 2,500	37	58	0.64
Total	100	100	
	N = 4,899		

[*]Bureau of the Census, 1910, Vol. I, Table 37.

TABLE 14B (Chap. 4)

Occupations and Types of Communities of Fathers of 1959 Civilian Federal Executives

Occupation of father	North Over 100,000	North Under 25,000	Midwest Over 100,000	Midwest Under 25,000	South Over 100,000	South Under 25,000	West Over 100,000	West Under 25,000	All Regions Over 100,000	All Regions Under 25,000
All Civilian Federal Executives										
Laborer	28%	24%	21%	18%	23%	14%	17%	19%	25%	18%
Owner of small business	19	16	14	14	12	14	15	12	16	14
White-collar worker	23	21	25	16	29	17	26	17	24	17
Major business executive or owner of large business	13	10	17	7	12	9	13	8	14	8
Professional man	16	18	20	16	22	19	25	16	19	17
Farmer	1	11	3	29	2	27	4	28	2	26
Total	100	100	100	100	100	100	100	100	100	100
Washington Civilian Federal Executives										
Laborer	26	24	17	16	24	12	16	17	23	17
Owner of small business	19	15	15	14	13	13	18	11	17	14
White-collar worker	23	21	24	14	28	17	22	17	25	17
Major business executive or owner of large business	15	10	20	7	13	8	11	8	15	8
Professional man	16	20	21	18	21	22	30	21	19	19
Farmer	1	10	3	31	1	28	3	26	1	25
Total	100	100	100	100	100	100	100	100	100	100

[continued]

TABLE 14B (Chap. 4)
[continued]

Field Civilian Federal Executives

Occupation of father	North Over 100,000	North Under 25,000	Midwest Over 100,000	Midwest Under 25,000	South Over 100,000	South Under 25,000	West Over 100,000	West Under 25,000	All Regions Over 100,000	All Regions Under 25,000
Laborer	32%	22%	25%	20%	22%	15%	19%	20%	28%	19%
Owner of small business	18	18	12	13	8	14	12	12	15	14
White-collar worker	22	22	25	17	31	17	29	18	24	18
Major business executive or owner of large business	11	10	16	6	12	10	14	8	13	8
Professional man	16	16	19	15	24	16	21	13	18	15
Farmer	1	12	3	29	3	28	5	29	2	26
Total	100	100	100	100	100	100	100	100	100	100

335

TABLE 15B (Chap. 4)

Ratio of Nativity of 1952 Business Leaders and 1959 Federal Executives and U. S. Population*

	Career civil service exec.	Political exec.	Foreign-service exec.	Civilian federal exec.	Business leaders	Military exec.
Executive foreign born	0.47	0.60	0.63	0.51	0.55	0.21
Executive U.S. born	1.19	1.15	0.95	1.15	1.01	0.64
Father and executive U.S. born Paternal grandfather, father, and executive U.S. born	1.01	1.00	1.05	1.01	1.06	1.16

*$\dfrac{1952 \text{ business leaders}}{1940 \text{ U.S. population}}$ = ratio.

$\dfrac{1959 \text{ federal executives}}{1950 \text{ U.S. population}}$ = ratio.

TABLE 16B (Chap. 4)

Occupational Mobility and Nativity: Occupations of Fathers of 1959 Civilian Federal Executives in Four Nativity Categories

Occupation of father	Executive foreign born	Executive U.S. born	Father and executive U.S. born	Father's father, father, and executive U.S. born	Percentage of all 1959 civilian federal executives
	All Civilian Federal Executives				
	(4% of total)	(20% of total)	(18% of total)	(58% of total)	
Unskilled and semi-skilled laborer	4%	8%	4%	2%	4%
Skilled laborer	17	24	19	14	17
Owner of small business	16	25	11	12	14
Clerk or salesman	6	6	12	10	9
Minor business executive	9	8	13	11	11
Major business executive	5	2	5	5	4
Owner of large business	8	7	7	5	6
Professional man	26	10	15	22	19
Farmer	6	9	13	17	15
Other	3	1	1	2	1
Total	100	100	100	100	100

[continued]

TABLE 16B (Chap. 4)
[continued]

Occupation of father	Executive foreign born	Executive U.S. born	Father and executive U.S. born	Father's father, father, and executive U.S. born	Percentage of all 1959 civilian federal executives
		Washington Civilian Federal Executives			
	(4% of total)	(21% of total)	(17% of total)	(58% of total)	
Unskilled and semi-skilled laborer	4%	6%	3%	2%	3%
Skilled laborer	20	25	18	13	17
Owner of small business	16	25	13	11	14
Clerk or salesman	5	7	12	9	9
Minor business executive	6	8	13	12	11
Major business executive	5	2	5	6	5
Owner of large business	9	8	7	6	6
Professional man	26	10	16	24	20
Farmer	5	8	12	16	14
Other	4	1	1	1	1
Total	100	100	100	100	100

TABLE 16B (Chap. 4)
[continued]

Occupation of father	Executive foreign born (4% of total)	Executive U.S. born (19% of total)	Father and executive U.S. born (18% of total)	Father's father, father, and executive U.S. born (59% of total)	Percentage of all 1959 civilian federal executives
		Field Civilian Federal Executives			
Unskilled and semi-skilled laborer	4%	10%	5%	2%	4%
Skilled laborer	15	23	20	15	18
Owner of small business	17	23	10	12	14
Clerk or salesman	6	6	11	10	9
Minor business executive	11	9	13	11	11
Major business executive	4	2	5	5	4
Owner of large business	7	7	7	5	6
Professional man	26	9	14	20	17
Farmer	7	11	14	18	16
Other	3	0*	1	2	1
Total	100	100	100	100	100

*Less than 0.5 per cent.

TABLE 17B (Chap. 4)

Distribution by Nativity and Occupation of 1959 Federal Executives' Fathers and of 1930 U. S. Adult Males*

Occupation of father	Foreign Born			U. S. Born		
	Fathers of civilian federal executives	Fathers of military executives	U.S. adult males in 1930	Fathers of civilian federal executives	Fathers of military executives	U.S. adult males in 1930
Unskilled or semi-skilled laborer	8%	4%	44%	2%	2%	26%
Skilled laborer	24	23	20	15	10	16
Clerk or salesman	6	5	8	10	10	15
Business owner or executive	42	41	14	35	39	12
Professional man	10	12	3	20	19	5
Farm laborer, owner, tenant	9	10	10	17	10	25
Uniformed service	1	5	1	1	10	1
Other						
Total	100	100	100	100	100	100

*Fifteenth Census, 1930, Vol. IV, Occupations by States, Table 11.

TABLE 18B (Chap. 4)

Comparisons among the Services of Native and Foreign-Born Executives' Fathers

	U.S. male adult working force in 1930*	Fathers of civilian federal executives	Fathers of career civil service executives	Fathers of political executives	Fathers of foreign-service executives	Fathers of business leaders	Fathers of U.S. male adult working force in 1920†
U.S. born	80.2	79.0	78.5	78.8	82.5	76.2	75.0
Foreign born	19.8	21.0	21.5	21.2	17.5	23.8	25.0

*Fifteenth Census, 1930, Vol. IV, Table 20.

†Warner and Abbegglen, Occupational Mobility, p. 93, Table 36.

TABLE 19B (Chap. 5)

Occupational Mobility in Three Generations: Occupations of Fathers and Paternal Grandfathers of 1959 Civilian Federal Executives

Occupation	Paternal Grandfather 22 occupational groups	Paternal Grandfather 8 occupational groups	Father 22 occupational groups	Father 8 occupational groups	Civilian Federal Executive 22 occupational groups	Civilian Federal Executive 8 occupational groups
Unskilled or semi-skilled laborer	4.6%	18%	3.5%	21%		
Skilled laborer	13.9		17.0			
Farm tenant or farm worker	2.1	44	0.4	15		
Tenant with paid help	1.4		0.7			
Farm owner without paid help	24.9		6.5			
Owner or manager with paid help	15.7		7.1			
Clerk or retail salesman	1.5	3	3.8	9		
Salesman	1.2		5.3			
Foreman	2.1	4	4.9	11		
Minor executive	1.8		5.9			
Major executive	1.7	2	4.6	4	100.0%	100%
Owner of small business	13.7	18	14.3	20		
Owner of medium business	3.0		4.3			
Owner of large business	1.1		1.9			
Doctor	1.9	10	2.5	19		
Engineer	0.9		3.1			
Lawyer	1.8		3.8			
Minister	3.0		2.8			
Other professional	2.7		6.3			
Uniformed service	0.6	1	0.7	1		
Government service	0.1		0.2			
Other occupations	0.3		0.4			
Total per cent	100.0	100	100.0	100	100.0	100
Total number		9,449		10,419		10,851

TABLE 20B (Chap. 5)

Movement of 1959 Civilian Federal Executives' Fathers out of Occupations of Paternal Grandfathers: Distribution of Fathers in Each of Ten Occupational Groups According to Occupation of Father's Father

Occupation of father's father	Semi-skilled or un-skilled laborer	Skilled laborer	Owner of small business	Clerk	Minor business executive	Major business executive	Owner of large business	Professional man	Farmer	Other	Distribution of fathers' fathers in occupational groups
Unskilled or semi-skilled laborer	35%	9%	3%	2%	5%	2%	1%	2%	1%	2%	4%
Skilled laborer	6	34	12	15	16	11	9	9	3	7	14
Owner of small business	8	8	29	20	14	14	19	12	4	12	14
Clerk	1	2	3	8	4	3	3	2	0	2	3
Minor business executive	0*	2	2	5	10	11	4	4	1	7	4
Major business executive	1	1	1	1	2	10	2	2	0*	6	2
Owner of large business	0*	1	2	4	4	7	24	5	1	4	4
Professional man	2	5	7	9	8	16	7	26	4	13	10
Farmer	46	37	40	35	36	25	31	37	86	34	44
Other	1	1	1	1	1	1	0	1	0*	13	1
Total	100	100	100	100	100	100	100	100	100	100	100

*Less than 0.5 per cent.

TABLE 21B (Chap. 5)

Ratios of Movement out of Occupations of 1959 Civilian Federal Executives' Paternal Grandfathers into Occupations of Fathers*

Occupation of father's father	Semi-skilled or unskilled laborer	Skilled laborer	Owner of small business	Clerk	Minor business executive	Major business executive	Owner of large business	Professional man	Farmer	Other	Mean mobility ratio out of occupation
Unskilled or semi-skilled laborer	<u>7.59</u>	2.02	0.74	0.52	1.09	0.35	0.35	0.35	0.22	0.37	0.67
Skilled laborer	0.43	<u>2.43</u>	0.87	1.10	1.14	0.82	0.61	0.63	0.23	0.55	0.71
Owner of small business	0.56	0.59	<u>2.13</u>	1.43	1.06	1.02	1.37	0.91	0.26	0.88	0.90
Clerk	0.22	0.78	0.96	<u>2.93</u>	1.44	1.26	1.07	0.93	0.19	0.63	0.83
Minor business executive	0.08	0.54	0.46	1.21	<u>2.59</u>	2.87	1.02	0.97	0.28	1.74	1.02
Major business executive	0.76	0.41	0.41	0.82	1.18	<u>6.06</u>	0.94	1.29	0.06	3.53	1.04
Owner of large business	0.07	0.27	0.49	0.98	0.95	1.63	<u>5.83</u>	1.17	0.15	1.02	0.75
Professional man	0.19	0.47	0.66	0.91	0.73	1.59	0.70	<u>2.53</u>	0.34	1.25	0.76
Farmer	1.05	0.85	0.92	0.78	0.82	0.56	0.71	0.83	<u>1.95</u>	0.78	0.81

*Mean = 0.83; diagonal mean = 3.78

Appendix B

TABLE 22B (Chap. 5)
Civilian Federal Executives: Sources and Channels of Mobility*

Father's father	Father	Major federal executive
Major business executive[†]	Major business executive	5.72
	Professional man	1.22
	White-collar worker	0.94
Professional man[†]	Professional man	2.50
	Major business executive	1.57
	White-collar worker	0.81
White-collar worker	Major business executive	2.18
	White-collar worker	2.00
	Professional man	0.94
Business owner[†]	Business owner	1.94
	Major business executive	1.16
	White-collar worker	1.16
	Professional man	0.96
Laborer[†]	Laborer	2.31
	White-collar worker	1.05
	Business owner	0.75
	Major business executive	0.70
Farmer[†]	Farmer	1.96
	Laborer	0.89
	Business owner	0.86
	White-collar worker	0.81

*A reinterpretation of the data used in Table 8 of the text, showing principal succession of occupation.

[†]Occupations in which there is occupational continuity from father's father to father's generation.

TABLE 23B (Chap. 5)

Occupational Mobility in Three Generations: Occupations of Fathers and Paternal Grandfathers of 1959 Military Executives

Occupation	Paternal Grandfather 22 occupational groups	Paternal Grandfather 9 occupational groups	Father 22 occupational groups	Father 9 occupational groups	Military Leader 22 occupational groups	Military Leader 9 occupational groups
Unskilled or semi-skilled laborer	3.4%	15%	1.9%	14%		
Skilled laborer	11.3		12.1			
Farm tenant or farm worker	1.4	41	0.4	10		
Tenant with paid help	1.0		0.6			
Farm owner without paid help	19.1		3.0			
Owner or manager with paid help	19.1		5.7			
Clerk or retail salesman	1.5	3	3.0	9		
Salesman	1.6		6.1			
Foreman	3.1	6	4.9	15		
Minor executive	3.3		9.8			
Major executive	2.6	2	5.5	5	100%	100%
Owner of small business	13.7	18	13.4	19		
Owner of medium business	3.0		4.0			
Owner of large business	0.9		1.8			
Doctor	2.4	13	3.9	18		
Engineer	0.8		2.8			
Lawyer	3.7		5.1			
Minister	3.1		1.7			
Other professional	2.9		5.1			
Uniformed service	1.9	2	8.5	9		
Government service	0.2	0*	0.4	1		
Other occupations	0.0		0.3			
Total per cent	100.0	100	100.0	100	100	100
Total number		1,854		2,015		2,078

*Less than 0.5 per cent.

Appendix B

TABLE 24B (Chap. 5)

Military Executives: Sources and Channels of Mobility*

Paternal grandfather	Father	Major federal executive
Major business executive†	Major business executive	4.35
	White-collar worker	1.35
	Professional man	0.77
	Business owner	0.77
	Uniformed service	0.73
Professional man	Professional man	1.95
	Uniformed service	2.06
	Major business executive	1.39
White-collar worker†	White-collar worker	2.07
	Uniformed service	1.37
	Major business executive	0.99
	Professional man	0.94
Business owner	Business owner	1.94
	White-collar worker	1.95
	Major business executive	1.56
	Uniformed service	1.03
Laborer†	Laborer	2.63
	White-collar worker	1.17
	Major business executive	0.90
	Business owner	0.74
Farmer†	Farmer	2.06
	Laborer	1.04
	Business owner	0.95
	Professional man	0.98
Uniformed service†	Uniformed service	7.16
	Professional man	1.05
	White-collar worker	0.47
	Business owner	0.47

*A reinterpretation of the data of Table 9 in the text, showing principal succession of occupations.

†Occupations in which there is occupational continuity from father's father to father's generation.

TABLE 25B (Chap. 5)

Big Business Leaders: Sources and Channels of Mobility

Father's father	Father	Business leader
Major business executive*	Major business executive	3.60
	Professional man	0.80
	White-collar worker	0.60
	Business owner	0.60
Professional man*	Professional man	2.70
	Major business executive	1.20
	White-collar worker	0.80
White-collar worker*	White-collar worker	2.20
	Major business executive	1.40
	Professional man	1.00
	Business owner	0.80
Business owner*	Business owner	1.56
	Major business executive	1.32
	White-collar worker	1.04
	Professional man	0.80
Laborer*	Laborer	2.65
	White-collar worker	1.10
	Business owner	0.70
Farmer*	Farmer	2.37
	Professional man	1.00
	White-collar worker	0.86
	Business owner	0.97

* Occupations in which there is occupational continuity from father's father to father's generation.

Appendix B

TABLE 26B (Chap. 6)

Occupations of Father's Father and Mother's Father
of 1959 Civilian Federal Executives

Occupation	Paternal Grandfather 22 occupational groups	Paternal Grandfather 8 occupational groups	Maternal Grandfather 22 occupational groups	Maternal Grandfather 8 occupational groups
Unskilled or semiskilled laborer	4.6%	18%	4.3%	19%
Skilled laborer	13.9		14.5	
Farm tenant or farm worker	2.1	44	1.7	39
Tenant with paid help	1.4		1.4	
Farm owner without paid help	24.9		21.4	
Owner or manager with paid help	15.7		14.3	
Clerk or retail salesman	1.5	3	2.2	4
Salesman	1.2		1.8	
Foreman	2.1	4	2.4	5
Minor executive	1.8		2.2	
Major executive	1.7	2	1.9	2
Owner of small business	13.7	18	15.6	20
Owner of medium business	3.0		3.5	
Owner of large business	1.1		1.4	
Doctor	1.9	10	1.9	10
Engineer	0.9		1.0	
Lawyer	1.8		2.0	
Minister	3.0		2.6	
Other professional	2.7		2.8	
Uniformed service	0.6	1	0.6	1
Government service	0.1		0.1	
Other occupations	0.3		0.4	
Total per cent	100.0	100	100.0	100
Total number		9,449		9,506

TABLE 27B (Chap. 7)

Occupations of Civilian Federal Executives' Fathers
and Occupations of Spouses' Fathers

Occupation	Spouse's father		Executive's father
Laborer		21%	21%
Unskilled or semiskilled	3%		
Skilled	18		
White-collar worker		9	9
Clerk or retail salesman	4		
Salesman	5		
Minor executive		11	11
Foreman	5		
Minor executive	6		
Major executive		4	4
Business owner		23	20
Small business	14		
Medium business	6		
Large business	3		
Professional man		16	19
Doctor	2		
Engineer	3		
Lawyer	3		
Minister	2		
Other profession	6		
Farmer		15	15
Farm worker or tenant	1		
Farm owner or manager	14		
Other occupations		1	1
Uniformed service	1		
Government service	0*		
Total per cent	100	100	100
Total number	9,601		

*Less than 0.5 per cent.

TABLE 28B (Chap. 7)

Comparison of Occupational Origins of Wives in the Several Services

Occupation	Political executives Father	Political executives Spouse's father	Career civil service executives Father	Career civil service executives Spouse's father	Foreign-service executives Father	Foreign-service executives Spouse's father	Military executives Father	Military executives Spouse's father	Civilian federal executives Father	Civilian federal executives Spouse's father	Business leaders Father	Business leaders Spouse's father
Laborer	15%	17%	23%	24%	14%	12%	14%	12%	21%	21%	15%	17%
White-collar worker	9	10	10	9	7	7	9	8	9	9	8	7
Minor executive	10	10	11	10	11	11	15	12	11	11	11	7
Major executive	6	5	4	3	9	9	5	7	4	4	15	8
Business owner	21	25	20	22	19	24	19	22	20	23	26	28
Professional	24	19	16	15	25	23	18	19	19	16	14	15
Farmer	13	12	15	16	12	11	10	8	15	15	9	15
Military executive							9	11				
Other	2	2	1	1	3	3	1	1	1	1	2	3
Total per cent	100	100	100	100	100	100	100	100	100	100	100	100
Total number		1,575		6,828		1,134		1,943		9,601		6,968

TABLE 29B (Chap. 7)

Education and Marriage of Civilian Federal Executives and Business Leaders when Both Father and Father's Father were Major Executives, Owners of Large Business, or Professional Men

	Education of Federal Executives and Business Leaders			
	College Graduation		H. S. Graduation or Some College	
Occupation of spouse's father	Federal executives	Business leaders	Federal executives	Business leaders
Laborer	9%	2%	17%	9%
White-collar worker or owner of small business	29	27	32	27
Major executive, owner of large business, or professional man	53	64	35	53
Farmer	9	7	16	11
Total	100	100	100	100

TABLE 30B (Chap. 7)

Marriage and Achievement Time: Mean Number of Years to Achieve Federal Position for Executives by Occupation of Father and Spouse's Father

	Occupation of Civilian Federal Executive's Father					
Occupation of spouse's father	Laborer	White-collar worker	Owner of small business	Major executive or owner of large business	Professional man	Farmer
Laborer	17.8	16.9	19.0	16.2	16.4	18.8
White-collar worker	17.4	16.9	16.9	15.0	16.3	18.6
Owner of small business	16.9	17.4	16.6	16.3	16.7	19.5
Major executive or owner of large business	15.7	15.5	16.0	14.9	14.6	18.3
Professional man	16.8	15.8	17.0	15.1	15.9	17.8
Farmer	19.2	17.6	19.5	17.8	16.6	19.3
Mean for background	17.5	16.7	17.4	15.5	16.0	18.8

TABLE 31B (Chap. 7)

Nativity and Marriage of 1959 Civilian Federal Executives

Occupation of spouse's father	Father's father U.S. born	Father U.S. Born	Executive U.S. born	Executive foreign born	Total
Laborer	18%	25%	26%	16%	22%
White-collar worker	20	22	18	17	20
Owner of small business	13	13	19	20	14
Major executive or owner of large business	13	11	13	18	13
Professional man	18	16	13	20	16
Farmer	18	13	11	9	15
Total	100	100	100	100	100

TABLE 32B (Chap. 7)

Nativity and Marriage of 1959 Military Executives

Occupation of spouse's father	Father's father U.S. born	Father U.S. born	Executive U.S. born	Executive foreign born	Total
Laborer	11%	15%	19%	14%	12%
White-collar worker	19	19	18	14	19
Owner of small business	13	12	9	11	12
Major executive or owner of large business	18	17	15	18	18
Professional man	19	18	18	25	19
Farmer	9	7	11	7	9
Uniformed service	11	12	10	11	11
Total	100	100	100	100	100

TABLE 33B (Chap. 8)

Comparison of Education of 1959 Federal Executives and 1952 Business Leaders with Population of the United States

Education of executive	U.S. adult males (30 years and over) in 1957	Civilian federal exec.	Career civil service exec.	Foreign-service exec.	Political exec.	Military exec.	U.S. adult males (30 years and over) in 1950	Business leaders
Less than high school	46%	0%*	0%*	0%*	0%*	0%*	55%	4%
Some high school	17	1	2	0*	1	0*	16	9
High school graduation	21	4	5	2	2	2	16	11
Some college	7	14	15	10	7	10	6	19
College graduation†	9	81	78	88	90	88	7	57
Total	100	100	100	100	100	100	100	100

*Less than 0.5 per cent.

†Includes four-year and more than four-year programs resulting in an earned degree.

TABLE 34B (Chap. 8)

Ratios of Educational Levels of Men in the Elites to Educational Levels of U.S. Adult Males[*]

Education of executive	Civilian federal exec.	Career civil service exec.	Foreign-service exec.	Political exec.	Military exec.	Business leaders
Less than high school	0.00	0.00	0.00	0.00	0.00	0.08
Some high school	0.06	0.19	0.00	0.06	0.00	0.56
High school graduation	0.19	0.24	0.09	0.09	0.09	0.69
Some college	2.00	2.14	1.43	1.00	1.43	3.17
College graduation	9.00	8.67	9.78	10.00	9.78	8.14

[*] $\dfrac{1952 \text{ business leaders}}{1950 \text{ U.S. adult males}}$ = ratio.

$\dfrac{1959 \text{ federal executives}}{1957 \text{ U.S. adult males}}$ = ratio.

TABLE 35B (Chap. 8)

Percentages, by Education of the Father, of Executives at Three Educational Levels

Executive	Less than high school	High school	College
Executives Who Went to College			
Civilian federal executives	91%	94%	98%
Career civil service executives	90	93	97
Foreign-service executives	98	97	99
Political executives	96	96	99
Military executives	98	97	99
Business leaders	63	80	91
Executives Who Went to High School			
Civilian federal executives	8	6	2
Career civil service executives	9	7	3
Foreign-service executives	2	3	1
Political executives	4	4	1
Military executives	2	3	1
Business leaders	29	19	8
Executives with Less than High School			
Civilian federal executives	1	0*	0*
Career civil service executives	1	0*	0*
Foreign-service executives	0*	0*	0
Political executives	0*	0*	0*
Military executives	0*	0	0
Business leaders	8	1	1

*Less than 0.5 per cent.

Appendix B

TABLE 36B (Chap. 8)

Executives Who Reported College Degrees

Executive	Bachelor's degree*	Master's degree	Doctor of Philosophy	Law degree	Doctor of Medicine
All civilian	70.7%	24.1%	10.5%	14.4%	2.7%
Career civil service	68.7	23.7	9.5	9.4	3.0
Political	72.5	19.8	12.5	39.9	2.1
Foreign service	80.6	32.7	12.9	8.0	1.4
Military	83.8	23.6	1.1	3.5	4.1

*The figures presented here for those who received bachelor's degrees are somewhat lower than the figure for "college graduation" shown in Table 33B, which is based on the total of all who reported that they had graduated from college. This table is based specifically on degrees reported and is therefore to some extent an underestimate. Some executives reported only the highest degree they held.

TABLE 37B (Chap. 8)

Sons of Fathers in Each Occupational Group Who Reported Master's Degrees

Occupation of father	Civilian federal exec.	Career civil service exec.	Political exec.	Foreign-service exec.	Military exec.
Unskilled or semi-skilled laborer	25.6%	22.6%	29.7%	45.7%	30.8%
Skilled laborer	19.8	18.9	17.2	34.8	23.8
Owner of small business	23.3	23.7	18.5	28.1	22.2
Clerk or salesman	22.9	21.6	24.0	32.9	30.1
Foreman	15.2	14.1	11.1	32.5	17.3
Minor or major business executive	22.2	22.1	17.5	27.3	27.1
Owner of large business	22.9	23.3	17.0	29.8	17.8
Professional man	29.3	30.5	20.6	36.4	24.2
Farm laborer	14.3	18.8	00.0	00.0	25.0
Farm tenant or owner	29.4	29.0	25.7	38.5	23.9
Uniformed service	20.5	21.9	29.4	13.6	16.9
All occupations*	24.1	23.7	19.8	32.7	23.6

*Percentages computed for all occupational categories combined.

Appendix B

TABLE 38B (Chap. 8)

Sons of Fathers in Each Occupational Group Who
Reported Doctor of Philosophy Degrees

Occupation of father	Civilian federal exec.	Career civil service exec.	Political exec.	Foreign-service exec.	Military exec.
Unskilled or semi-skilled laborer	8.6%	7.4%	13.5%	14.3%	0.0%
Skilled laborer	7.1	6.3	10.0	10.4	0.4
Owner of small business	10.5	9.7	10.1	17.3	0.7
Clerk or salesman	9.2	7.0	12.3	20.0	1.1
Foreman	5.4	5.5	5.6	2.5	2.0
Minor or major business executive	7.9	6.7	11.5	7.6	0.6
Owner of large business	9.9	8.9	9.8	12.8	0.8
Professional man	14.8	14.7	14.8	13.8	2.7
Farm laborer	9.5	9.4	14.3	0.0	0.0
Farm tenant or owner	14.6	13.7	17.3	17.6	1.6
Uniformed service	5.5	3.1	17.6	0.0	0.0
All occupations*	10.5	9.5	12.5	12.9	1.1

*Percentages computed for all occupational categories combined.

TABLE 39B (Chap. 8)

Sons of Fathers in Each Occupational Group Who Reported Medical Degrees

Occupation of father	Civilian federal exec.	Career civil service exec.	Political exec.	Foreign-service exec.	Military exec.
Unskilled or semi-skilled laborer	3.1%	3.5%	0.0%	2.9%	15.4%
Skilled laborer	2.0	2.1	1.8	0.7	4.9
Owner of small business	2.6	2.9	1.8	1.4	2.2
Clerk or salesman	2.3	2.4	1.9	1.2	2.7
Foreman	2.5	3.0	1.4	0.0	3.1
Minor or major business executive	1.9	2.4	1.4	1.0	1.3
Owner of large business	2.7	2.9	2.0	2.1	5.1
Professional man	3.8	4.1	3.7	2.6	7.3
Farm laborer	2.4	3.1	0.0	0.0	0.0
Farm tenant or owner	3.0	3.9	0.4	0.0	5.9
Uniformed service	9.6	12.5	11.8	0.0	1.7
All occupations[*]	2.7	3.0	2.1	1.4	4.1

[*]Percentages computed for all occupational categories combined.

Appendix B

TABLE 40B (Chap. 8)

Sons of Fathers in Each Occupational Group
Who Reported Law Degrees

Occupation of father	Civilian federal exec.	Career civil service exec.	Political exec.	Foreign- service exec.	Military exec.
Unskilled or semi-skilled laborer	15.4%	10.2%	43.2%	8.6%	0.0%
Skilled laborer	12.8	8.7	41.2	8.1	2.5
Owner of small business	16.5	11.8	43.6	9.4	3.3
Clerk or salesman	13.3	8.6	39.6	4.7	4.9
Foreman	11.9	9.3	26.4	10.0	4.1
Minor or major business executive	15.4	10.1	42.4	4.0	3.5
Owner of large business	18.1	10.7	41.8	9.6	5.9
Professional man	17.8	10.0	45.0	10.2	3.8
Farm laborer	9.5	0.0	42.9	50.0	25.0
Farm tenant or owner	9.8	6.8	25.7	8.1	2.7
Uniformed service	6.8	3.1	23.5	0.0	1.2
All occupations[*]	14.4	9.4	39.9	8.0	3.5

[*]Percentages computed for all occupational categories combined.

TABLE 41B (Chap. 8)

Degrees and Area of Specialization of 1959 Civilian Federal Executives*

Area of Specialization

Degree	Human-ities	Behav. science	Phys. science	Biol. science	Educa-tion	Bus. admin.	Pub. admin.	Medi-cine†	Law†	Engi-neering	Military science	Total no. of degrees
Four-year level	14.5%	19.1%	12.3%	8.7%	2.6%	10.2%	2.7%	0.8%	0.9%	27.6%	0.6%	7,640
Master's level	8.7	20.4	16.4	10.2	6.2	9.1	9.7	0.6	1.6	16.9	0.2	2,598
Doctoral level	8.3	25.9	33.8	13.6	5.2	1.3	5.0	0.9	0.5	5.5	0.0	1,132
Second degree, all levels	7.9	8.1	4.5	2.7	3.6	7.7	8.6	1.8	35.7	18.7	0.7	465
Medical degree, all levels								100.0				289
Law degree, all levels									100.0			1,582
Total degrees held by civilian executives												13,706

*Degrees included here are only those for which the area of specialization was reported. Some executives reported degrees without indicating areas of specialization, and these degrees are not included in the totals.

†At the bachelor, master's, and doctoral levels executives reported some degrees as in the subject areas of law and medicine, but not leading to professional standing. These degrees have been analyzed at the three academic levels, but not included in the figures for law and medical degrees.

TABLE 42B (Chap. 8)

Degree and Area of Specialization of 1959 Career Civil Service Executives*

Area of Specialization

Degree	Human-ities	Behav. science	Phys. science	Biol. science	Educa-tion	Bus. admin.	Pub. admin.	Medi-cine†	Law†	Engi-neering	Military science	Total no. of degrees
Four-year level	9.3%	15.7%	13.7%	9.7%	2.7%	12.1%	1.7%	0.8%	0.5%	33.3%	0.5%	5,227
Master's level	6.3	18.5	18.4	11.5	5.4	10.0	8.5	0.8	1.3	19.2	0.1	1,805
Doctoral level	6.5	24.2	35.1	17.5	5.0	1.3	4.2	1.2	0.3	4.7	0.0	721
Second degree, all levels	7.5	8.2	4.1	4.5	4.5	9.7	8.2	2.2	26.1	24.6	0.4	278
Medical degree, all levels								100.0				230
Law degree, all levels									100.0			721
Total degrees held by career civil servants												8,982

* Degrees included here are only those for which the area of specialization was reported. Some executives reported degrees without indicating areas of specialization, and these degrees are not included in the totals.

† At the bachelor, master's, and doctoral levels executives reported some degrees as in the subject areas of law and medicine, but not leading to professional standing. These degrees have been analyzed at the three academic levels, but not included in the figures for law and medical degrees.

TABLE 43B (Chap. 8)

Degree and Area of Specialization of 1959 Political Executives*

Area of Specialization

Degree	Human-ities	Behav. science	Phys. science	Biol. science	Educa-tion	Bus. admin.	Pub. admin.	Medi-cine	Law†	Engi-neering	Military science	Total no. of degrees
Four-year level	21.5%	24.0%	11.9%	5.0%	1.7%	6.5%	3.7%	0.4%	2.4%	21.8%	1.1%	1,340
Master's level	4.8	23.6	23.8	5.1	4.5	7.7	5.7	0.6	2.0	21.6	0.6	361
Doctoral level	4.0	25.7	46.4	6.3	1.4	0.9	3.1	0.9	0.5	10.8	0.0	229
Second degree, all levels	2.3	6.2	7.0	0.0	1.5	3.9	3.1	0.8	63.6	10.1	1.5	134
Medical degree, all levels								100.0				37
Law degree, all levels									100.0			751
Total degrees held by political executives												2,852

*Degrees included here are only those for which the area of specialization was reported. Some executives reported degrees without indicating areas of specialization, and these degrees are not included in the totals.

†At the bachelor, master's, and doctoral levels executives reported some degrees as in the subject areas of law and medicine, but not leading to professional standing. These degrees have been analyzed at the three academic levels, but not included in the figures for law and medical degrees.

364

TABLE 44B (Chap. 8)

Degree and Area of Specialization of 1959 Foreign-Service Executives*

Area of Specialization

Degree	Human-ities	Behav. science	Phys. science	Biol. science	Educa-tion	Bus. admin.	Pub. admin.	Medi-cine†	Law†	Engi-neering	Military science	Total no. of degrees
Four-year level	32.1%	30.1%	3.8%	8.4%	3.7%	5.4%	6.3%	1.1%	1.2%	7.5%	0.4%	1,021
Master's level	21.8	25.8	1.0	9.3	10.5	6.7	18.2	0.0	2.4	3.8	0.5	415
Doctoral level	23.2	36.1	4.5	7.8	11.6	1.9	12.3	0.0	1.3	1.3	0.0	166
Second degree, all levels	26.1	13.0	0.0	0.0	4.4	6.5	26.1	2.2	13.0	8.7	0.0	52
Medical degree, all levels								100.0				17
Law degree, all levels									100.0			102
Total degrees held by foreign-service men												1,773

*Degrees included here are only those for which the area of specialization was reported. Some executives reported degrees without indicating areas of specialization, and these degrees are not included in the totals.

†At the bachelor, master's, and doctoral levels executives reported some degrees as in the subject areas of law and medicine, but not leading to professional standing. These degrees have been analyzed at the three academic levels, but not included in the figures for law and medical degrees.

365

TABLE 45B (Chap. 8)

Degree and Area of Specialization of 1959 Military Executives*

Area of Specialization

Degree	Human-ities	Behav. science	Phys. science	Biol. science	Educa-tion	Bus. admin.	Pub. admin.	Medi-cine†	Law†	Engi-neering	Military science	Total no. of degrees
Four-year level	5.5%	5.0%	4.0%	3.9%	1.6%	6.9%	0.4%	1.0%	0.2%	11.7%	59.8%	1,740
Master's level	3.7	4.3	5.1	1.4	5.3	19.0	3.9	0.8	0.0	53.6	2.9	492
Doctoral level	13.0	13.0	8.7	8.7	13.0	4.4	17.4	0.0	0.0	17.4	4.4	23
Second degree, all levels	9.6	3.6	7.2	4.8	1.2	10.8	1.2	4.8	6.0	38.7	12.1	84
Medical degree, all levels								100.0				89
Law degree, all levels									100.0			74
Total degrees held by military leaders												2,502

*Degrees included here are only those for which the area of specialization was reported. Some executives reported degrees without indicating areas of specialization, and these degrees are not included in the totals.

†At the bachelor, master's, and doctoral levels executives reported some degrees as in the subject areas of law and medicine, but not leading to professional standing. These degrees have been analyzed at the three academic levels, but not included in the figures for law and medical degrees.

TABLE 46B (Chap. 9)

Types of Institutions from Which Master's Level Degrees Were Received

Type of institution	Civilian federal exec.	Career civil service exec.	Political exec.	Foreign-service exec.	Military exec.
Private colleges and universities	44.8%	41.4%	47.0%	58.5%	45.2%
Public colleges and universities	45.0	47.8	38.0	37.7	23.8
Technical institutions and U.S. Academies	6.0	6.6	8.6	0.8	30.6
Miscellaneous U.S. institutions	2.2	2.8	0.6	1.1	0.0
Foreign institutions	2.0	1.4	5.8	1.9	0.4
Total degrees reported with name of institution	2,492[*]	1,751	347	372	482

[*]Includes twenty-two degrees reported by men not classifiable into one of the three civilian services.

TABLE 47B (Chap. 9)

Types of Institutions from Which Doctoral Level Degrees Were Received

Type of institution	Civilian federal exec.	Career civil service exec.	Political exec.	Foreign-service exec.	Military exec.
Private colleges and universities	51.2%	49.2%	51.4%	60.2%	68.3%
Public colleges and universities	38.1	42.8	29.8	28.5	22.7
Technical institutions and U.S. Academies	4.4	3.9	8.7	0.6	4.5
Miscellaneous U.S. institutions	0.6	0.3	0.0	2.5	4.5
Foreign institutions	5.7	3.8	10.1	8.2	0.0
Total degrees reported with name of institution	1,085*	693	218	158	22

*Includes sixteen degrees reported by men not classifiable into one of the three services.

Appendix B

TABLE 48B (Chap. 9)

Types of Institutions from Which Law Degrees Were Received

Type of institution	Civilian federal exec.	Career civil service exec.	Political exec.	Foreign- service exec.	Military exec.
Private colleges and universities	71.1%	72.1%	69.4%	76.4%	59.7%
Public colleges and universities	24.1	19.2	29.3	17.7	37.3
Technical institutions and U.S. Academies	0.0	0.0	0.0	0.0	0.0
Miscellaneous U.S. institutions	4.2	8.2	1.0	2.4	1.5
Foreign institutions	0.6	0.5	0.3	3.5	1.5
Total degrees reported with name of institution	1,378*	596	689	85	67

* Includes eight degrees reported by men not classifiable into one of the three services.

TABLE 49B (Chap. 9)

Types of Institutions from Which Medical
Degrees Were Received

Type of institution	Civilian federal exec.	Career civil service exec.	Political exec.	Foreign-service exec.	Military exec.
Private colleges and universities	48.2%	44.1%	66.6%	64.0%	49.4%
Public colleges and universities	47.4	51.7	30.6	28.6	49.4
Technical institutions and U.S. Academies	0.0	0.0	0.0	0.0	0.0
Miscellaneous U.S. institutions	0.7	0.5	0.0	7.1	1.2
Foreign institutions	3.7	3.7	2.8	0.0	0.0
Total degrees reported with name of institution	270*	215	36	14	18

* Includes five degrees reported by men not classifiable into one of the three services.

Appendix B

TABLE 50B (Chap. 9)

Types of Institutions from Which Second Degrees
at All Levels Were Received

Type of institution	Civilian federal exec.	Career civil service exec.	Political exec.	Foreign-service exec.	Military exec.
Private colleges and universities	58.4%	51.5%	71.2%	60.0%	33.3%
Public colleges and universities	26.2	32.5	16.8	17.5	26.0
Technical institutions and U.S. Academies	7.0	8.8	5.6	0.0	37.0
Miscellaneous U.S. institutions	3.1	4.8	0.8	0.0	1.2
Foreign institutions	5.3	2.4	5.6	22.5	2.5
Total degrees reported with name of institution	415*	249	125	40	81

* Includes one degree reported by men not classifiable into one of the three services.

TABLE 51B (Chap. 9)

Thirty Institutions Which Produced the Largest Number of Four-Year Degrees Reported by Civilian Federal Executives

All civilian federal executives		Career civil service executives		Political executives		Foreign-service executives	
George Washington	3*	George Washington	3*	George Washington	4*	Harvard	5*
City Col. of N.Y.	6	City Col. of N.Y.	6	Harvard	8	Princeton	10
California	8	California	8	City Col. of N.Y.	13	Yale	14
Harvard	10	Ohio State	10	Yale	11	California	17
Minnesota	12	Minnesota	12	California	16	George Washington	20
Illinois	14	Illinois	14	Princeton	18	Stanford	22
Michigan	15	Washington	16	Michigan	20	Georgetown	24
Wisconsin	17	Wisconsin	17	Pennsylvania	22	Illinois	26
Ohio State	19	Mass. Inst. of Tech.	19	Mass. Inst. of Tech.	24	Chicago	28
Washington	20	Michigan	21	Minnesota	25	Wisconsin	29
Mass. Inst. of Tech.	22	New York	22	Wisconsin	27	Columbia	31
Princeton	23	Cornell	24	Washington	28	Dartmouth	32
Yale	25	Benjamin Franklin	25	Chicago	30	Michigan	34
New York	26	Purdue	26	Georgetown	31	Minnesota	35
Cornell	28	Missouri	27	Illinois	32	Cornell	37
Benjamin Franklin	29	Nebraska	29	Iowa	34	Oklahoma State	38
Pennsylvania	30	Penn. State	30	Cornell	35	Northwestern	39
Missouri	31	Colorado	31	Northwestern	36	Utah	40
Purdue	32	Pennsylvania	32	Ohio State	37	Oberlin	41
Georgetown	33	Iowa State	33	Kansas	38	South Dakota State	42

[continued]

TABLE 51B (Chap. 9)
[continued]

All civilian federal executives		Career civil service executives		Political executives		Foreign-service executives	
Nebraska	34	Harvard	34	New York	40	Washington	43
Chicago	35	Kansas State	35	North Carolina	40	Pennsylvania	44
Stanford	36	Maryland	35	Purdue	41	North Carolina	45
Penn. State	37	Tennessee	36	Missouri	42	Missouri	46
Colorado	38	Cincinnati	37	Stanford	43	Syracuse	47
Iowa	39	Syracuse	38	Columbia	44	Mass. Inst. of Tech.	48
Iowa State	39	Stanford	38	Alabama	44	Benjamin Franklin	48
Columbia	40	Alabama Polytech.	39	Texas	45	Brown	49
Kansas	41	Georgetown	40	Brown	46	Ohio State	50
Syracuse	42	Oregon State	41	South Dakota State	46	U.S. Naval Academy	51

*Percentage of total accumulated through the rankings.

TABLE 52B (Chap. 9)

Thirty Institutions Which Produced the Largest Number of Master's Level Degrees Reported by Civilian Federal Executives

Number	Accumulative number	Accumulative percentage	Institution
173	173	6.7	Harvard
105	278	10.7	George Washington
104	382	14.7	Columbia
86	468	18.1	Chicago
81	549	21.1	Ohio State
69	618	23.8	Wisconsin
69	687	26.4	California
65	752	29.0	Mass. Inst. of Tech.
62	814	31.3	Michigan
61	875	33.8	Minnesota
50	925	35.6	Illinois
50	975	37.5	American University
49	1,024	39.4	Iowa State
45	1,089	41.9	New York
44	1,133	43.6	Yale
43	1,176	45.3	Cornell
42	1,218	46.9	Iowa
41	1,259	48.5	Pennsylvania
38	1,297	49.9	Missouri
38	1,335	51.4	Syracuse
35	1,370	52.8	Stanford
33	1,403	54.0	Nebraska
32	1,435	55.3	Benjamin Franklin
31	1,466	56.4	Maryland
28	1,494	57.5	Kansas State
23	1,517	58.4	Northwestern
23	1,540	59.3	Purdue
23	1,557	59.9	Colorado
23	1,580	60.8	Princeton
22	1,602	61.7	City Col. of N.Y.

Total master's level degrees: 2,597

Appendix B

TABLE 53B (Chap. 9)

Thirty Institutions Which Produced the Largest Number of Federal Executives with Law Degrees at All Levels

Number	Accumulative number	Accumulative percentage	Institution
294	294	18.6	George Washington
109	403	25.5	Georgetown
104	508	32.1	Harvard
48	556	35.1	Southeastern
43	599	37.9	Columbia
36	635	40.1	Catholic Univ. of Amer.
33	668	42.2	Michigan
28	696	44.0	Washington
28	724	45.8	New York
27	751	47.5	Yale
26	777	49.1	Chicago
26	803	50.8	American University
24	827	52.3	Fordham
23	850	53.7	Pennsylvania
22	872	55.1	Northwestern
17	884	56.2	Texas
17	906	57.3	Wisconsin
16	922	58.3	Virginia
14	936	59.2	Iowa
12	948	60.0	Maryland
11	955	60.4	Illinois
11	966	61.1	Minnesota
11	977	61.6	Nebraska
10	987	62.4	California
10	997	63.0	Boston
9	1,006	63.6	Alabama
9	1,015	64.1	Oklahoma
9	1,024	64.7	Kansas
9	1,033	65.3	St. Johns (New York)
9	1,042	65.9	Creighton

Total law degrees: 1,582

TABLE 54B (Chap. 9)

Institutions Attended by American Business Leaders[*]

Institution	First or only college attended	Graduate or second undergraduate college attended
Yale	36	9
Harvard	27	28
Princeton	20	1
Cornell	18	2
University of Pennsylvania	16	4
University of Illinois	13	3
Mass. Inst. of Tech.	13	6
University of Michigan	13	6
New York University	12	4
University of Minnesota	11	4
Williams College	10	0
Univ. of California (Berkeley)	10	0
University of Chicago	9	7
Columbia University	8	13
Total	216	87
Northwestern University	7	7
Pennsylvania State	7	0
Stanford University	7	2
University of Wisconsin	7	2
Western Reserve University	7	1
Dartmouth	6	2
University of Washington	6	0
University of North Carolina	5	0
University of Pittsburgh	5	2
University of Texas	5	1
Total	62	17

[*]Warner and Abegglen, Big Business Leaders in America.

Appendix B

TABLE 55B (Chap. 9)

Men from Three Occupational Origins Who Received Law Degrees from Twenty Institutions

Father's Occupation

Lower range*		Middle range†		Upper range‡	
Southeastern	37%§	Iowa	77%§	Maryland	55%§
Fordham	32	Texas	76	Michigan	53
American	31	Catholic	64	Harvard	52
Catholic	27	Chicago	62	Pennsylvania	50
New York	27	Wisconsin	53	Virginia	50
Geo. Washington	20	Georgetown	53	Northwestern	41
Wisconsin	20	Southeastern	50	Yale	41
Georgetown	19	Washington	50	Columbia	36
Washington	19	Fordham	50	Geo. Washington	31
Columbia	14	Northwestern	50	Washington	31
Chicago	11	Virginia	50	Georgetown	28
Yale	11	Columbia	49	Chicago	27
Maryland	9	Geo. Washington	49	American	27
Pennsylvania	9	Yale	48	Wisconsin	27
Northwestern	9	New York	46	New York	27
Iowa	8	American	42	Fordham	18
Michigan	7	Harvard	42	Texas	18
Harvard	6	Pennsylvania	40	Iowa	15
Texas	6	Michigan	39	Southeastern	13
Virginia	0	Maryland	36	Catholic	9

*Includes unskilled and skilled workers, and farm workers and tenants without paid help.

†Includes white-collar workers, minor business executives, foremen, small business owners, farm owners, and tenants with paid help.

‡Includes major business executives, professional men, and owners of medium and large business.

§Percentage of all executives holding four-year degrees from each institution, by occupational origin group.

TABLE 56B (Chap. 10)

Career Sequence of 1959 Career Civil Service Executives

Occupation of civil service executive	First occupation	Five years later	Ten years later	Fifteen years later
Laborer	16%	7%	4%	3%
White-collar worker	27	20	9	4
Minor executive	4	15	29	27
Major executive	0*	1	6	20
All professions	43	45	44	40
Uniformed service	5	7	5	3
Business owner	1	2	1	1
Other occupation	4	3	2	2
Total	100	100	100	100
The professions in detail				
Engineer	17	20	19	18
Lawyer	2	3	3	3
Medical doctor	2	2	2	2
Professor	3	3	3	1
Public school teacher	6	2	1	0*
Scientist	6	7	8	8
Accountant	1	2	2	2
Management analyst	1	2	2	2
Other profession	5	4	4	4

*Less than 0.5 per cent.

TABLE 57B (Chap. 10)

Career Sequence of 1959 Political Executives

Occupation of political executive	First occupation	Five years later	Ten years later	Fifteen years later
Laborer	11%	4%	2%	1%
White-collar worker	21	11	4	1
Minor executive	5	12	17	13
Major executive	0*	2	8	20
All professions	53	60	62	59
Uniformed service	6	7	4	2
Business owner	1	1	2	3
Other occupation	3	3	1	1
Total	100	100	100	100
The professions in detail				
Engineer	11	12	10	9
Lawyer	22	27	33	33
Medical doctor	1	2	2	1
Professor	4	4	3	3
Public school teacher	5	2	0*	0*
Scientist	6	8	9	9
Accountant	1	0*	0*	0*
Management analyst	1	2	2	2
Other profession	2	3	3	2

*Less than 0.5 per cent.

TABLE 58B (Chap. 10)

Career Sequence of 1959 Foreign-Service Executives

Occupation of foreign-service executive	First occupation	Five years later	Ten years later	Fifteen years later
Laborer	9%	2%	2%	1%
White-collar worker	25	11	5	1
Minor executive	15	35	47	43
Major executive	1	4	12	28
All professions	38	31	24	20
Uniformed service	6	12	6	3
Business owner	1	1	1	1
Other occupation	5	4	3	3
Total	100	100	100	100
The professions in detail				
Engineer	5	4	4	4
Lawyer	4	3	2	1
Medical doctor	1	1	1	1
Professor	7	6	5	3
Public school teacher	7	3	1	1
Scientist	2	3	3	3
Accountant	0*	0*	0*	0*
Management analyst	3	3	4	3
Other profession	9	8	4	4

*Less than 0.5 per cent.

TABLE 59B (Chap. 10)

Career Sequence of 1959 Military Executives

Occupation of military executive	First occupation	Five years later	Ten years later	Fifteen years later
Laborer	7%	1%	0%*	0%*
White-collar worker	10	3	0*	0*
Minor executive	3	4	3	1
Major executive	0*	0*	1	1
All professions	12	9	6	4
Uniformed service	65	81	89	94
Business owner	1	1	1	0*
Other occupation	2	1	0*	0*
Total	100	100	100	100
The professions in detail				
Engineer	4	3	2	1
Lawyer	2	1	1	1
Medical doctor	2	2	1	1
Professor	0*	1	0*	0*
Public school teacher	3	1	1	0*
Scientist	0*	0*	0*	0*
Management analyst	0*	0*	0*	0*
Other profession	1	1	1	1

*Less than 0.5 per cent.

TABLE 60B (Chap. 10)

Career Sequence of 1952 Business Leaders[*]

Occupation of business leader	First occupation	Five years later	Ten years later	Fifteen years later
Laborer	14%	3%	1%	0%
White-collar worker	44	29	11	4
Minor executive	9	35	43	25
Major executive	1	6	26	57
Business owner	1	2	3	3
All professions	24	21	14	10
Uniformed service	2	2	1	1
Government service	1	1	1	0
Training program	3	0	0	0
Other occupation	1	1	0	0
Total	100	100	100	100

[*]From Occupational Mobility, revised.

TABLE 61B (Chap. 10)

Father's Occupation and Career Pattern of Military Executives*

Occupation of father	Laborer	White-collar worker	Profes-sional man	Minor execu-tive	Major execu-tive	Uniformed service	Other occupa-tion	Total
				First Occupation				
Laborer	13%	12%	11%	4%	0%	55%	5%	100%
White-collar worker or minor executive	8	9	11	4	0	66	2	100
Owner of small business	8	10	16	2	0	60	4	100
Farmer	10	7	15	4	0	58	6	100
Professional man	4	7	15	2	0	69	3	100
Major executive or owner of large business	5	11	14	5	0	61	4	100
				Five Years Later				
Laborer	3	4	10	8	0	72	3	100
White-collar worker or minor executive	3	2	7	4	0*	82	2	100
Owner of small business	0	1	10	5	0*	82	2	100
Farmer	1	3	11	5	1	76	3	100
Professional man	1	2	13	3	0	80	1	100
Major executive or owner of large business	1	3	7	10	0	75	4	100
				Ten Years Later				
Laborer	0*	0*	7	4	2	87	0	100
White-collar worker or minor executive	1	0*	3	1	6	88	1	100
Owner of small business	0	0	5	1	1	91	2	100
Farmer	0	2	8	4	2	83	1	100
Professional man	0	0	8	2	1	88	1	100
Major executive or owner of large business	1	0*	2	6	2	85	4	100
				Fifteen Years Later				
Laborer	0*	0	5	1	1	92	1	100
White-collar worker or minor executive	0*	0*	3	0*	1	96	0*	100
Owner of small business	0	0	3	0	0*	97	0	100
Farmer	0	0	5	2	1	91	1	100
Professional man	0	0	4	1	1	94	0*	100
Major executive or owner of large business	1	0*	3	2	2	91	1	100

*Asterisks indicate less than 0.5 per cent. Percentages of 10 and over are underlined.

TABLE 62B (Chap. 10)

Father's Occupation and Years Required to Achieve Present Position after Entering Public Service

Years to Achieve Position

Occupation of father	Civilian federal executives	Career civil service executives	Political executives	Foreign-service executives	Military executives	Business leaders
Laborer	17.6 +0.7	17.8 +0.4	16.8 +2.1	17.2 −0.4	24.0 −1.4	26.0 +2.1
Clerk or salesman	16.9 0.0	17.2 −0.2	16.3 +1.6	16.2 −1.4	24.1 −1.3	24.8 +0.9
Minor business executive	16.5 −0.4	16.8 −0.8	14.9 +0.2	17.4 −0.2	25.6 +0.2	25.0 +1.1
Owner of small business	17.2 +0.3	17.6 +0.2	15.5 +0.8	17.2 −0.4	25.0 −0.4	22.6 −1.3
Owner of large business	15.6 −1.3	16.8 −0.6	12.4 −2.3	17.0 −0.7	24.4 −1.0	21.2 −2.7
Major business executive	14.9 −2.0	15.6 −1.8	11.8 −2.9	16.7 −0.9	25.1 −0.3	20.6 −3.3
Professional man	15.8 −1.1	16.3 −1.1	13.7 −1.0	17.3 −0.3	26.2 +0.8	22.5 −1.4
Farmer	18.8 +1.9	19.2 +1.8	15.7 +1.0	19.8 +2.2	24.7 −0.7	25.1 +1.2
Uniformed service					28.0 +2.6	
Average time for elite	16.9	17.4	14.7	17.6	25.4	23.9
Difference between extreme averages	3.9	3.6	5.0	3.6	4.0	5.4

Appendix B

TABLE 63B (Chap. 10)

Comparison of Age at Entry and Time to Achieve Present Position by Men in Each of the Elites

	Civilian federal exec.	Career civil service exec.	Political exec.	Foreign-service exec.	Military exec.	Business leaders
1. Age entered service or business	27.9	27.2	30.2	28.2	22.5	21.4
2. Years to achieve present position	16.9	17.4	14.7	17.6	25.4	23.9
Age of entry into present position (1 plus 2)	44.8	44.6	44.9	45.8	47.9	45.3

TABLE 64B (Chap. 10)

Average Age of Executives by Occupation of the Fathers

Present Age of Executives

Occupation of father	Civilian federal executives	Career civil service executives	Political executives	Foreign-service executives	Military executives	Business leaders
Laborer	48.7 −0.7	48.8 −0.8	49.2 −0.2	48.0 −0.3	49.5 −0.4	53.7 0.0
Clerk or salesman	48.6 −0.8	48.8 −0.8	48.4 −0.1	47.1 −1.2	49.1 −0.8	53.5 +0.2
Minor business executive	48.5 −0.9	48.8 −0.8	47.8 −1.6	47.4 −0.9	49.6 −0.3	53.4 −0.3
Owner of small business	49.4 0.0	49.6 0.0	48.9 +0.3	48.5 +0.2	49.8 −0.1	54.2 +0.5
Owner of large business	50.0 +0.6	50.3 +0.7	50.3 +0.9	48.5 +0.2	50.8 +0.9	53.2 −0.3
Major business executive	48.4 −1.0	49.0 −0.6	47.8 −1.6	47.3 −1.0	50.0 +0.1	50.6 −3.1
Professional man	49.4 0.0	49.8 +0.2	49.3 −0.1	48.4 −0.3	50.6 +0.7	53.2 −0.5
Farmer	51.5 +1.1	51.5 +0.9	51.6 +2.2	50.7 +2.4	50.1 +0.2	56.3 +2.6
Uniformed service					49.5 −0.4	
Average age for elite	49.4	49.6	49.4	48.3	49.9	53.7
Difference between extreme means	3.1	1.7	3.8	3.6	0.7	3.1

TABLE 65B (Chap. 10)

Number of Organizations Associated with as an Executive

Number of organizations	Civilian federal exec.	Career civil service exec.	Political exec.	Foreign- service exec.	Military exec.	Business leaders
1	33%	35%	27%	22%	65%	48%
2	24	25	25	21	20	26
3	17	16	18	17	7	14
4	11	10	13	15	4	6
5	6	6	7	10	1	3
6 or more	9	8	10	15	3	3
Total	100	100	100	100	100	100

TABLE 66B (Chap. 10)

Interorganizational Mobility and Speed of Career

Years to Achieve Position after Entering Public Service

No. of organizations executive has been associated with	Civilian federal exec.	Career civil service exec.	Political exec.	Foreign-service exec.	Military exec.	Business leaders
1	18.2	18.8	14.8	18.4	27.4	22.4
2-3	16.9	17.3	14.5	17.4	23.0	24.0
4-6	16.5	16.8	14.8	17.2	21.8	25.3
7 or more	17.7	17.9	16.9	18.8	22.9	27.7
Average years	16.9	17.4	14.7	17.5	25.3	23.9

Years before Entering Present Organization*

1	1.3	1.4	1.1	0.8	0.6	0.0
2-3	4.2	3.8	4.7	6.1	2.3	9.4
4-6	6.5	6.1	6.9	8.4	2.3	15.3
7 or more	10.4	9.9	11.3	12.1	4.1	20.0
Average years	5.8	5.5	6.2	7.8	1.4	7.2

*Difference between age when first self-supporting and age at which present organization was entered.

Appendix B

TABLE 67B (Chap. 10)

Experience in Private Enterprise and Speed of Career

Years to Achieve Position after Entering Public Service

Number of private organizations executive has been associated with	Civilian federal executives	Career civil service executives	Political executives	Foreign-service executives
1	17.9	18.2	16.1	18.7
2-3	16.0	16.4	13.7	16.8
4-6	15.4	16.0	13.8	13.8
7 or more	15.1	16.3	13.6	11.9
Average years	16.9	17.4	14.7	17.5

Years before Entering Public Service[*]

1	5.9	5.4	6.4	8.4
2-3	5.6	5.4	5.8	7.1
4-6	6.1	5.7	7.3	6.3
7 or more	7.2	7.1	8.0	8.0
Average years	5.8	5.4	6.2	7.8

[*]Difference between age when first self-supporting and age at which present organization was entered.

TABLE 68B (Chap. 10)

Occupational Mobility and Types of Public Organizations
of 1959 Civilian Federal Executives

Department or agency	Average age executive entered public service	Average years to achieve position	Average present age
Executive Office of the President	26.5	16.4	47.0
Department of Defense	27.9	14.8	46.8
Departments of 19th century	27.1	18.9	50.4
Departments of 20th century	27.8	18.3	52.0
Regulatory commissions and agencies	28.5	16.6	50.7
Major agencies	28.8	15.9	49.2
Miscellaneous agencies	38.5	11.7	56.6
Average of all civilian federal executives	27.9	16.9	49.4

Appendix B

TABLE 69B (Chap. 11)

Proportions of Women Executives and of Total Civilian Executives in 1959, at the GS Levels

GS level	All civilian federal executives	Women executives
Above GS–18	3%	2%
GS–18	3	2
GS–17	4	1
GS–16	11	7
GS–15	42	22
GS–14	37	66
Total per cent	100	100
Total number	10,851	145

TABLE 70B (Chap. 11)

Departments and Agencies in Which 1959 Civilian Federal Executives and 1959 Civilian Federal Women Executives Served

Department or agency	All 1959 civilian federal executives	1959 civilian federal women executives
Department of State	13.07%	14.58%
Treasury Department	6.99	4.17
Department of Defense	23.19	4.86
Department of Justice	2.64	3.47
Post Office Department	1.57	0.00
Department of Interior	4.83	0.69
Department of Agriculture	8.17	10.43
Department of Commerce	6.42	6.25
Department of Labor	1.67	10.43
Department of Health, Education, and Welfare	3.64	25.69
Executive Office of the President	1.52	2.09
U.S. Atomic Energy Commission	2.43	1.39
Civil Service Commission, U.S.	0.99	3.47
Federal Reserve System	0.41	0.69
General Services Administration	1.36	0.00
Housing and Home Finance Agency	1.95	2.09
U.S. Information Agency	2.12	3.47
Tennessee Valley Authority	1.67	0.00
Veterans Administration	3.90	2.78
Federal Communication Commission	0.58	0.69
National Labor Relations Board	0.71	0.00
Federal Trade Commission	0.44	0.00
Interstate Commerce Commission	0.42	0.00
Securities and Exchange Commission	0.58	0.00
Federal Power Commission	0.57	0.00
Civil Aeronautics Board	0.62	0.69
Federal Aviation Committee	2.19	0.00
Air Coordinating Committee	0.77	0.00
National Aeronautics and Space Agency	1.88	0.00
National Science Foundation	0.35	0.00
Railroad Retirement Board, U.S.	0.30	0.00
The Renegotiation Board	0.35	0.00
Small Business Administration	0.15	0.00
Federal Deposit Insurance Corporation	0.26	0.00
Miscellaneous*	1.29	2.07
Total	100.00	100.00

*All independent agencies with fewer than 30 total mailings.

Appendix B

TABLE 71B (Chap. 11)

1959 Civilian Federal Women Executives by Line and Staff Position in the Federal Hierarchy

Line and staff	Number	Percentage
Line	62	46
Staff	68	51
Line and staff	4	3
Total	134	100
Unknown	11	
Grand total	145	100

TABLE 72B (Chap. 11)

Occupations of Fathers of 1959 Civilian Federal Women Executives

Occupation of father		
Laborer		13%
Unskilled or semiskilled	2.1%	
Skilled worker or mechanic	10.7	
White-collar worker		7
Clerk or retail salesman	3.6	
Salesman	3.6	
Business executive		18
Foreman	2.9	
Minor executive	7.1	
Major executive	7.9	
Business owner		13
Small business	7.9	
Medium business	1.4	
Large business	3.6	
Professional man		34
Doctor	3.6	
Engineer	5.0	
Lawyer	5.0	
Minister	2.1	
Other profession	18.5	
Farmer		14
Farm tenant or farm worker	0.7	
Tenant with paid help	0.0	
Farm owner without paid help	3.6	
Owner or manager with paid help	10.0	
Other occupations		1
Uniformed service	0.0	
Government service	0.0	
Other occupation	0.7	
Total per cent	100.0	100
Total number		145

TABLE 73B (Chap. 11)

Ratios of Women Executives and of Total Executives in the Several Services to Adult Male Population in 1930*

Occupation	Total adult male U.S. population in 1930	Women exec.	1959 women exec.	All 1959 civilian federal exec.	Career civil service exec.	Political exec.	Foreign-service exec.
Unskilled or semiskilled laborer	33%	2%	0.06	0.12	0.12	0.06	0.09
Skilled laborer	15	11	0.73	1.13	1.27	0.87	0.73
Owner of small business	7	8	1.14	2.00	2.14	1.86	1.71
Clerk or salesman	12	7	0.58	0.75	0.83	0.75	0.58
Foreman	2	3	1.50	2.50	2.50	2.00	1.50
Minor or major executive; owner of large business	3	20	6.67	5.67	4.67	6.67	8.00
Professional man	4	34	8.50	4.75	4.00	6.00	6.25
Farm laborer	6	1	0.17	0.00	0.00	0.00	0.00
Farm tenant or owner	16	13	0.81	0.88	0.94	0.81	0.75

*Fifteenth Census, 1930, Vol. IV, Occupations by States, Table 11.

TABLE 74B (Chap. 11)

The Professions as Sources of Women Executives: Ratios of Women Executives and of Executives in the Several Elites to Adult Male Population in 1920*

Profession	1920 male adult population	1959 women exec.	All 1959 civilian federal exec.	Career civil service exec.	Political exec.	Foreign-service exec.
Lawyer	0.46%	10.87	8.44	5.56	20.44	10.00
Minister	0.41	5.12	6.67	5.71	6.90	11.90
Engineer	0.52	9.62	4.77	4.77	5.08	4.92
Doctor	0.51	7.06	5.95	5.24	7.14	8.09
Other professions	2.47	7.49	2.74	2.52	2.61	3.87

*Warner and Abegglen, Occupational Mobility.

TABLE 75B (Chap. 11)

The Professions as Sources of 1959 Civilian Federal Women Executives

Profession	Percentage
Lawyer	5.0
Minister	2.1
Engineer	5.0
Doctor	3.6
Accountant with degree	10.0
Management analyst	0.7
Scientist	0.7
Professor	2.1
Public school teacher	0.0
Professional artist and author	0.7
Secondary medical professional	1.4
Other professionals	2.9
Total	34.2

Appendix B

TABLE 76B (Chap. 11)

Occupational Mobility in Three Generations: Occupations of Fathers and Paternal Grandfathers of 1959 Civilian Federal Executives and of 1959 Civilian Federal Women Executives

Occupation	Paternal Grandfather All	Paternal Grandfather Women	Father All	Father Women	1959 Executives All	1959 Executives Women
Laborer	18%	10%	21%	13%		
Farmer	44	50	15	14		
Clerk or salesman	3	3	9	7		
Minor business executive	4	8	11	10		
Major business executive	2	1	4	8	100%	100%
Business owner	18	17	20	13		
Professional man	10	10	19	34		
Other occupation	1	1	1	1	—	—
Total	100	100	100	100	100	100

TABLE 77B (Chap. 11)

Ratios of 1959 Civilian Federal Executives and of Civilian Federal Women Executives by Region of Birth to 1910 Adult Population by Region of Residence

Region	Percentage of 1910 U.S. population living in region	1959 civilian federal women executives Per cent	1959 civilian federal women executives Ratio	All 1959 civilian federal executives Per cent	All 1959 civilian federal executives Ratio
New England	7	10	1.43	8	1.14
Middle Atlantic	21	22	1.05	22	1.05
East North Central	20	16	0.80	19	0.95
West North Central	13	19	1.46	16	1.23
South Atlantic	13	16	1.23	13	1.00
East South Central	9	4	0.44	6	0.67
West South Central	9	3	0.33	6	0.67
Mountain	3	5	1.67	5	1.67
Pacific	5	5	1.00	5	1.00
Total	100	100		100	

TABLE 78B (Chap. 11)

Ratios of Size of Birthplace of 1959 Civilian Federal Executives and of 1959 Civilian Federal Women Executives by Size of Community of Residence to 1910 U. S. Population

Size of community	Percentage of 1910 U.S. population living in community	1959 civilian federal women executives born in community Per cent	Ratio	All 1959 civilian federal executives born in community Per cent	Ratio
400,000 and over	11	21	1.91	21	1.91
100,000–400,000	8	9	1.13	12	1.50
25,000–100,000	8	15	1.88	12	1.50
2,500–25,000	15	23	1.53	21	1.40
Under 2,500	58	32	0.55	34	0.59
Total	100	100		100	

TABLE 79B (Chap. 11)

Nativity of 1959 Civilian Federal Executives and of 1959 Civilian Federal Women Executives and U. S. Population in 1950[*]

Nativity	All civilian federal executives	Civilian federal women executives	U.S. white population in 1950
Executive foreign born	3.8%	0.7%	7.5%
Executive U.S. born	20.2	18.1	17.5
Father and executive U.S. born	17.7	15.3	75.0
Paternal grandfather, father, and executive U.S. born	58.3	65.9	
Total	100.0	100.0	100.0

[*]Bureau of the Census, 1950, Special Report, PE no. 3A, Table 3.

Appendix B

TABLE 80B (Chap. 11)

Ratios of Educational Levels of Women Executives and of the Three Civilian Elites to the Adult Male Population*

Education	U.S. adult males (30 years and over) in 1957	1959 civilian federal women executives Per cent	Ratio	Career civil service exec.	Foreign-service exec.	Political exec.
Less than high school	46	0	0.00	0.00	0.00	0.00
Some high school	17	1	0.06	0.19	0.00	0.06
High school graduation	21	1	0.05	0.24	0.09	0.09
Some college	7	10	1.43	2.14	1.43	1.00
College graduation	9	88	9.78	8.67	9.78	10.00

*$\dfrac{1959 \text{ federal executives}}{1957 \text{ U.S. adult males}}$ = ratio. Bureau of the Census, Current Population Reports, Series p-20, no. 77, 1957, "Population Characteristics; Educational Attainment: March 1957."

TABLE 81B (Chap. 11)

Present Age of Women Executives and of Executives in the Three Civilian Services by GS Level

GS level	Women executives	Career civil service executives	Foreign-service executives	Political executives
Above GS-18	58.0	00.0	55.2	52.7
GS-18	59.7	52.0	49.8	50.2
GS-17	58.0	50.4	00.0	48.2
GS-16	53.0	50.4	48.3	49.2
GS-15	52.1	49.2	48.8	48.8
GS-14	51.9	49.9	47.2	50.3

TABLE 82B (Chap. 11)

Marital Status of All 1959 Civilian Federal Executives
and of 1959 Civilian Federal Women Executives

Marital status	All 1959 civilian federal executives	1959 civilian federal women executives
Married	95.6%	34.7%
Not married	4.4	65.3
Total	100.0	100.0

Index

Appendixes A and B are not included in the index

Achievement time, 164–76, 187. *See also* Age, Agencies, Organizational mobility, Years
Age: and achievement time, 164–76, 187; of business executives, 20; of entrance into business, 20, 165–67; of entrance into public service, 13, 15, 17, 165–67; of government executives, 13, 15, 17, 187; and personality structure, 200–01; and occupation of father, 20, 164–69. *See also* Achievement time, Years
Agencies, federal, 6, 9; and career speeds, 175–76; women executives in, 180–81. *See also* Organizational mobility
Air Force. *See* Military executives
Army. *See* Military executives
Attitudes, 221–36; on career in government, 223–29; causal factors of, 155–56; and moral code, 232; to outsiders, 224, 230; on social image of self, 229–36. *See also* Bureaucracy, Personality structure

Birthplace, 56–60; of business executives, 19, 58–60; and geographical mobility, 50, 52–55, 73; of government executives, 11, 58–66; size of, 11, 19, 57–58. *See also* Foreign born, Geographical mobility, Nativity, Region of birth
Bureaucracy, public, 1–23, 237–50; attitudes of, 155–56, 221–36; compared to business, 155–56; executive role in, 237–50; personality structure in, 191–220; representative, 4–6, 17, 22, 25–67, 54–55, 58, 67, 109; role demands in, 243–50. *See also* Public service
Business executives *(1952):* age and achievement time, 20–21, 164 ff., 173; birthplace and geographical movement, 52–55; birthplace and nativity, 19, 58–60, 62–67; career patterns, 154–56; compared to government executives, 10–23; education, 19–20, 99, 109, 111, 113–15, 141; marriage and mobility, 90, 92, 99–103; occupation of father, 18–19, 35–38, 63, 65–67, 110–12, 164–69; occupation of father's father and intergenerational mobility, 81–83; organizational mobility, 170 ff.; personality structure, 191; profile of, 18–21; regional movement, 47, 50–55; region of birth, 19, 45–46
Business firms. *See* Definitions, Organizational mobility

Career civil service executives *(1959)*, 6; age and achievement time, 13, 164 ff.; birthplace and geographical movement, 53; birthplace and nativity, 58, 62–66; career patterns, 151–53, 156; compared to business executives, 12–13, 18–23; compared to other government executives, 12–18; education, 109, 111, 115–19, 120–25, 127–31, 135–36; endogamy and exogamy, 84–89; marriage and mobility, 91–103; occupation of father, 35, 37–38, 65–67, 110–12, 117–20, 164–69; occupation of father's father and intergenerational mobility, 81–83; occupation of father's father and mother's father, 86–89; occupation of mother's father, 92 ff.; organizational mobility, 170 ff.; personality structure, 190–97; profile of, 12–13; region of birth, 45–46. *See also* Civilian federal executives, Public service
Career patterns, 148–76, 184–87; and age and achievement time, 164–76; and attitudes, 155–56; business executives, 155–56; and career speeds, 164–76; executives' concepts of, 223–29; of government executives, 148–76, 184–87, 223–29; and lateral entry, 169–76; and marriage, 187; and occupation of father, 157–69; and occupation of father and scalar position,

Career Patterns (Cont.)
161–64; and organizational mobility, 169–76; private experience of government executives, 15, 169–76; the professions and, 157–58, 186–87; and scalar position, 161–64, 168–69; sequences in, 149–56, 184–86. See also Occupational mobility
Census data, 30–31, 41 n., 43, 58, 62, 66, 109, 163
Civil service. See Public service
Civilian federal executives, as a whole (1959): age and achievement time, 101, 164–76, 173–74; attitudes, 221–36; birthplace and geographical movement, 52–55; birthplace and nativity, 58–66; career patterns, 149–76, 184–87; compared to business executives, 10–23; compared to military executives, 17–18; education, 11, 96–101, 104–46; endogamy and exogamy, 84–89; environment of, 237–50; marriage and mobility, 10–103; occupation of father, 28–32, 35, 37–38, 63–67, 74–77, 110–12, 116–20, 141–46, 157–61, 164–69; occupation of father and scalar position, 161–64; occupation of father's father and intergenerational mobility, 71–83; occupation of father's father and mother's father, 86–89; occupation of mother's father, 84–89, 92 ff.; organizational mobility, 170–76; personality structure, 191–220; profile of, 10–11; regional movement, 47–55; region of birth, 41–49; role demands on, 243–50; scalar position, 161–64; scalar position and personality structure, 201–05. See also Career civil service executives, District of Columbia, Foreign-service executives, Political executives, Public service, Women executives
Classification grade. See Scalar position
Colleges and universities. See Education

Definitions: of "areas of educational specialization," 120–21 n.; of "dependency," 194 n.; of "executive," 6, 31–32; of "law degree," 121 n.; of "levels," 6; of "medical degree," 121 n.; of "organization" and "firm," 169–70 n.; of "other profession," 29 n.; of "second degree," 122 n.
Departmental service. See District of Columbia
Departments, federal. See Agencies
District of Columbia: birthplace and nativity in, 57, 59–60, 64; education in, 133, 139–41, 146; as region of birth, 43–45; and regional movement, 47–48. See also Field service

Education, 104–46; areas of undergraduate specialization, 11, 120–25; of business executives, 19–20, 99, 109, 111, 113–15; colleges and universities, 11, 14, 15, 17, 126–46; of executive compared to father, 113; of government executives, 11 ff., 17, 18, 96–101, 104–46, 184; at graduate level, 115–20, 129–30, 136–41, 144–45; at graduate level and father's occupation, 116–20; levels of, 107–10, 113–16, 184; and marriage and mobility, 96–101; and occupational mobility, 20, 141–46; and occupation of father, 20, 110–13, 141–46; in the professions, 11, 14, 15, 17, 115–16, 119–20, 129–30, 140, 145–46, 186; and type of institution, 126–41. See also Definitions, District of Columbia, Professional training
Elite, civil service as an, 229–30
Endogamy, 21, 84–89
Environment, executive, 237–50
Ethnic groups. See Foreign born, Nativity
Executive, definition of, 6, 31–32
Executive branch, development of, 6–10. See also Public service
Executives. See Business executives, Public service
Exogamy, 21, 84–89

Family, influence of, 69–103. See also Marriage
Fathers. See Occupation of father
Federal executives. See Civilian federal executives, Military executives, Public service
Federal government: development of, 6–10; executive role in, 243–50. See also Bureaucracy, Public service
Field service: birthplace and nativity, 57, 59–60, 64; region of birth, 43–45; and regional movement, 46–47. See also District of Columbia
Foreign born, 11, 13, 15, 17, 61–67, 101–03, 183–84. See also Nativity
Foreign-service executives (1959), 6; age and achievement time, 15, 163 ff.; birthplace and geographical movement, 53; birthplace and nativity, 58, 61–66; career patterns, 152–53, 156; compared to business executives, 14–15, 18–23; compared to other government executives, 10–18; education, 15, 109, 111, 115–19, 120–25, 127–31, 135–36; endogamy and exogamy, 84–89; marriage and mobility, 91–103; oc-

Index

Foreign-Service Executives (Cont.)
cupation of father, 35, 37–38, 65–67, 110–12, 117–20, 164–69; occupation of father's father and intergenerational mobility, 81–83; occupation of father's father and mother's father, 86–89; occupation of mother's father, 92 ff.; organizational mobility, 170 ff.; personality structure, 191–95; profile of, 14–15; region of birth, 45–46. *See also* Civilian federal executives, Public service

General Schedule. *See* Scalar position
Geographical mobility, 39–67; business executives, 19–21, 47–55, 58–60, 62–67; as factor in vertical mobility, 21, 51–55, 63–67, 73; government executives, 11, 39–67, 73. *See also* Birthplace
Grade levels. *See* Scalar position
Graduate work. *See* Education
Grandfather. *See* Occupation of father's father, Occupation of mother's father

Henry, W. E., 191

Ideology, 221–36
Interorganizational mobility, 169–76
Interviews, 191–93

Lateral entry, 170–76
Legal training. *See* Definitions, Occupation of father, Professional training

Marine Corps. *See* Military executives
Marriage, 21, 90–103; and achievement time, 101; of business executives, 90; and education and mobility, 96–101; of government executives, 90, 187; and nativity and geographic origins, 101–03; and occupational mobility, 21. *See also* Occupation of wife's father
Medicine. *See* Definitions, Occupation of father, Professional training
Methods. *See* Research methods
Military executives *(1959)*, 6, 12; age and achievement time, 17, 164 ff.; birthplace and nativity, 58, 61–66; career patterns, 153–54, 160; compared to business executives, 15–23; compared to civilian federal executives, 15–18; education, 17, 18, 109, 111, 115–19, 120–25, 127–31; endogamy and exogamy, 84–89; marriage and mobility, 91–103; occupation of father, 31–33, 37–38, 65–67, 77–80, 110–12, 117–20, 160–61, 164–69; occupation of father's father and intergenerational mobility, 77–83; oc-

cupation of father's father and mother's father, 86–89; occupation of mother's father, 92 ff.; organizational mobility, 170 ff.; profile of, 15–17; region of birth, 44–46. *See also* Public service
Mobility. *See* Occupational mobility, Personality structure
Mothers, 84–89. *See also* Occupation of mother's father

Nativity, 60–67; of business executives, 58–60, 62–67; and geographic origins and marriage, 101–03; of government executives, 11, 13, 15, 17, 58–66; and occupation of father, 63–67; and vertical mobility, 63–67. *See also* Birthplace
Navy. *See* Military executives
Neutrality, political, 228–29, 231–32

Occupation of father: and age and achievement time, 164–69; of business executives, 18–19, 35–38, 63, 65–67, 110–12, 164–69; and career patterns, 157–61, 164–69; compared to U. S. population, 30; and education, 110–13, 116–20; and father's father, 71–83; government and business compared, 35–38; of government executives, 11 ff., 16 ff., 28–33, 63–67, 71–83, 110–13, 116–20, 141–46, 156–64, 164–69, 182–83; and nativity, 60–67; profession and birthplace, 60; profession and nativity, 67; a profession as, 14, 16, 18, 33–35, 117–18, 183; public service as, 14, 15–16, 33, 80, 83; and scalar position, 161–64; and wife's father and mother's father, 91–96
Occupation of father's father, 71–83, 183; of business executives, 71, 81–83; of government executives, 71–83, 183; and intergenerational mobility, 71–83; and mother's father, 86–89
Occupation of mother's father, 84–89; and father's father, 86–89; of government executives, 84–89, 92–96; and wife's father and father, 91–96
Occupation of wife's father, 90–103; and achievement time, 101; of business executives, 92, 99–101; and education and mobility, 96–101; of government executives, 90–103; and mother's father and father, 91–96; and nativity and geographic origins, 101–03
Occupational mobility, 2–6, 12, 20–23, 31, 64–67, 81–83, 95–96, 101, 107, 141–46, 148–76, 184–87

Occupational sequence. *See* Career patterns
Occupational succession. *See* Occupational mobility
Organizational mobility, and career speed, 169–76

Personality structure, 191–220; of career and political executives, 195–98; and grade, 201–03; method for evaluating, 191–93; of the mobile and nonmobile, 198–99; of the older and younger executive, 200–01, and scalar position, 201–03; styles of, 195–205; summary on, 203–05; three profiles of, 206–20; variations in, 193–95. *See also* Attitudes
Political affiliation, 61 n.
Political executives *(1959)*, 6; age and achievement time, 13, 164 ff.; birthplace and geographical movement, 53; birthplace and nativity, 58, 62–66; career patterns, 152–53, 156; compared to business executives, 13–14, 18–23; compared to other government executives, 13–18; education, 14, 109–111, 115–19, 120–25, 127–31, 135–36; endogamy and exogamy, 84–89; marriage and mobility, 91–103; occupation of father, 35, 37–38, 65–67, 110–12, 117–20, 164–69; occupation of father, 35, 37–38, 110–12, 117–20, 164–69; occupation of father's father and intergenerational mobility, 81–83; occupation of father's father and mother's father, 86–89; occupation of mother's father, 92 ff.; organizational mobility, 170 ff.; personality structure, 191–98; profile of, 13–14; region of birth, 45–46. *See also* Civilian federal executives, Public service
Politics and policy: and executive role, 239–42; neutrality in, 228–29, 231–32
Professional training: of business executives, 155–56; and career sequences, 150–51, 157–58; and executive perspective, 155–56; of government executives, 11, 14, 15, 17, 115–16, 119–20, 129–30, 140, 145–46, 157–58, 184–87; and occupational mobility, 119–20, 157–58. *See also* Definitions, Education, Occupation of father
Public service U. S., 1–23, 237–50; agencies in, 9, 175–76, 180–81; civilian and military comparisons, 10–17; compared to business, 10–23; development of civilian, 6–9; development of military, 9–10; employment data, 8, 10, 11, 179; environment in, 237–50; increasing power of, 1–2, pay, 1; role demands in, 243–50; summary profiles of executives in, 10–17. *See also* Bureaucracy, Career civil service executives, Civilian federal executives, District of Columbia, Military executives, Political executives, Women federal executives

Questionnaire. *See* Research methods

Rank. *See* Scalar position
Region of birth, 39–55; business executives, 19, 45–46; government executives, 11, 13, 14, 16, 41–52, 183–84; importance of, 39–41; movement in and out of, 47–55; and size of birthplace, 50, 52–55; states and, 44–45; and U. S. population, 43. *See also* Birthplace, District of Columbia
Religion, 61 n.
Representative bureaucracy, 4–6, 17, 22, 25–67, 54–55, 58, 67, 109
Research methods: agencies, 6, 9; on foreign born, 63 n.; interviews, 191–93; for personality study, 191–93; purpose of research, 2–4; questionnaire, 41, 57, 61; religion and political affiliation, 61 n.; respondents, 6; sample, 6, 9, 192; statistical presentation, 12, 192–93; Thematic Apperception Test, 191–92. *See also* Census data, Definitions
Residence. *See* District of Columbia, Geographical mobility, Nativity, Region of birth
Respondents. *See* Research methods
Role, executive, 243–50
Rural origins. *See* Birthplace

Sample. *See* Research methods
Scalar position, 6; and occupation of father, 161–64; and personality structure, 201–03
Service. *See* Public service
Social mobility, 2–6, 22–23, 54–55. *See also* Occupational mobility
States. *See* Region of birth
Status, 22–23

Territorial mobility. *See* Geographical mobility
Thematic Apperception Test, 191–92

Universities. *See* Education
Urban origins. *See* Birthplace

Values, in Service career, 221–36
Vertical mobility. *See* Occupational mobility

Index

Washington, D.C. *See* District of Columbia

Wives, 80–103. *See also* Marriage, Occupation of wife's father

Women federal executives *(1959)*, 177–87; age and achievement time, 187; career patterns, 184–87; education, 12, 184; marriage of, 187; nativity, 183–84; occupation of father, 182–83; occupation of father's father, 183; profile of, 11–12, 177–87; region of birth, 183–84; types of positions held by, 180–81. *See also* Civilian federal executives, Public service

Years to achieve present position: in business, 20, 101, 168; in government, 13, 15, 17, 101, 167–68; and marriage, 101; and occupation of father, 20–21, 161–69. *See also* Age

Years with firm or agency: business executives, 173; government executives, 173–74. *See also* achievement time